Women and the Subversion of the Community

A Mariarosa Dalla Costa Reader

Women and the Subversion of the Community: A Mariarosa Dalla Costa Reader
© 2019 PM Press.

ISBN: 978-1-62963-570-5
Library of Congress Control Number: 2018931531

Cover by Josh MacPhee
Interior design by briandesign
All photos from the personal archives of Mariarosa Dalla Costa and from the Archivio di Lotta Femminista per il salario al lavoro domestico. Donazione Mariarosa Dalla Costa

10 9 8 7 6 5 4 3 2 1

PM Press
PO Box 23912
Oakland, CA 94623
www.pmpress.org

Printed in the USA by the Employee Owners of Thomson-Shore in Dexter, Michigan.
www.thomsonshore.com

Contents

Preface

May 1, 1976, demonstration against unpaid domestic labor organized by the WHH committee in Trieste.

When Mariarosa asked me to write a preface for this collection, my first thought was to draft a piece on "Reading Dalla Costa." But after reading Camille Barbagallo's introduction, I decided that she has provided a useful enough sketch of the ideas in this collection to make such a draft redundant. However, in her introduction Camille also notes how studying Mariarosa's ideas and political activities changed her life, narrowly, in giving her an intellectual focus for her doctoral thesis, and then more broadly, in providing a political prospective that helped her cope with personal day-to-day challenges. Although her comments about the personal impact of the ideas and history behind the essays gathered here are few, they made me think about how rarely reading another's writing results in appropriations so profound as to change one's life: even among those dedicated to bringing about change—in the world and in their own lives. Precisely because such dedication often involves a great deal of reading in the search for new and better ideas, strategies, and tactics, militants too often wind up replicating the experience of many academics—acquiring an extensive erudition but little actual appropriation that changes how they think and act.[1] I think Camille's evocation of the effects on her life of studying Mariarosa's work—as a woman, an intellectual, a militant, and a mother—should provide every bit as much encouragement to readers to study these collected essays as her sketch of their contents.

Rather than add to Camille's comments on that content, I'd like to complement her account of how her life was affected by these essays with some parallel reflections on their impact on my own life and work, as a man, an intellectual, a militant, and a father.

First, however, some necessary background. As a boy child, and then as a young man, I was reared in a middle-class family in a rural Ohio countryside, where the traditional, patriarchal gender roles of the nuclear family obtained. My father worked for the U.S. Air Force in a salaried administrative position, overseeing contract negotiations with private industry. My mother—despite having graduated from the same university as my father and having worked briefly for a wage—accepted the typical burdens of a rural housewife: cooking, housekeeping, rearing children, patching up her husband, helping build a house, landscape a yard, and tend an extensive garden, eventually taking on the caring labor required when my father's parents moved in with us during their final years. In the absence of any alternative gender relationships, I assumed that this division of labor was natural and did not question it—all the way through high school and into college.

Grasping the limitations of these relationships, perceiving alternatives, and getting beyond them took several shocks, including discovering Mariarosa's writings.

The first shock occurred while I was studying in France, at the Université de Montpellier (1964–1965). Despite the way many French family traditions and laws at that time imposed even more limitations on women than in the United States, feminists were on the march against "*les servitudes de la maternité*." Birth rates were dropping, and women were beginning to achieve new legal rights and had little patience for patriarchal values. At the time, I was both appalled at the laws limiting women's rights and impressed with the demands that French women were making.[2] I encountered their impatience when a fellow student I had started dating called me on my very traditional views of gender relationships. She issued an ultimatum: either I would sit down and seriously read Simone de Beauvoir's *Le Deuxième Sexe*, volumes 1 and 2 or she would never speak with me again. Challenged, I undertook what at first seemed a Herculean task; I was still struggling to read French and the two volumes contained several hundred pages. After many, many hours with the texts and my *Petit Larousse*, not only was my French vocabulary considerably expanded, but I got the point. The results were profound. Reading de Beauvoir and recognizing the cogency of her analysis forced me to confront the limitations of my prior assumptions about gender and to embrace feminism—at least in theory. It wasn't long before I was calling myself a 'theoretical feminist,' theoretical because accepting the theory was one thing, changing more than twenty years of habitual thinking and modes of behavior was something else entirely. It was the beginning of a long, rough road.

That said, what I took away from that first reading and the discussions that followed primarily concerned issues of gender equality. By that time,

I had read Sartre's plays, novels, and *Being and Nothingness* and was study-ing Hegel's *Phénoménologie de L'Esprit* in a course at the Université, so I understood de Beauvoir's evocation of woman as *l'Autre* (the Other) and the limited parallel she drew with the relations between masters and slaves. But I had not yet begun to read Marx. Whatever elements of his analysis had shaped her essay, I missed entirely.[3]

The second shock, or series of shocks, came with the rise of feminism within the American anti–Vietnam War movement, in which I became deeply engaged while a graduate student at Stanford University. In the Bay Area of California, protests were intense, fueled not only by outrage but by serious research into the involvement of the university and surrounding industry in the war efforts in Southeast Asia. As our efforts grew to confront the entire Pacific Basin strategy of American capital, some of us created a radical think tank that we called the Pacific Studies Center (PSC) to carry out part of that research. Because both men and women were engaged in that project, doing the research, writing, and churning out leaflets and arti-cles for the local underground newspaper (the *Midpeninsula Observer*) and sometimes for *Ramparts* magazine, confrontations over gender politics were recurrent. While none of the men involved were overtly anti-feminist, and some of us were ardently pro-feminist, our language and behaviors were repeatedly challenged by women in the group. They forced us to con-front contradictions between the feminist theory we claimed to accept and our actual practice. In those years of the late 1960s and early 1970s, such con-tradictions were becoming more and more obvious as the feminist move-ment solidified, became more autonomous from men, and began producing an ever more voluminous literature detailing the unacceptable behaviors of men, even of men who supported women's struggles. The more we men were confronted, both in print and in regular weekly T-group encounters,[4] the more we recognized that we needed to figure out new ways to be, not only within the anti-war movement but in our lives more generally.

In my case, 'more generally,' those years meant figuring out how to live with a graduate student wife (the French woman who had introduced me to de Beauvoir) and a daughter. Sharing and informed by feminist theory, my wife and I sought to evenly divide our time for study and time for house-keeping, including caring for our daughter. With respect to our daughter, we sought both to set an example of equal gender relationships and to create learning experiences in which she was encouraged to pursue whatever curiosity moved her, in whatever direction, with no gender bias. As she learned to listen to stories, we read her those in which girls were strong and independent. Alongside feminist rewrites of traditional myths and fairy tales, such as Atalanta, included in the 1972 book and album *Free to be . . . You and Me*, I remember reading her Maoist propaganda comic books with a feminist slant, e.g., an illustrated story about a little girl who proved more capable than her older brother in producing anti-Japanese leaflets.[5] As she began to read on her own, we sought out and provided her with novels and comic books of a similar character. When she became interested in dolls, we refused to buy a Barbie and instead found a more realistic girl doll for whom I crafted mountain climbing gear (something I was into at the time), complete with appropriate clothing, ice axe, ropes, carabiners, hammer, and pitons. Such were some of our efforts to translate theory into daily practice and play.

The third shock came from my encounter with the Wages for Housework movement, and with Mariarosa's writings in particular, after years of reading quite different interpretations of Marx's theory. Engagement in political struggle in the 1960s meant, among other things, casting about for intellectual moorings to ground choices of tactics and strategies. Alternatives proliferated. The anti-war movement surged in the wake of the Civil Rights Movement and in tandem with the rise of autonomous movements for women's, African American, and then Mexican American empowerment. So, pacifism vied with militant confrontations with the police in the streets, at draft centers, university campuses, and corporate offices. Confronting economic exploitation and COINTELPRO repression at home and imperialism abroad required learning and interpreting the histories that had given rise to those movements, from patriarchy and racism in the U.S. to colonialism overseas. The American New Left of those years was *new* because we drew less on orthodox Marxism-Leninism, including Maoism (despite widespread propaganda about the virtues of the Cultural Revolution in China), and more on the neo-Marxism of the *Monthly Review* variety, radical bottom-up and revisionist histories of grassroots struggles and the Cold War, and various currents of critical theory and Western Marxism. Despite the common origin of various struggles that arise within the exploitation and alienations of capitalism, the assertion of autonomy in self-organization supported notions of separate 'social movements' as distinct from earlier, narrow Marxist concepts of 'class' that relegated every struggle outside of those of the waged industrial proletariat to secondary status. As the title of a well-known essay by Heidi Hartmann—"The Unhappy Marriage of Marxism and Feminism"—suggested, working out a useful relationship between the two perspectives was no simple matter and the subject of intense debate.

Unlike Camille's work, my own dissertation research did not benefit from exposure to Mariarosa's writings but was focused on American policy makers' efforts to contain rural revolution, efforts that ultimately resulted—alongside military intervention—in the attempted technological 'fix' of the Green Revolution, based on new high-yielding strains of rice and wheat. Instead, it was framed by concepts of modes of production and the structuralism characteristic of French Marxist anthropology in the 1970s.

However, while putting the finishing touches on that dissertation, and during my first semester teaching in the Graduate Program of the New School for Social Research in the fall of 1974, I joined the Zerowork Collective that was just then producing the first issue of a journal with that title. Both the editors and several of the articles were heavily influenced by the Wages for Housework (WFH) movement and perspective. As a result, I started reading Mariarosa's essays, other things written by the women in that movement, and a few bits and pieces of English translations of texts produced by the Italian workerist movement in which Mariarosa had been involved prior to founding the International Feminist Collective and the Wages for Housework campaign.[6] Feminists, of course, had been critiquing housework for decades, but not, in my experience, demanding to be paid for it.[7]

Before long, I no longer accepted the theory that had framed my dissertation. Needless to say, I didn't reveal this contradiction to my committee but defended it anyway. After the defense, however, I needed to return to Marx's theory of value and discover whether it could provide an alternative to mode of production analysis for understanding the history I had discovered while working on my dissertation and whether the new interpretations of Marx developed by Mariarosa, her comrades, those in Zerowork, and the Italian workerists were consistent with that theory of value or provided an alternative.

In the process, I undertook two parallel projects. The first was reading everything Marx had written on value in the two languages then at my disposal, English and French. The second was the close study of Mariarosa's foundational essay "Women and the Subversion of the Community," whose influence was obvious throughout the Wages for Housework literature. The results of the first project was a set of notes for my students presenting my interpretation of Marx's value theory.[8]

The results of the second project included the following. I found her analysis consistent with my interpretation of Marx but also a great contribution to repairing his failure to thoroughly analyze the labor of producing and reproducing labor power. Basically, she not only amplified Marx's recognition of how the largely unwaged labor of producing and reproducing labor power is every bit as essential to capitalist accumulation as waged and salaried labor but went further in demonstrating how, therefore, the struggle by women against the unwaged reproductive work is also essential to any effective strategy to overthrow and get beyond capitalism. Those aspects of her analysis were fundamental not only to the demands for wages for housework but countered the long-standing Marxist bias toward seeing the struggles of the unwaged as secondary and subordinate to those of wage-workers, long viewed as the vanguard of working-class struggle against capitalism. To someone who had been involved in student struggles and had long acted in support of the struggles of both women and peasants— most of whom were unwaged—this made Marxism more relevant than ever.

As Camille points out in her introduction, these insights were not universally appreciated. Rather, they caused a tremendous uproar among Marxists for many reasons, including a perceived contradiction with Marx's concepts of value and the origin of surplus value, i.e., the central process of exploitation in accumulation. Mariarosa's assertion that the amount of housework had an impact on the amount of surplus value appeared to contradict Marx's analysis that only labor that produced commodities sold in the market, upon which profit was realized, produced surplus value. Yes, reproductive labor produced the commodity labor power, but its sale, Marx had argued, earned only the wage—the cost of reproducing the commodity—but did not generate any surplus value. Indeed, while rethinking Marx's value theory in conjunction with studying Mariarosa's essay and presenting my interpretation in lectures to students at the New School, I was repeatedly confronted by this counterargument by both more orthodox Marxists and my colleague Heidi Hartmann.

This particular objection, I concluded, was based on a misreading of Mariarosa's reasoning, a position I eventually spelled out in an essay on "Domestic Labor and Value" in 2005, based on my own interpretation of Marx's theory. A proper reading, I argued, recognizes Mariarosa to be contending that the greater the amount of housework, the lower the amount of necessary labor required to produce the means of subsistence, and therefore, *ceteris paribus*, the greater the surplus value. This argument, with parallels to his analysis of relative surplus value, does not contradict Marx's argument but supplements it by exploring more closely than he did the relationship between reproductive labor, the value of labor power, and the amount of surplus value.

This insight also provides a theoretical foundation for grasping not only housework but also other unwaged activities essential to the production and reproduction of labor power, e.g., schoolwork, the work of the job hunt, and peasant subsistence agriculture, as integral aspects not only of capitalist accumulation but also of class struggle against the imposition of the capitalist way of organizing society around endless work. In other words, recognizing the necessity of unwaged labor to capital and the consequent potential for its refusal to rupture accumulation makes the struggles by waged and salaried workers, the unemployed, unwaged housewives, unwaged students, and subsistence peasants at least potentially complementary. That was precisely what we sought during the anti-war movement as we chanted "Ho, Ho, Ho Chi Minh, the NLF is going to win!" in solidarity with the resistance of Vietnamese peasants to first French colonialism and then American neocolonialism. Whereas at the time, solidarity for most of us was primarily emotional—identifying with others fighting for freedom under quite different circumstances—this new reading of Marxist theory provides material grounds of that solidarity in a common enemy.[9]

Besides the objection to a perceived contradiction with Marx's theory of surplus value, there was another complaint raised against Mariarosa's essay: its failure to analyze any positive aspects of the human relationships involved in those various domains shaped by capital to produce labor power, e.g., families, schools, communities. The complaint was raised most vociferously by those who had long viewed the family as a relative safe haven from the domain of capitalist exploitation and by some who had found solidarity in student struggles and among *campesinistas* and who touted the virtues of traditional indigenous community solidarity. In my interpretation, these objections were similar to those I had long raised against Marx's *relative* neglect both of working-class struggles against capitalism and of attempts to develop alternatives—despite his obvious efforts to contribute to the former and open the way for the latter. The WFH literature that responded to these objections—debunking the visions of the family as safe haven, by detailing how schools are subordinated to capital, and by emphasizing the internal conflicts inflicted upon those domains—did little to douse the fire of criticism.

Just as Marx had devoted most of his energy to revealing the depredations of capital, so too did Mariarosa and those who draw upon her writing devote themselves to revealing the ways in which the relations between spouses or partners, between parents and children, among children, between children and teachers, and so on had been poisoned by capital. In other words, this whole approach emphasized what needed to be fought against, rather than what one might fight for. While fighting against capitalism was clearly designed to reduce and ultimately sweep away obstacles, there was a failure to theorize efforts to create alternatives. Given the central role of Marxist analysis, this was not terribly surprising. Marx, after all, had eschewed utopian speculation and mostly pointed to marginal gains won by workers in struggle, e.g., a reduction in work hours here, an increase in wages there, with little attention to the creation, however temporary, of concrete alternative forms of social organization. There were exceptions, of course; he did praise worker cooperatives as foreshadowing broader transformations and praised the Paris Commune for having experimented with a new form of self-government. But overall, in Marx, in Mariarosa's essay, and in much of what followed in support of its basic thesis, there was little of that.

This was an absence that I didn't entirely understand, partly because within both Italian *operaismo* and the earlier movements on which it had drawn, there had been efforts to recognize and theorize moments and spaces in which workers and students did create concrete alternatives.[10] Partly too because in those years a wave of squatting, in which young workers and students seized vacant buildings and created autonomous *centri sociali*, free radio stations, e.g., Radio Alice, and even a European Counter Network of computer communication, was sweeping Italy.

When I visited in 1978, before meeting Mariarosa in Padua, I met Toni Negri, an important figure in Italian operaismo, in Milan. In discussions and later in reading his lectures on the *Grundrisse* to students at L'Ecole Normale in Paris—gathered in the book *Marx beyond Marx*—I discovered his appropriation of Marx's concept of self-valorization. Reversing Marx's usage, which referred to capital's own self-expansion, Negri used the term to denote precisely those acts in which workers moved beyond capital by creating concrete alternatives.[11] His effort to theorize such creativity struck me as both reflecting some of what was happening in Italy and resonating with many American experiences in the countercultural movements in the 1960s. In response, I did two things. First, I raised the concept with some in the Wages for Housework movement, including Mariarosa, and their supporters. Because of differences with Toni on several issues, they did not share my appreciation of his concept of self-valorization and, as far as I have seen, have never adopted it for their own purposes.

Second, uninvolved in those conflicts, and despite disagreeing with Toni's centering of self-valorization on labor, I not only appropriated the concept but used it as a lens to reexamine Mariarosa's essay.[12] When I did so, I discovered some eleven passages in which she evoked various kinds of desirable relationships quite different from those shaped by capital. Primarily focused on revealing the distortions caused by capitalist interference in our lives, she did not explore those relationships, nor did she classify them under one rubric, such as self-valorization. But the visions are there, however briefly evoked. The upshot for me was finding the concept of self-valorization complementary to the analysis in her essay, and both providing—in conjunction with Marx's analysis of production—analytical points of departure for examining our concrete experiences of daily life to figure out *to what degree* they have been shaped by capital for its purposes and *to what degree* we have been successful at subverting those purposes and creating something different. Since writing that essay in 1971, she has both reflected on the limitations of her original essay and spent more time exploring moments of creative invention by various groups of people in struggle.[13]

As was the case for Camille, finding these new analytical tools had implications for my daily life. To limit my illustration of those implications, I will restrict myself to the consequences for my work as a salaried professor and my relationship with unwaged students.[14] The recognition of how capital has sought to colonize all aspects of our lives and shape them to be compatible with its own reproduction demands not only a 'worker's inquiry' to identify those shapes but also parallel evaluations of any and all possibilities for rupturing the patterns capital has sought to impose *and* for creating alternatives.

While at the New School I wrote a draft essay examining work in schools by both salaried professors and unwaged students and how this process of colonization could be resisted. Although there was some useful discussion among student and faculty participants in a study group we organized that met outside of classes, from those students who were invested in more orthodox Marxist analyses and hell-bent on getting degrees that would get them academic jobs the resistance I got was to the ideas in that draft. During my second year of teaching, a ragtag coalition of Maoists, Trotskyists, and Marxologists formed to lobby against my being rehired for a third year.[15] Despite sharp ideological conflicts among them, they were united in opposing the kind of autonomist Marxist analysis I was presenting in lectures, in that essay, and in suggestions about the politics of class struggle in schools.

Fortunately, a quite different set of less ideological students, who had been engaged in three years of struggle to get a Marxist hired at the University of Texas at Austin, solicited and then welcomed me there, where I taught from 1976 until I retired in 2012. In those years, discussion and debate continued to be partially shaped by the influence of Mariarosa's analysis, which I shared with my students, especially in my courses on Marx. Despite the role played by students in getting me hired, our efforts at collaboration, inside and outside of courses, repeatedly came up against the structural difference in power conferred by my status as a salaried professor versus their status as largely unwaged students. From the point of view of the university administration, the primary mandate in my job was not helping students learn, but rather turning in a rank-ordering of students' willingness to work in the form of grades. For unwaged students, most of whom considered their future to be at least partially dependent on grades, this structural divide between the grader and the graded was an unavoidable obstacle to collaboration with any professor. Because I recognized and repeatedly raised with students the way things were set up to divide us and pit us against one another, ways of minimizing conflict and maximizing collaboration for mutual learning was a recurrent theme of discussion and frequently of collusion, semester after semester, year after year.

Those struggles led both to the revision of the essay I had drafted at the New School and to repeated experiments to find ways to subvert grading and maximize the opportunities for students to self-valorize, i.e., to fulfill their own self-defined learning objectives.[16] The experiments were too numerous to recount but included everything from student refusal to take tests to collaborative efforts to create new courses designed specifically to meet students' self-defined needs—both individual conference courses and full-scale elective courses open to everyone interested. One example of a course co-designed by my students and myself was "The Political Economy of Education," the direct result of over a dozen activist students seeking opportunities to study materials germane to their struggles with the university administration. Both the original selection of readings and then those chosen each semester were determined by the interests of students signed up for the course. Unable to avoid grading (and still keep my job), I first replaced the multiple-choice and short-answer tests typical of my department with essay questions, often formulated by the students themselves, then by papers on self-selected subjects, and eventually I refounded grading on students' personal assessments of what they were seeking and what they were able to appropriate from the courses we designed together.[17] Throughout the evolution of such experimentation, we explicitly discussed how to minimize *the degree to which* our activity met capital's desire for measures of students' willingness to work and maximize *the degree to which* we were able to achieve our own self-determined, autonomous objectives that did not contribute to the mere production of our labor power.[18]

To conclude, I recommend the essays in this volume not only because they constitute serious contributions to the development of Marxist thinking about both theory and political struggle, but because, as I have tried to illustrate, the appropriation of ideas developed in those essays may change your life. As a professor, I eventually realized that one of my essential tasks was to separate the wheat from the chaff in my reading, to share with my students both what I considered to have been time well spent and what I considered to have been largely a waste of time and effort. Having hopefully conveyed some sense of my own priorities, they could then judge the likelihood that my recommendations were salient to their own interests. This preface is, therefore, intended to provide the same service. Yours to choose.

Harry Cleaver
Austin, Texas
December 2017

Notes

1 In 1851, Arthur Schopenhauer warned against reading that does not contribute either to new ways of thinking or new kinds of action. See his essays "On Learning and the Learned" and "On Reading and Books," in *Parega and Paralipomena: Short Philosophical Essays*, vol. 2 (Oxford: Clarendon Press, 1974).

2 Married women only obtained the right to work without their husband's consent in 1965. Contraception was illegal until 1967, and abortion would not be legalized until 1975. Mothers only obtained legal rights over their children in 1970; their right to administer their children's property was not obtained until 1985. One of the consequences of the struggles of French women for control over procreation that only became clear to me a decade later, upon reading one of Mariarosa's essays, was the

connection to the influx of immigrant workers from North Africa and French West Africa. See her "Reproduction and Emigration" (1974) in this volume.

3   For example, her analysis in the first volume of the failings of Engels' *Origin of the Family, Private Property and the State* (1884) to adequately explain the particularity of women's situation made sense to me, but having yet to study Marx, I could not see the influence of his analysis of alienation on her critique.

4   A T-group or training group (sometimes also referred to as sensitivity-training group, human relations training group or encounter group) is a form of group training where participants . . . learn about themselves (and about small group processes in general) through their interaction with each other. They use feedback, problem solving, and role play to gain insights into themselves, others, and groups; see T-groups, *Wikipedia*, accessed September 16, 2018, https://en.wikipedia.org/wiki/T-groups.

5   Although set in the years of the Chinese resistance to Japanese imperialism, with a distinctly nationalist framing, our interest was solely on the gender dynamics portrayed.

6   Those few translations could be found mostly in *Radical America* and *Telos*. When I visited Europe in 1978 in search of more information on *operaismo*, I discovered the translations by Red Notes in London, a few more in France, and a vast untranslated literature in Italy, dating back to the early 1960s. Learning to read Italian became essential to taking on that literature. I provided a brief sketch in the introduction to my *Reading* Capital *Politically* (Austin: University of Texas Press, 1979), but it was not until Steve Wright published *Storming Heaven: Class Composition and Struggle in Italian Autonomist Marxism* (London: Pluto Press, 2002) that an in-depth study became available.

7   One then current example, "Housework," was included on Marlo Thomas and Friends, *Free to Be . . . You and Me*, Bell Records, 1972. The poem—designed to debunk advertisements portraying housework as enjoyable—can be found on YouTube. As Mariarosa discovered, while working on her 1983 book *Family, Welfare and the State: Between Progressivism and the New Deal* (Brooklyn, NY: Common Notions, 2015), some feminists were demanding remuneration from the state for housework early in the twentieth century. See her comment in note 21 of "Women and the Subversion of the Community," included in this volume.

8   Those notes became the theoretical core of my book *Reading* Capital *Politically*. It was published in 1979, but only after extensive research, including the trip to Europe referenced in footnote 5 above, made it possible for me to write an introduction situating the theory in the history of what I came to call autonomist Marxism.

9   In retrospect, despite the chant, sympathies in the anti-war movement lay more with the peasants suffering from napalm, carpet bombing, mass killings, CIA assassinations, and Agent Orange than with Ho Chi Minh or the political factions making up the National Liberation Front (NLF). While at the time, some Trotskyists had enunciated serious critiques of the Vietnamese Communist Party, its eventual imposition of state capitalism and its opening of the "liberated" country to multinational corporate investment forced a clear differentiation between Communist Party leaders and those who had been exploited by foreign powers. See, for example, Philip Mattera, "National Liberation, Socialism and the Struggle against Work: The Case of Vietnam," *Zerowork: Political Materials* 2 (Fall 1977): 71–89.

10 I am referring here to the council communists, who took their name from the German worker's councils formed during the ill-fated 1918 revolution, to the Johnson-Forest Tendency, and to the Socialisme ou Barbarie group in France; both of the latter valorized workers' self-activity and pointed not only to the German workers' councils but also the Russian Soviets and the workers' councils formed during the Hungarian Revolution of 1956 as examples of the ability of workers to create new organizational forms, to craft 'the future in the present.' Their writings were translated and informed the emergence of operaismo in Italy.

11 In time, drawing on Spinoza and Deleuze, Negri would reformulate the concept of self-valorization as "constituent power"—the power of constituting newness, as opposed to the (very capitalist) power to impose sameness. See his books *The Savage Anomaly: The Power of Spinoza's Metaphysics and Politics* (Minneapolis: University of Minnesota Press, 1991) and the collection *Le Pouvoir constituant: Essai sur les alternatives de la modernité* (Paris: Presses Universitaires de France, 1992).

12 My reexamination can be found in "Self-valorization in Mariarosa Dalla Costa's 'Women and the Subversion of the Community,'" accessed July 26, 1018, https://la.utexas.edu/users/hcleaver/357k/HMCDallaCostaSelfvalorization2.htm.

13 On her reflections of the limits, see her 2002 essay "The Door to the Garden" in this volume. On her subsequent explorations, see many of her more recent writings, including *Our Mother Ocean: Enclosure, Commons, and the Global Fishermen's Movement* (Brooklyn, NY: Common Notions, 2014).

14 This leaves out not only the implications for the rest of my life, e.g., for relations with my children and friends, but also those for my relationships with partially waged graduate teaching assistants, university administrators, and activist students engaged in many moments of direct protest within the university and beyond.

15 The same coalition also opposed the rehiring of Heidi Hartmann. Neither of us were catering to their political priorities, and we had to go.

16 "On Schoolwork and the Struggle against It," accessed July 26, 2017, https://www.google.com/search?q=Schoolwork+and+the+Struggle+Against+It&oq=Schoolwork+and+the+Struggle+Against+It&aqs=chrome..69i57j0l2.432j0j4&sourceid=chrome&ie=UTF-8.

17 The ideas behind this approach are laid out in "Learning, Understanding and Appropriating," accessed July 26, 2018, https://la.utexas.edu/users/hcleaver/Appropriation.htm.

18 As you might imagine, the degree to which all these things unfolded depended on who was taking the courses. As at the New School in New York, there were plenty of students totally uninterested in any concerted effort to undermine the capitalist organization of their studies and simply interested in obtaining degrees with the least effort necessary. Such attitudes, of course, illustrated the natural tendency of students to refuse schoolwork they had not designed, regardless of how they framed their refusal.

Introduction

May 1, 1976, demonstration of WFH network in Naples.

The present conditions of womanhood keep pushing us toward the past. From the overrepresentation of women in low-paid and low-status jobs and the structural and interpersonal violence that women face to the continued attacks on women's sovereignty over their bodies and the fact that women still do the vast amount of unwaged childcare, eldercare, and housework: the insights from 1970s feminism keep reappearing. One of the reasons that 1970s feminism continues to be relevant is because when we analyze the contemporary conditions of life and labor for the vast majority of women, what currently passes for mainstream feminism not only misses the point, it reads more like a slap in the face. This is not least because when we consider that women are overrepresented in welfare lines, in the growing numbers of the working poor, the dispossessed, and the highly exploited, there is something violent in the distance between the conditions of life and labor for the majority of women and the concerns that currently constitute mainstream feminism.

Mainstream feminism today—much of it corporate sponsored, coated in pink, incorporated into forms of repressive legislation, and providing justification for military operations—is more interested in 'saving' and 'rescuing' vulnerable women than in dismantling the economic and political systems that produce our vulnerability and exploitation. The emergence and popularity of a corporate feminism that calls for women to 'lean in' to get ahead in the workplace conveniently locates the problem at the level of women's individual lack of aspiration and ambition. As a number of feminist scholars have pointed out, one of the problems is that so much of mainstream gender politics sings from the same song sheet as neoliberalism. "The future is female," we are told, with an emphasis on the individual female self, who is always making 'choices' and possessing that much-needed entrepreneurial spirit. Women's individual capacity to adapt and succeed in historically male-dominated arenas of power is a barometer of this new entrepreneurialism—with the usual outcome being women exploiting other women. We are told we just need to feminize capitalism and things will get better—so much so that a systematic and structural analysis of how gender operates in and through capitalism has been abandoned in favor of feminist celebrities and being the next female Bill Gates in the making. There is a constant celebration of individual women's success stories in their start-up businesses, sporting events, or parliament, with that obligatory paragraph about how she amazingly manages to balance it all with marriage and motherhood.

There is a political fatigue that haunts the ideas and campaigns animating mainstream feminism: breaking through glass ceilings, ending male violence, tackling gender pay gaps, getting more women into parliament, and the so-called 'mommy wars.' When we talk about gender and what it means to be a woman today, the conversation never seems to get around to issues such as the lack of affordable and safe housing, immigration raids, cuts to legal aid, hospital closures, the privatization of eldercare—all of which negatively affect women. But let's be clear: they disproportionately affect working-class women.

Contemporary mainstream feminist politics is trapped in a loop—or, perhaps more correctly, can be said to have reached an impasse. It is not just that feminism today appears hopelessly out of touch and is too often racist and transphobic. It's more than that: it's that mainstream feminism is actually part of the problem. To be blunt, focusing on getting more and more women into the waged workforce as the primary way to address questions of gender inequality has certainly benefitted a few women at the top, but it has been disastrous for the rest of us—especially migrants, women of color, and those of us too poor to pay another woman to do the reproductive work that we don't like doing or don't have time to do. In global cities across the world, a growing army of working-class women, many of them migrants and women of color, work to clean homes and offices, cook and prepare food, staff hospitals and schools, and take care of elders and children. They are the women who perform ever more of the reproductive labor that is fundamental for the maintenance of life, but their labor continues to be devalued, degraded, and considered low-skilled. They do this labor for ridiculously low wages and in exploitative conditions, denied basic work rights like holiday pay, maternity leave, pensions, and dignity at work.

The globalized context of women's exploitation is such that the current conditions of womanhood are marked by an ever-increasing polarization of the experiences, opportunities, and struggles that different communities and households face. Whether the difference lies in how our children are policed when they are on the streets, whether we walk into work as a cleaner or manager, or whether we worry about how to get our kids across the border in a boat or how to take them on a holiday during school term, these differences make it clear that how we experience womanhood is produced as much by race and class as it is by relations of gender. The continued inability—and let's be clear that at times it's an unwillingness—to understand the ways that race and class produce gender and the reverse, how gender produces and intersects with race and class, has meant that mainstream feminism ends up talking about and to a very particular group of women: overwhelmingly white, middle-class women who live in global cities in developed countries.

The destruction of decent wages and employment conditions over the last forty years has meant that all adults are now expected and compelled to be 'active' in the labor market. The normalization of the 'adult worker model' has occurred at the same time as the nation-state has consistently withdrawn support and funding for social services that make the conditions for a decent life and women's labor market participation bearable. When you add into the mix that the gendered organization of domestic and care work in most households has remained pretty much the same as it was in the 1970s, it becomes clear why there has been a renewed and sustained interest not only in 1970s feminism, but specifically in the political tendency of Marxist feminism and the contributions of Mariarosa Dalla Costa. For the vast majority of us who will never have the opportunity or the desire to be a female CEO, the problem with mainstream feminism is that it obscures the class and race antagonisms that are central to how gender is organized and experienced under capitalism. If women's struggles for empowerment and equality continue to be built on the backbreaking and devalued reproductive labor of other women, feminism will remain part of the problem. The reason Marxist feminism, of which Mariarosa's work is emblematic, is useful is that it gives us a mobile compositional lens that acknowledges the bifurcated experiences of class, race, and gender as they intersect and provides a radical orientation for a life beyond capitalism.

•

I can say without hyperbole that the political and intellectual work of Mariarosa Dalla Costa changed my life. Her intellectual contribution, spanning five decades, has danced both center stage and in the shadows of my personal and intellectual life for nearly twenty years. I spent seven years writing a doctoral thesis that analyzed her work in nearly every chapter. I survived a crisis of motherhood by eventually wrapping my head around the contradictions that occur when you produce the capitalist commodity of labor power and, at the same time, life. As a result, I spend time thinking about the complexity of housework under capitalism while picking up toys or scrubbing the bathroom, transforming the tasks into a worker's enquiry rather than only a burden to be escaped.

This edited volume brings together a collection of Mariarosa's essays that focus on the politics of reproduction, feminist movements, and the question of women's autonomy. After I agreed to edit this volume, and during the long hours of agonizing over writing this introduction, it became clear that what should be a relatively straightforward task of situating her contribution within both the traditions of Italian operaismo and women's liberation movements was, in fact, going to be anything but simple. In part it is a complicated task because there is something nearly impossible to grasp in Mariarosa's work. She pushes us toward thinking and analyzing the conditions of women in a way that feels like things might just break if we follow her thoughts to their conclusion. In sharp contrast to the mainstreaming of neoliberal gender politics, the ungovernability and radical potential of her ideas lie in the injunction not just that things *could* break but that they *should*. When I think about what her work does, its effect often feels like a dusty heavy curtain being pulled back. What I mean by that is that her work helps us to make visible many of the key dynamics and contradictions inherent to capitalism and to make sense of the notion that there is nothing 'natural' about the way we reproduce life and labor under capitalism.

At a meeting in Padua in 1972, Mariarosa Dalla Costa, Selma James (London), Silvia Federici (New York), and Brigitte Galtier (Paris) formed the International Feminist Collective to develop a militant feminist politics and to promote debate on reproductive work, the woman as its subject, and the family as a place of production and reproduction of labor power. Through the coordination of self-organized women's collectives and actions in various countries, a vast international network formed: Wages for Housework groups and committees.

Their political work played a leading role in the development of a political tendency within 1970s feminism that promoted and organized major struggles with an anti-capitalist perspective. Central to the political work of the Wages for Housework campaign was the demand for a transformation in the organization of production and a society that would produce the conditions for women to gain personal autonomy, starting with women's economic autonomy. However, their politics broke with previous feminist theories and with the dominant ideas of women's emancipation at the time. Women's autonomy, they argued, would never be realized through women taking on additional jobs outside the home. Instead, they demanded recognition of the economic value of reproductive work, encapsulated in the demand for wages for housework. In addition, they demanded that the workweek be reduced to twenty hours—so that all people, including men, could have the time to undertake the burdens of reproductive labor, have the space for emotional exchanges, and equally experience the pleasures of reproducing life and being together.

It was a totally self-organized feminism, its activity funded through dues collected from activists. In this sense it had considerable autonomy and power and did not depend on anyone nor was it constrained by the bureaucratic commitments of funded projects like those that would come to dominate feminism in the 1980s and 1990s. Theirs was a feminism that distrusted institutions, keeping a distance from them, even if many of their victories would determine major changes at institutional levels: the legalization of abortion, legal reforms concerning divorce, the establishment of family planning clinics, and new developments in family law. Equally, this was a feminism that was not at all enthusiastic about the politics of women's equality. They were critical of a politics that viewed women's liberation as equality with men, who themselves were exploited through the wage relation. Why would women want to be equal to a wage slave? They made the crucial point that any notion of women's equality remained empty talk if the contradictions and problems of how reproduction is organized under capitalism remained unresolved.

Mariarosa had a prominent role in this militant anti-capitalist feminism. The texts collected in this volume trace developments in her thinking that begin with insights she gained during years of militancy in Potere Operaio (Workers' Power) in Italy. Through her involvement in the workers' and students' struggles of the late 1960s and early 1970s she located silences and gaps in the political action and thought of the time. From these experiences it became clear to her that the discomfort, abuse, and suffering of women, which had not yet started to be articulated through the feminist movement, were absent in political discourse. These silences and gaps became the new terrain for her reflections during a time when the beginnings of a women's movement were emerging in Italy.

These developments in her political education and activity occurred alongside her academic career. In July 1967, she graduated from the University of Padua with a degree in law, having completed a thesis in philosophy of law under Professor Enrico Opocher. Soon after, Opocher appointed her to archive all the documents relating to the Italian resistance during World War II, which were stored at the Institute of History of the Resistance at the University of Padua, and during the 1970s Mariarosa held various temporary teaching positions at the university. It was during this time that she began to work with Antonio Negri, a former assistant to Opocher, who was on his way to becoming a professor of state doctrine at the Faculty of Political Science. Mariarosa's encounter with Negri entailed her discovery of the works of Marx, especially *The Class Struggles in France from 1848 to 1850* and *Capital*. It also entailed her discovery of factory militancy, which later became the basis of her political work in Porto Marghera. As she recounts in an interview in 2005 in *Derive Approdi*, "This was the experience I had been looking for and which responded to my need to understand and to act . . . method, determination, and passion in wanting to take action to transform the existing situation. These were only three basic elements of that experience, but I found them all in the other territories that I crossed over to in the following periods."

The late 1960s and early 1970s had a deep and longstanding impact on Mariarosa as well as her generation as a whole. The students discovered the workers, the workers discovered the students, and a circuit of intellectuals became involved in these encounters. In short, sites of power were discovered, especially in the university and the factory, but also their mutual relation to a mobile global capital. The experiences of those years were fundamental to Mariarosa's political training and would guide what she considered to be of importance in her activity in the feminist movement.

In the 1970s, she travelled to the United States and Canada on several occasions to deliver lectures at universities and meet with feminist activists. During this time, she turned down a teaching position in New York, at Richmond College, Staten Island, deciding she could not stop the political work she had begun with women's groups in Europe. By the late 1970s, political repression in Italy had effectively silenced the radical political movements of the previous decade. This was certainly true in the case of the radical feminist movement. Demands for wages for housework were either totally ignored or strongly opposed. More broadly, since the 1980s, institutional responses to radical feminist movements have centered upon limiting the scope of gender politics to demands for equal opportunity and anti-discrimination policies. This new dominant 'post-feminist' politics was anathema to the convictions of Wages for Housework activists, who distanced themselves from it definitively. They continued their more radical political enquiry and activity by turning their sights to the analysis of capitalist accumulation and the status of women in the Global South. Indeed, on several occasions, Mariarosa travelled along with others to various countries in the Global South to meet with activists and learn from their struggles. In stark contrast to the turmoil and scope of political activity of the previous period in the Global North, any chance of pursuing radical politics that aimed at making great changes appeared to be over by the 1980s.

Mariarosa's intellectual work and political activity in the 1970s and 1980s was centered upon the concepts of *time* and *money*. She undertook many research projects and engaged in militant study, particularly on the relationship between women and welfare, as well as investigating the connections between women and emigration/immigration, the activity of the women's movement, and labor and social policies. Some of her most important research is her systematic study, published in 1983, of the 1930s in the United States, in which she analyzes the relationship between the emergence of the welfare system and the redefinition of women's role in the urban nuclear family. Her interest in this period was motivated by the fact that (albeit with some significant differences, such as the lack of a public health care system) the 1930s in the United States provides the model of reproduction for the modern family in times of crisis.

From the early 1990s onward, Mariarosa's analysis of the sustained and ongoing attacks on the commons brought another issue to the fore in her research: land and the connected issue of food sovereignty. In her more recent works she has paid considerable attention to the struggles of indigenous people and communities around land, water, and the maintenance of subsistence economies and biodiversity. In the winter of 1992–1993, she travelled to Chiapas, Mexico, where she could already see in the various posters praising the heroes of the epic Zapatista guerrillas warnings and the radical potential of a movement that would explode the following year, on January 1, 1994. One such indication was that as early as 1993 the Maya women had already drafted their Women's Revolutionary Law.

In 1994, Mariarosa was invited to Japan to host a series of conferences on the theme of women and ecology. In Hiroshima she met atomic bomb victims; in Okinawa she met women's groups that were active in the struggle against the exploitation of sex workers around military bases, and who campaigned for compensation for Korean women who had been abducted and forced to provide sex services for Japanese soldiers during the war. Her tour of major Japanese cities provided the opportunity for a fruitful meeting with several European ecofeminist scholars. With these women, including Maria Mies (Germany) and Vandana Shiva (India), Mariarosa spoke at the Women's Day on Food in Rome, a conference that ran parallel to the UN Food and Agriculture Organization's 1996 summit meeting, where Via Campesina launched its program for food sovereignty.[1]

More and more, land (conceptualized within a versatility of meanings) and food policy have become central to Mariarosa's reflections on how social reproduction is organized and structured at a global level. As she points out in various writings, we need to grasp the strategic nature of current global food policies: it is via these policies that a new formula of domination over humanity is being enacted in which capital is able to continuously diminish freedom and self-sufficiency. In contrast to this and to a life that is increasingly a product of the laboratory is the fight to safeguard the sources and cycles of the spontaneous reproduction of life—the first of which are land, water, and seeds. We need to pay urgent attention to the ways that food is produced, starting with the knowledge that food is not just any old commodity. In this way Mariarosa's thinking connects to contemporary political tendencies that call for a universal basic income. She argues that the guarantee of human reproduction cannot reside only in the guarantee of money, even in the form of a guaranteed income. What are we to do with the money if we can only buy poison? It is not a question of just having enough hard currency to buy food on the global market, as argued by those who campaign for 'food security': we should, as Mariarosa argues, exercise food sovereignty as a right to decide what to eat and how to produce it.

The essays collected in this volume also discuss another often neglected issue that Mariarosa has been researching since the 1990s, one that she calls the third great battle that the female body has to face in its maturity, after those of childbirth and abortion: the abuse of hysterectomy. This procedure often means the unjustified castration of the reproductive powers of the 'female body,' just as often happens in the case of the earth. Mariarosa has publicly denounced this abuse in a series of debates with different participants, including doctors and lawyers, which she organized in various Italian cities. With a dedication and force of will that has characterized her political organizing since the late 1960s, she has sought to raise consciousness among women and the medical profession, bringing about considerable positive change on this issue.

In bringing together these essays, we return to the archives of Marxist feminism and to the moments of struggle and the stories of women's resistance that are too often erased from history lessons. Our return to the past is not only to understand the present but also to address the urgent need to find ways to disrupt the continued brutalizing and devastating effects of capitalism. Unlike the forces of reaction, our past is not wrapped up with soft sentimentalities, nor are we nostalgic for a postwar era that never existed. Instead, we return to a defiant and rebellious past, one in which, thankfully, women behaved badly. It is a past in which moments of considerable rupture occurred at the level not only of the political but also of the personal. Women's movements across the world took aim at everything from the nuclear family and idealized motherhood to women's limited employment opportunities and the normalization of sexual violence. Of the vast literature of critique and complaint that women produced in the 1970s, one of the threads historically—one that continues today—that binds women's political and personal lives together is reproductive work: the untold hours of unwaged cleaning, care, sex, and domestic work that produces and reproduces both the possibility of life and the current and future workforce.

Mariarosa's insistence on understanding the tasks, activities, and processes of reproduction as a labor process has been at the heart of considerable feminist debate and continues to animate much of the feminist theory that seeks to understand the role of domesticity and motherhood. The centrality of women's domestic destiny to feminist concerns in the 1970s cannot be overstated. From the women's movement we have inherited a theoretical and political definition of domestic labor. "Women and the Subversion of the Community," written by Mariarosa in 1971, is widely acknowledged as being the spark that initiated the 'domestic labor debate' by redefining housework as work that, while necessary to the functioning of capital, is rendered invisible by its removal from the wage relation. Insofar as the text was influential and provocative at the time of publication, its publication date in the early 1970s intersects with two important historical developments: the emergence of an international women's movement in the years immediately prior to the elections of Margaret Thatcher and Ronald Reagan, and their ascendancy to power in Britain and the United States, which saw the birth of what is now called neoliberalism.

By returning to the politics of reproduction and women's struggles for autonomy over our bodies and lives, another line of inquiry is opened: one that necessitates digging around in older conflicts and histories of capitalism and the wage labor system and tracing the interconnections between waged and unwaged labor in societies dominated by the logics of capitalist social relations. In doing so, it is useful to consider how unwaged reproductive labor and many of the elements that organize reproduction were forged during the long prehistory of capitalism, the period that Marx refers to in volume 1 of *Capital* as 'primitive accumulation.' However, to recognize one's debt and the wealth of inherited knowledge is not to perform the role of the dutiful daughter. Indeed, the definition of reproduction that we have inherited from Marxist feminism is one that critiques orthodox Marxist accounts of the processes of valorization of reproductive labor and draws our attention to some of the specificities of the processes and practices at play in the terrain of reproduction. At the same time that reproductive labor produces and reproduces people, it also produces and reproduces the commodity of labor power—a process that Marxist feminism articulates as the 'dual characteristic of reproduction.' In positing reproduction as possessing a duality, it becomes possible to revalue reproduction and at the same time identify the practices and processes of reproduction as implicated and foundational in the reproduction of capitalist social relations.

Insofar as reproductive work involves working on bodies and relationships, it involves producing and maintaining people. The dual characteristic of reproduction draws our attention to the tensions and contradictions at the center of reproductive processes and practices: a tension that is directly related to what reproduction does within capitalism and how it operates. In societies dominated by capitalist social relations, people are reproduced as workers but, at the same time, as people whose lives, desires, and capabilities exceed the role of 'worker.' People are more than their economic role; they are irreducible to it. People struggle, have conflicts, and at times are capable of resistance. In this way reproductive labor can be said to have two functions: it maintains capitalism, in that it produces the most important commodity of all—labor power—and at the same time has the potential to undermine the smooth flow of accumulation of profit by producing subjects who can and do resist the rule of capitalism.

If we are to confront both the ongoing economic and ecological crisis that continues to bring devastation and harm to millions across the planet and overcome the impasse that feminism faces, we need to reclaim the clarity and courage of women behaving badly. We need to ask ourselves what possibilities exist for radical politics and action, given the global conditions of womanhood and contemporary class composition under neoliberal capitalism. Recent feminist attempts to reimagine what an international women's strike might look like today are just one example of how Mariarosa's analysis of the general strike in the 1970s locates the memory of the past as an essential element of the struggles of the present. The uneven processes of automation and widespread ecological destruction present contemporary terrains of struggle that produce urgent moments of anxiety and vulnerability and new forms of exploitation. We need to take seriously the necessity not only to behave in ungovernable ways but also to bring the politics of reproduction to the center of our plans for a life beyond the brutalizing effects of capitalism. It is hoped that this volume of Mariarosa Dalla Costa's work will contribute to the necessary innovations in feminist modes of thoughts that are needed to make feminism dangerous again.

Camille Barbagallo
London, UK
December 2017

Notes

1   Via Campesina is an international peasants'movement, with an international secretariat based in Harare, Zimbabwe, see *La Via Campesina*, accessed September 17, 2018, https://viacampesina.org/en/.

Preface to the Italian Edition of Women and the Subversion of the Community (March 1972)

Translated by Richard Braude

Mariarosa Dalla Costa at an October 17–20, 1975, conference in Toronto of the WFH network.

t was just over a year ago that the feminist movement began to emerge in Italy. Groups of women began to spring up spontaneously, usually coming from the student movement, as well as through the extraparliamentary left or party politics—or sometimes from among those immune to any kind of 'political activism.'

Their common experience, however, lay in not having found in any of these places—from the student assemblies through the meetings of extraparliamentary groups or political parties to the four walls of the kitchen—any location where their struggle, or their life, was something other than a mere 'appendix.'

This situation was also imposed upon female workers—despite, being, as 'workers,' inscribed into the very definition of the historical subject of exploitation par excellence, the 'working class'—irrespective of the subject claiming to be the organizer of the struggle in the factory.

The confrontation of the female experience with what has passed for Marxism obliges us to analyze of the situation of women in a way that responds not only to the problem of *how* women have been degraded but *why*.

The literature of the feminist movement, after outlining how women are conditioned to be subordinate to men, described the family as a social arena in which the young are forced to accept the discipline of capitalist relations, which from a Marxist point of view begins with labor discipline. Some women have identified the family as the center of consumption, while others have identified housewives as a hidden reserve of labor power. These 'unemployed' women work behind the closed doors of the home until once again called outside when capital needs them.

We agree with all of this, but see it differently: under capitalism, the family is a center of consumption and a reserve of labor power—but first of all it is a *center of production*. When 'Marxists' say that the capitalist family does not produce for capitalism, that it is not a factor in social production, they are effectively rejecting the potential social power of women. Or better still, in assuming that the women at home have no social power, they are unable to conceive of these women as producers. If your production is vital to capitalism, *the refusal to produce*, the refusal to *work*, is a fundamental leveraging of social power.

The commodity that women produce, unlike all other commodities produced under capitalism, is the human being: the worker. Social context is thus not a separate element, an auxiliary of the factory, but is itself *integral* to the capitalist mode of production, which like the factory is ever more regimented, which is why we call it the 'social factory.'

The seclusion of women in the home has historically been and remains greater in Italy than in other industrialized countries. It is precisely this situation that has deteriorated despite the few legislative provisions designed to 'protect' women. The wage in Italy has thus managed to encompass a great deal of 'housework.' Italian capital, more than in other industrialized countries, has 'freed' the man from domestic services and made him available for maximum exploitation in the factory.

For the postwar 'Italian road to socialism' it was understood that the power of women would derive from higher female employment, which in turn would be accompanied by ever increasing democratic freedoms and the inevitable progressive conquest of equality by the female citizen. But in the meantime, this mass of female 'citizens' had to choose between the alternative of endless work in the countryside or moving to the city without any certainty of work.

In the end the least insecure positions were destined for men, while women were routed into the sectors that had been hardest hit by the failing economy, that is, the backward sectors. When they entered the factory, women were the last to be hired and the first to be fired.

The recession of 1963–1964, just like today's, provided useful, salient lessons—but for the bosses more than for the left, insomuch as our planners think they will have *no problem* keeping the ratio of female employment to overall employment low over the coming years.

If women had waited to enter the workplace until they could begin to struggle, there would have been no end to work in the fields, nor the struggle against price hikes, nor squatting. On the other hand, the limited power that women have in confronting the current price hikes only goes to show the general vulnerability of the class in the context of inflation. This is the only way to explain why the Italian working class has been defenseless on a social level when faced with the violence of the recession.

In England and the USA—as is certainly the case with other countries in the West—the women's liberation movement had to fight against the left's refusal to consider any area of struggle that was not in the metropolitan factory.

In Italy, the women's liberation movement, while forging its own autonomy with respect to the left and the student movement, collided with them on an issue that they were apparently also discussing: how to organize the struggle on a social level. The left's proposal for the social struggle was simply the mechanical extension and projection of the factory struggle: the male worker continued to be its central figure. The women's liberation movement considers the social level to be first and foremost *the home*, and thus views the figure of the *woman* as central to social subversion. In this way, women pose themselves as a contradiction to *their* political framework, reopening the entire question of the perspective for political struggle and revolutionary organization.

This time it is the entire female population that is 'coming to its senses,' not so much 'stunned by the noise and turmoil of production,' but rather by the ideological noise of the left around 'production.'[1]

Padua, January 1972

Notes

1   Karl Marx, *Capital: A Critique of Political Economy*, vol. 1 (Harmondsworth: Penguin Books, 1976), chapter 10.

Women and the Subversion of the Community (1972)

Mariarosa Dalla Costa holding a banner at a May 1, 1975, demonstration in Mestre, Venice.

These observations are an attempt to define and analyze the 'Woman Question' and to locate this question in the entire 'female role' as it has been created by the capitalist division of labor. We place foremost in these pages the housewife as the central figure in this female role. We assume that all women are housewives, and that even those who work outside the home continue to be housewives. What is, on a world level, particular to domestic work, not only measured as number of hours and nature of work but as the quality of life and the quality of relationships that it generates, is that it determines a woman's place wherever she is and whatever class she belongs to. We concentrate here on the position of the working-class woman, but this is not to imply that only working-class women are exploited. Rather it is to confirm that the role of the working-class housewife, which we believe has been indispensable to capitalist production, is *the* determinant for the position of all other women. Every analysis of women as a caste must proceed from an analysis of the position of working-class housewives.

In order to see the housewife as central, it is first of all necessary to analyze briefly how capitalism has created the modern family and the housewife's role in it by destroying the types of family group or community that previously existed. This process is by no means complete. While we are speaking of the Western world, and Italy in particular, we wish to make clear that to the extent that the capitalist mode of production also brings the Third World under its command the same process of destruction must be and is taking place there. Nor should we take for granted that the family as we know it today in the most technically advanced Western countries is the final form the family can assume under capitalism. But the analysis of new tendencies can only be the product of an analysis of how capitalism created this family and what woman's role is today, each as a moment in a process.

We will complete our observations on the female role by also analyzing the position of the woman who works outside the home, but this is for a later date. We wish merely to indicate here the link between two apparently separate experiences: that of housewife and that of working woman.

The day-to-day struggles of women since World War II run counter to the organization of both the factory and the home. The 'unreliability' of women both in the home and outside of it has grown rapidly since then, and directly opposes the factory as regimentation organized in time and space and the social factory as organizational form of the reproduction of labor power. This trend toward more absenteeism, less respect for timetables, and higher job mobility is shared by young men and women workers alike. But where the man for crucial periods of his youth will be the sole support of a new family, women who on the whole are not restrained in this way, and who must always consider the job at home, are bound to be even more disengaged from work discipline, forcing disruption of the productive flow and therefore higher costs for capital. This is one excuse for the discriminatory wages that make up for capital's loss many times over. It is this same trend of disengagement that groups of housewives express when they leave their children with their husbands at work.[1] This trend is and will increasingly be one of the decisive forms of the crisis in the systems of the factory and of the social factory.

•

In recent years, especially in the advanced capitalist countries, there have developed a number of women's movements of different orientations and ranges, from those that believe the fundamental conflict in society is between men and women to those focusing on the position of women as a specific manifestation of class exploitation.

If at first sight the position and attitudes of the former are perplexing, especially to women who have previously participated in militant political struggles, it is, we think, worth pointing out that women for whom sexual exploitation is the basic social contradiction provide an extremely important index of the degree of frustration experienced by millions of women both inside and outside the movement. There are those who define their own lesbianism in these terms. Here we refer to views expressed by a section of the movement in the U.S. in particular: "Our associations with women began when, because we were together, we could acknowledge that we could no longer tolerate relationships with men, that we could not prevent these from becoming power relationships in which we were inevitably subjected. Our attentions and energies were diverted, our power was diffused and its objectives delimited." This rejection constitutes the basis for a movement of gay women that asserts the possibility of relationships free of a sexual power struggle and of the biological social unit, while at the same time asserting our need to open ourselves to a wider social and therefore sexual potential.

Now, in order to understand the frustrations women are expressing in ever increasing forms, we must make clear what in the nature of the family under capitalism precipitated a crisis on this scale. The oppression of women, after all, did not begin with capitalism. What began with capitalism was both the more intense exploitation of women as women and the possibility at last of their liberation.

The Origins of the Family under Capitalism

In precapitalist patriarchal society, *the home and the family* were central to agricultural and artisanal production. With the advent of capitalism, the socialization of production was organized with *the factory* at its center. Those who worked in the new productive center, the factory, received a wage. Those who were excluded did not. Women, children, and the aged lost the relative power that derived from the family's dependence on their labor, *which was seen to be social and necessary*. Capital, destroying the family, the community, and production as a whole, on the one hand, has concentrated basic social production in the factory and the office and, on the other, has in essence detached the man from the family and turned him into a *wage laborer*. It has put on the man's shoulders the burden of financial responsibility for women, children, the old, and the ill: in a word, all those who do not receive wages. That marked the beginning of the expulsion from the home of all those who did not *procreate and service those who worked for wages*. After men, the first to be excluded from the home were children; they were sent to school. The family not only ceased to be the productive but also the educational center.[2]

To the extent that men had been the despotic heads of the patriarchal family, based on a strict division of labor, the experiences of women, children, and men are the contradictory experiences that we inherit. But in precapitalist society the work of each member of the community of serfs was seen to be directed to a purpose: either to the prosperity of the feudal lord or to our survival. To this extent the whole community of serfs was compelled to be cooperative in a unity of unfreedom that involved to the same degree women, children, and men, cooperation that capitalism had to break.[3] In this sense the *unfree individual* and *the democracy of unfreedom*[4] entered into a crisis. The passage from serfdom to free labor power separated the male from the female proletarian and both of them from their children. The unfree patriarch was transformed into the 'free' wage earner, and upon the contradictory experience of the sexes and the generations was built a more profound estrangement and, therefore, a more subversive relation.

We must stress that this separation of children from adults is essential to an understanding of the full significance of the separation of women from men, to grasp fully how the organization of the struggle on the part of the women's movement, even when it takes the form of a violent rejection of any possibility of relations with men, can only aim to overcome the separation that is based on the 'freedom' of wage labor.

The Class Struggle in Education

The analysis of the school that has emerged during recent years, particularly with the advent of the students' movement, has clearly identified the school as a center of ideological discipline and of the shaping of the labor force and its masters. What has perhaps never emerged, or at least not in its profundity, is precisely what precedes all this; the usual desperation of children on their first day of nursery school, when they see themselves dumped into a class and their parents suddenly desert them. *But it is precisely at this point that the whole story of school begins.*[5]

Seen in this way, elementary school children are not those append-ages who, merely by the demands for 'free lunches, free fares, free books' learned from the older ones, can in some way be united with the students in the higher schools.[6] In elementary school children, in those who are the sons and daughters of workers, there is always an awareness that school is in some way setting them against their parents and their peers, and conse-quently there is an instinctive resistance to studying and to being 'educated.' This is the resistance for which black children are confined to educationally subnormal schools in Britain.[7] The European working-class child, like the black working-class child, sees in the teacher somebody who is teaching her something against her mother and father, not as a defense of the child but as an attack on the class. Capitalism is the first productive system where the children of the exploited are disciplined and educated in institutions organized and controlled by the ruling class.[8]

The final proof that this alien indoctrination that begins in nursery school is based on the splitting of the family is that those (few) working-class children who arrive at university are so brainwashed that they are no longer able to talk to their community.

Working-class children are the first who instinctively rebel against schools and the education provided in schools. But their parents carry them to schools and confine them to schools because they are concerned that their children should 'have an education,' that is, be equipped to escape the assembly line or the kitchen to which they, the parents, are confined. If a working-class child shows particular aptitudes, the whole family immediately concentrates on this child, gives him the best conditions, often sacrificing the others, hoping and gambling that he will carry them all out of the working class. This in effect is the way capital moves through the aspirations of the parents to enlist their help in disciplining fresh labor power.

In Italy parents are less and less successful in sending their children to school. Children's resistance to school is constantly increasing, even when this resistance is not yet organized. At the same time that the resistance of children to being educated in schools grows, so does *their refusal to accept the definition* that capital has given of their *age*. Children want everything they see; they do not yet understand that in order to have things one must pay for them, and in order to pay for them one must have a wage, and therefore one must also be an adult. No wonder it is not easy to explain to children why they cannot have what television has told them they cannot live without.

But something is happening among the new generation of children and youth that is making it steadily more difficult to explain to them the arbitrary point at which they reach adulthood. Rather the younger generation is demonstrating their age to us: in the 1960s, six-year-olds have already come up against police dogs in the South of the United States. Today we find the same phenomenon in southern Italy and Northern Ireland, where children have been as active in the revolt as adults. When children (and women) are recognized as integral to history, no doubt other examples will come to light of very young people's (and of women's) participation in revolutionary struggles. What is new is the autonomy of their participation, *in spite of, and because of,* their exclusion from direct production. In the factories youths refuse the leadership of older workers, and in the revolts in the cities they are the diamond point. In the metropolis generations of the nuclear family have produced youth and student movements that have initiated the process of shaking the framework of constituted power; in the Third World unemployed youth are often in the streets before the working class organized in trade unions.

It is worth recording what the *Times of London* (June 1, 1971) reported concerning a head teachers' meeting called because one of them was admonished for hitting a pupil: "Disruptive and irresponsible elements lurk around every corner with the seemingly planned intention of eroding all forces of authority." This "is a plot to destroy the values on which our civilization is built and of which our schools are some of the finest bastions."

The Exploitation of the Wageless

We wanted to make these few comments on the attitude of revolt that is steadily spreading among children and youth, especially from the working class, and particularly black people, because we believe this to be intimately connected with the explosion of the women's movement and that it is something that the women's movement must take into account. We are dealing here with the revolt of those who have been excluded, who have been separated by the system of production, and who express in action their need to destroy the forces that stand in the way of their social existence, but who this time are coming together as individuals.

Women and children have been excluded. The revolt of the one against exploitation through exclusion is an index of the revolt of the other. To the extent that capital has recruited the man and turned him into a wage laborer, it has created a fracture between him and all the other proletarians without a wage who, not participating directly in social production, were thus presumed incapable of being the subjects of social revolt.

Since Marx, it has been clear that capital rules and develops through the wage, that is, that the foundation of capitalist society was the wage laborer and his or her direct exploitation. What has been neither clear nor understood by the working-class organizations is that it is precisely through the wage that the exploitation of the non-wage laborer is organized. This exploitation has been even more effective because the lack of a wage hides it. That is, the wage pays for more labor than factory bargaining makes obvious. *Where women are concerned, their labor appears to be a personal service outside of capital.* The woman seems only to be suffering from male chauvinism, being pushed around because capitalism meant general 'injustice' and 'bad and unreasonable behavior'; the few (men) who noticed convinced us that this was 'oppression' but not exploitation. But 'oppression' hid another and more pervasive aspect of capitalist society. Capital excluded children from the home and sent them to school not only because they are in the way of others' more 'productive' labor nor only to indoctrinate them. The rule of capital through the wage compels every able-bodied person to function under the law of division of labor, and to function in ways that are if not immediately then ultimately profitable to the expansion and extension of the rule of capital. That is the fundamental meaning of school. *Where children are concerned, their labor appears to be learning for their own benefit.*

Proletarian children have been forced to undergo the same education in the schools: this is capitalist levelling against the infinite possibilities of learning. Woman on the other hand has been isolated in the home, forced to carry out work that is considered unskilled, the work of giving birth to, raising, disciplining, and servicing the worker for production. Her role in the cycle of social production remained invisible because only the product of her labor, *the laborer*, is visible. She herself is thereby trapped within precapitalist working conditions and never paid a wage.

And when we say 'precapitalist working conditions' we do not refer only to women who have to use brooms to sweep. Even the best equipped American kitchens do not reflect the present level of technological development; at most they reflect the technology of the nineteenth century. If you are not paid by the hour, within certain limits, nobody cares how long it takes you to do your work.

This is not only a *quantitative* but also a *qualitative* difference from other work, and it stems precisely from the kind of commodity that this work is destined to produce. Within the capitalist system generally, the productivity of labor doesn't increase unless there is a confrontation between capital and class: technological innovations and cooperation are at the same time moments of attack for the working class and moments of capitalistic response. But if this is true for the production of commodities generally, this has not been true for the production of that special kind of commodity, labor power. If technological innovation can lower the limit of necessary work, and if the working-class struggle in industry can use that innovation for gaining free hours, the same cannot be said of housework; to the extent that she must procreate, raise, and be responsible for children in isolation, a high mechanization of domestic chores doesn't free any time for the woman. She is always on duty, for the machine doesn't exist that makes and minds children.[9] A higher productivity of domestic work through mechanization, then, can be related only to specific services, for example, cooking, washing, cleaning. Her workday is unending not because she does not have machines but because she is isolated.[10]

Confirming the Myth of Female Incapacity

With the advent of the capitalist mode of production, women were relegated to a condition of isolation, enclosed within the family cell, dependent in every aspect on men. The new autonomy of the free wage slave was denied to her, and she remained in a precapitalist stage of personal dependence, but this time more brutalized, because her situation contrasted with the prevailing large-scale highly socialized production. Woman's apparent incapacity to do certain things, to understand certain things, originated in her history, which is a history very similar in certain respects to that of 'backward' children in special educational needs classes. To the extent that women were cut off from direct socialized production and isolated in the home, all possibilities of social life outside the neighborhood were denied them, and hence they were deprived of social knowledge and social education. When women are deprived of wide experience of organizing and collectively planning industrial and other mass struggles, they are denied a basic source of education, the experience of social revolt. And this experience is primarily the experience of learning your own capacities, that is, your power, and the capacities, the power, of your class. Thus, the isolation from which women have suffered has confirmed to society and to them the myth of female incapacity.

First, this myth has hidden the fact that to the degree that the working class has been able to organize mass struggles in the community, rent strikes, and struggles against inflation generally, the basis has always been the unceasing informal organization of women; second, in struggles in the cycle of direct production, women's support and organization, formal and informal, has been decisive. At critical moments this unceasing network of women surfaces and develops through the talent, energy, and strength of the incapable female. But the myth does not die. Where women could join the men in claiming victory—to survive (during unemployment) or to survive and win (during strikes)—the spoils of the victor belonged to the class 'in general.' Women rarely if ever got anything specifically for themselves; rarely if ever did the struggle have as an objective in any way altering the power structure of the home and its relation to the factory. Strike or unemployment, a woman's work is never done.

The Capitalist Function of the Uterus

Never as with the advent of capitalism has the destruction of the woman as a person also meant the immediate diminution of her *physical integrity*. Before the emergence of capitalism, feminine and masculine sexuality had already undergone a series of regimes and forms of conditioning. Previously there had also been efficient methods of birth control, which have unaccountably disappeared. Capital established the family as the nuclear family and within it subordinated the woman to the man, as the person who, not directly participating in social production, does not present herself independently on the labor market. Just as it cuts off her possibilities for creativity and the development of her working activity, it also cuts off the expression of her sexual, psychological, and emotional autonomy.

We repeat: never before had such a stunting of the physical integrity of woman taken place, affecting everything from the brain to the uterus. Participating with others in the production of a train, a car, or an airplane is not the same thing as using the same broom in the same few square feet of kitchen in isolation for centuries.

This is not a call for equality of men and women in the construction of airplanes; it is merely to assume that the difference between the two histories not only determines the differences in the actual forms of struggle but also finally brings to light what has been invisible for so long—the different forms women's struggles have assumed in the past. In the same way as women are robbed of the possibility of developing their creative capacity, they are robbed of their sex life, which has been transformed into a function for reproducing labor power: the same observations that we made on the technological level of domestic services apply to birth control (and, by the way, to the whole field of gynecology)—research into which until recently has been continually neglected, while women have been forced to have children, being forbidden the right to have abortions when, as was to be expected, the most primitive techniques of birth control failed.

From this complete diminution of woman, capital constructed the female role and has made the man of the family the instrument of this reduction. The man as wageworker and head of the family was the specific instrument of this particular exploitation, the exploitation of women.

The Homosexuality of the Division of Labor

In this sense, we can explain to what extent the degraded relationships between men and women are determined by the rift that society has imposed between man and woman, subordinating woman as object, the 'complement' of man. And in this sense, we can see the validity of the explosion of tendencies within the women's movement in which women want to conduct the struggle against men as such[11] and no longer even wish to use their strength to sustain sexual relationships with them, since these relationships are always frustrating. A power relation precludes any possibility of affection and intimacy. Yet, between men and women, power with its prescriptions *commands* sexual affection and intimacy. In this sense, the gay movement is the most massive attempt to disengage sexuality and power.

But homosexuality generally is, at the same time, rooted in the framework of capitalist society itself: women at home and men in factories and offices, separated one from the other for the whole day; or a typical factory of one thousand women with ten foremen; or a typing pool (of women, of course) which works for fifty professional men. All these situations are already a homosexual framework of living.

Capital, while it elevates heterosexuality to a religion, at the same time makes it impossible for men and women to be in touch with each other; physically and emotionally it undermines heterosexuality except as a sexual, economic, and social discipline.

We believe that this is a reality from which we must begin. The explosions of the gay tendencies have been and are important for the movement precisely because they pose the urgency to claim for itself the specificity of women's struggle and, above all, to clarify in all their depths all facets and connections of the exploitation of women.

Surplus Value and the Social Factory

At this point we would like to begin to clear the ground of a certain point of view that orthodox Marxism, especially in the ideology and practice of so-called Marxist parties, has always taken for granted. And this is the idea that when women remain outside social production, that is, outside the socially organized productive cycle, they are also outside social production. The role of women, in other words, has always been seen as that of a psychologically subordinated person who, except where she is marginally employed outside the home, is outside of production; essentially a supplier of a series of use values in the home. This basically was the viewpoint of Marx, who, observing what happened to women working in the factories, concluded that it would have been better for them to be at home, where resided a morally higher form of life. But the true nature of the role of housewife never emerges clearly in Marx. Yet observers have noted that Lancashire women, cotton workers for over a century, are more sexually free and receive more help from men in domestic chores. On the other hand, in the Yorkshire coal mining districts where a lower percentage of women worked outside the home, women are more dominated by the figure of the husband. Even those who have been able to define the exploitation of women in socialized production were unable to then go on to understand the exploited position of women in the home; men are too compromised in their relationship with women. For that reason, only women can define themselves and move on the woman question.

We have to make clear that within the wage domestic work not only produces use value but is essential to the production of surplus value.[12] This is true of the entire female role as a person who is subordinated at all levels—physical, psychological, and occupational—and who has had and continues to have a precise and vital place in the capitalist division of labor and in the pursuit of productivity at the social level. Let us examine more specifically the role of women as a source of social productivity, that is, of surplus value—first, within the family.

Part A: The Productivity of Wage Slavery Based on Unwaged Slavery

It is often asserted that within the definition of wage labor women in domestic labor are not productive. In fact, precisely the opposite is true if one thinks of the enormous amount of social service that capitalist organization transforms into privatized activity, putting it on the backs of housewives. Domestic labor is not essentially 'feminine work'; a woman doesn't fulfil herself more or get less exhausted than a man from washing and cleaning. These are social services inasmuch as they serve the reproduction of labor power. And capital, precisely by instituting its family structure, has 'liberated' the man from these functions so that he is completely 'free' for direct exploitation; so that he is free to 'earn' enough for a woman to reproduce him as labor power.[13] It has made men wage slaves to the degree that it has succeeded in allocating these services to women in the family, while at the same time controlling the flow of women onto the labor market. In Italy, women are still necessary in the home and capital still needs this form of the family. At the present level of development in Europe generally, and in Italy in particular, capital still prefers to import labor power in the form of millions of men from underdeveloped areas—while consigning women to the home.[14]

And women are of service not only because they carry out domestic labor *without a wage and without going on strike*, but also because they always receive back into the home all those who are periodically expelled from their jobs by economic crisis. The family, a maternal cradle that is always ready to help and protect in time of need, has been in fact the best guarantee that the unemployed do not immediately become a horde of disruptive outsiders.

The organized parties of the working-class movement have been careful not to raise the question of domestic work. Aside from the fact that they have always treated women as a lower subject, even in the factories, to raise this question would be to challenge the whole basis of the trade unions as organizations that deal (a) only with the factory; (b) only with a measured and 'paid' work day; (c) only with that side of wages that is given to us and not with the side of wages which is taken back, that is, inflation. Women have always been forced by the working-class parties to put off their liberation until some hypothetical future, making them dependent on the gains that men, limited in the scope of their struggles by these parties, win for 'themselves.'

In reality, every phase of working-class struggle has cemented the subordination and exploitation of women at a higher level. The proposal of pensions for housewives[15] (and this makes us wonder why not a wage) serves only to show the complete willingness of these parties to further institutionalize women as housewives and men (and women) as wage slaves.

Now it is clear that not one of us believes that emancipation can be achieved through work. Work is still work, whether inside or outside the home. The independence of the wage earner means only being a 'free individual' for capital, no less for women than for men. Those who advocate that the liberation of the working-class woman lies in her getting a job outside the home are part of the problem not the solution. Slavery to an assembly line is not a liberation from slavery to a kitchen sink. To deny this is also to deny the slavery of the assembly line itself, proving again that if you don't know how women are exploited, you can never really know how men are. But this question is so crucial that we will deal with it separately. What we wish to make clear here is that when we produce in a capitalistically organized world and are not paid a wage, the figure of the boss is concealed behind that of the husband. He appears to be the sole recipient of domestic services, and this gives an ambiguous and slave-like character to housework. The husband and children, through their loving involvement and their loving blackmail, become the first foremen, the immediate controllers of this labor.

The husband tends to read the paper and wait for his dinner to be cooked and served, even when his wife goes out to work as he does and comes home with him. Clearly, the specific form of exploitation represented by domestic work demands a corresponding specific form of struggle, namely, women's struggle, *within the family.*

If we fail to grasp completely that it is precisely this family that is the very pillar of the capitalist organization of work, if we make the mistake of regarding it only as a superstructure, dependent for change only on the stages of the struggle in the factories, then we will be moving in a limping revolution—one that will always perpetuate and *aggravate a basic contradiction in the class struggle, and a contradiction that is functional to capitalist development.* We would, in other words, be perpetuating the error of considering ourselves as producers of use value only and the error of considering housewives external to the working class. As long as housewives are considered external to the class, the class struggle at every moment and any point is impeded, frustrated, and unable to find full scope for its action. To elaborate this further is not our task here. To expose and condemn domestic work as a masked form of productive labor, however, raises a series of questions concerning both the aims and the forms of women's struggle.

Socializing the Struggle of the Isolated Laborer

In fact, the demand that would follow, namely, "pay us wages for housework," would run the risk of looking, in the light of the present balance of power in Italy, as though we wanted further to entrench the conditions of institutionalized slavery that are produced with the condition of housework, and therefore such a demand could scarcely operate in practice as a mobilizing goal.[16]

The issue is, therefore, to develop forms of struggle that do not leave the housewife peacefully at home, at most ready to take part in occasional demonstrations in the streets, waiting for a wage that would never pay for anything; rather we must discover forms of struggle that immediately break the whole structure of domestic work, rejecting it absolutely, rejecting our role as housewives and the home as the ghetto of our existence, since the problem is not only to stop doing this work but to smash the entire role of housewife. *The starting point is not how to do housework more efficiently but how to find a place as protagonists in the struggle: that is, not a higher productivity of domestic labor but a higher subversiveness in the struggle.*

We must immediately overthrow the relationship between 'time given to housework' and 'time not given to housework': it is not necessary to spend time each day ironing sheets and curtains, cleaning the floor until it sparkles, or dusting. And yet many women still do. Obviously, it is not because they are stupid: once again we are reminded of the parallel we drew earlier with the special educational needs schools. In reality, it is only in this work that they can realize an identity, precisely because, as we said before, capital has cut them off from the process of socially organized production.

But it does not automatically follow that to be cut off from socialized production is to be cut off from socialized struggle: struggle, however, demands time away from housework, and at the same time it offers an alternative identity to the woman who before found it only at the level of the domestic ghetto. In the sociality of struggle women discover and exercise a power that effectively gives them a new identity. *The new identity is and can only be a new degree of social power.*

The possibility of social struggle arises out of the *socially productive character* of women's work in the home. It is not only or mainly the social services provided in the home that make women's role socially productive, even though at this moment these services are in fact identified with women's role. But capital can technologically improve the conditions of this work. What capital does not want to do for the time being, in Italy at least, is to destroy the pivotal role of the housewife in the nuclear family. For this reason, there is no point in our waiting for the automation of domestic work, because this will never happen: the maintenance of the nuclear family is incompatible with 'the automation of these services.' To really automate them, capital would have to destroy the family as we know it; that is, it would be driven to *socialize* in order to *automate* fully. But we know all too well what their socialization means: it is always at the very least the opposite of the Paris Commune!

The new leap that capitalist reorganization could make, and one that we can already smell in the United States and in the more advanced capitalist countries generally, is to destroy the precapitalist isolation of production in the home by constructing a family that more closely reflects capitalist equality and its domination through cooperative labor. In doing so, capital could transcend 'the incompleteness of capitalist development' in the home, with the precapitalist, unfree woman as its pivot, and instead make the family more closely reflect its capitalist productive function, which is the reproduction of labor power.

To return then to what we said above: women as housewives, identifying themselves with the home, tend to a compulsive perfection in their work. We all know the saying too well; you can always find work to do in a house.

They don't see beyond their own four walls. The housewife's situation as a precapitalist mode of labor, and consequently this 'femininity' imposed upon her, makes her see the world, the others, and the entire organization of work as a something that is obscure, essentially unknown and unknowable; not lived; perceived only as a shadow behind the shoulders of the husband who goes out each day and meets this something. So when we say that women must overthrow the relation of 'domestic work time' to 'non-domestic time' and must begin to move out of the home, we mean their point of departure must be precisely this willingness to destroy the role of housewife, in order to begin to come together with other women, not only as neighbors and friends but as workmates and anti-workmates; thus breaking the tradition of the privatized female, with all its rivalry, and reconstructing a real solidarity among women: not solidarity for defense but solidarity for attack and for the organization of the struggle—a common solidarity against a common form of labor. In the same way, women must stop meeting their husbands and children only as wife and mother, that is, at mealtimes after they have come home from the outside world.

Precisely because *every sphere of capitalist organization presupposes the home*, every place of struggle outside the home offers a chance for attack by women; factory meetings, neighborhood meetings, and student assemblies are all legitimate places for women's struggle, places where women can encounter and confront men—women versus men, if you like, but as individuals, rather than mother-father or son-daughter, with all the possibilities this offers to blow open the contradictions outside of the home, the frustrations that capital had wanted to see implode within the family.

A New Compass for Class Struggle

If women demand in workers' assemblies that the night shift be abolished because at night, besides sleeping, one wants to make love—and it's not the same as making love during the day if the women work during the day—they would be advancing their own independent interests as women against the social organization of work, refusing to be unsatisfied mothers for their husbands and children.

But in this new intervention and confrontation women are also saying that their interests as women are not, as they have been told, separate and alien from the interests of the class. For too long political parties, especially of the left, and trade unions have determined and confined the areas of working-class struggle. To make love and to refuse night work so as to be able to make love *is the interest of the class.* To explore why it is women and not men who raise the question is to shed new light on the whole history of the class.

To meet your sons and daughters at a student assembly is to discover them as individuals who speak with other individuals; it is to present yourself to them as an individual. Many women have had abortions and very many have given birth. We can't see why they should not express their point of view as women first in an assembly of medical students, whether or not they are students. (We do not give the medical faculty as an example by accident. In the lecture hall and in the clinic, we can see once more the exploitation of the working class, and not only when it is exclusively the third-class patients who are made the guinea pigs for research. Women especially are the prime objects of experimentation and also of the sexual contempt, sadism, and the professional arrogance of doctors.)

To sum up: the most important thing becomes precisely this explosion of the women's movement as an expression of the specificity of female interests hitherto castrated from all its connections by the capitalist organization of the family. This struggle has to be waged in every quarter of this society, each of which is founded precisely on the suppression of such interests, since the entire class exploitation has been built upon the specific mediation of women's exploitation. And so as a women's movement we must pinpoint every single area in which this exploitation takes place, that is, we must regain the whole specificity of the female interest in the course of waging the struggle.

Every opportunity is a good one: housewives of families threatened with eviction can object that their housework has more than covered the rent of the months they didn't pay. On the outskirts of Milan, many families have already taken up this form of struggle. Electric appliances in the home are lovely things to have, but the workers who mass produce them must spend their time and wear themselves out doing so. That every wage has to buy all of them creates difficulties, and it presumes that every wife must be the sole user all her appliances; this only means that she is stuck in the home, but now on a more mechanized level. Lucky worker, lucky wife!

However, the issue is not to have communal canteens. We must remember that capital makes Fiat for the workers before the canteen. For this reason, to demand a communal canteen in the neighborhood without integrating this demand into a practice of struggle against the organization of labor, against labor time, risks giving the impetus for a new leap that, on the community level, would regiment none other than women into some alluring work, which would create the option for us to eat a bad meal together at lunchtime in the canteen.

We want them to know that this is not the canteen we want, nor do we want play centers or nurseries of the same order.[17] We want canteens and nurseries and washing machines and dishwashers, but we also want choices: to eat in privacy with a few people when we want, to have time to be with children, to be with the old people, with the sick, when and where we choose. To 'have time' means to work less. To have time to be with the children, the old, and the sick does not mean running to pay a quick visit to the garages where you park children, old people, and invalids. It means that we, the first to be excluded, are taking the initiative in this struggle so that all those other excluded people, the children, the old, and the ill, can reappropriate social wealth; to be reintegrated with each other and all of us with men, not as dependents but autonomously—as we women want for ourselves—since, like ours, their exclusion from the directly productive social process and from social existence has been created by capitalist organization.

The Refusal of Work

Hence, we must refuse housework as women's work, as work imposed upon us, which we didn't invent, which has never been paid for, and in which they have forced us to cope with an absurd number of hours of work, twelve or thirteen a day, in order keep us at home.

We must get out of the house; we must reject the home, so we can unite with other women to struggle against any situation that presumes that women will stay at home and to link ourselves to the struggles of all those who live in ghettos, whether that ghetto is a nursery, a school, a hospital, an old-age home, or a slum. To abandon the home is already a form of struggle, since the social services we provide would then cease to be carried out under these conditions, and all those who work out of the home would then demand that the burden carried by us until now be thrown squarely where it belongs—onto the shoulders of capital. This alteration in the terms of struggle will be all the more violent the more the refusal of domestic labor on the part of women is violent, determined, and on a mass scale.

The working-class family is more difficult to break through, because it supports the worker, but as worker, and for that reason it also supports capital. The support of the class, the very survival of the class, depends on the working-class family—but *at the woman's expense and against the class itself*. The woman is the slave of a wage slave, and her slavery ensures the slavery of her man. Like the trade union, the family protects the worker, while ensuring that he or she will never be anything but a worker. And that is why the struggle of the woman of the working class against the family is so crucial.

To meet other women who work inside and outside their homes provides us with other opportunities to struggle. To the extent that our struggle is a struggle against work, it is inscribed in the struggle that the working class wages against capitalist work. But to the extent that the exploitation of women through domestic work has had its own specific history, tied to the survival of the nuclear family, the specific course of this struggle must therefore pass through the destruction of the nuclear family as established by the capitalist social order, and this adds a new dimension to the class struggle.

Part B: The Productivity of Passivity

However, the woman's role in the family is not only that of a hidden supplier of social services who does not receive a wage. As we said at the beginning, the imprisonment of women in a purely complementary role and subordinate to men within the nuclear family has been premised on the stunting of their physical integrity. In Italy, with the successful help of the Catholic Church, which has always defined her as an inferior being, a woman is compelled before marriage into sexual abstinence and after marriage into a repressed sexuality destined only to bear children and obliging her to do so. It has created a female image of 'heroic mother and happy wife' whose sexual identity is pure sublimation, whose function is essentially that of receptacle for other people's emotional expression, and who is the cushion for familial antagonism. What has been defined, then, as female frigidity has to be redefined as an imposed passive receptivity in the sexual function as well.

Now this passivity of the woman in the family is itself 'productive.' First, it makes her the outlet for all the oppressions that men suffer in the world outside the home and at the same time the object on whom the man can exercise a hunger for power that the domination of the capitalist organization of work implants in him. In this sense, the woman becomes productive for capitalist organization by acting as a safety valve for the social tensions it causes. Second, the woman becomes productive inasmuch as the complete denial of her personal autonomy forces her to sublimate her frustration in a series of continuous needs that are always centered in the home, a kind of consumption that is the exact parallel of her compulsive perfectionism in her housework. Clearly, it is not our job to tell women what they should have in their homes. Nobody can define the needs of others. Our interest is to organize the struggle that will make this sublimation unnecessary.

Dead Labor and the Agony of Sexuality

We use the word 'sublimation' advisedly. The frustrations of monotonous and trivial chores and of sexual passivity are only separable in words. Sexual creativity and creativity in labor are both areas where human need demands we give free scope to our "interplaying natural and acquired activities."[18] For women (and therefore men) natural and acquired powers are repressed simultaneously. The passive sexual receptivity of women creates the compulsively tidy housewife and can make a monotonous assembly line therapeutic. The trivia of most of housework and the discipline that is required to perform the same work over and over every day, every week, every year, double on holidays, destroys the possibilities of uninhibited sexuality. Our childhood is a preparation for martyrdom: we are taught to derive happiness from clean sex on whiter than white sheets—to sacrifice sexuality and other creative activity at one and the same time.

So far the women's movement has exposed the physical mechanism that allowed women's sexual potential to be strictly defined and limited by men, most notably by destroying the myth of the vaginal orgasm. Now we can begin to reintegrate sexuality with other aspects of creativity, to see that sexuality will always be constrained unless the work we do does not mutilate us and our individual capacities and unless the persons with whom we have sexual relations are not our masters and are not also mutilated by their work. To explode the vaginal orgasm myth is to demand female autonomy as opposed to subordination and sublimation. But it is not only the clitoris versus the vagina. It is both versus the uterus. Either the vagina is primarily the passage for the reproduction of labor power sold as a commodity, the capitalist function of the uterus, or it is part of our natural powers, our social equipment. Sexuality after all is the most social of expressions, the deepest human communication. It is in that sense the dissolution of autonomy. The working class organizes as a class to transcend itself as a class; within that class we organize autonomously to create the basis to transcend autonomy.

The 'Political' Attack against Women

But while we are finding our way of being and of organizing ourselves in struggle, we discover we are confronted by those who are only too eager to attack women, even as we form a movement. In defending herself against obliteration through work and through consumption, they say the woman is responsible for the lack of unity of the class. Let us make a partial list of the sins of which she stands accused. They say:

1. She wants more of her husband's wages to buy clothes for herself and her children, for example, not based on what he thinks she needs but on what she thinks she and her children deserve. He works hard for the money. She only demands a different distribution of their lack of wealth, rather than assisting his struggle for more wealth, for higher wages.

2. She is in a rivalry with other women to be more attractive, to have more things, and to have a cleaner and tidier house than her neighbors. She doesn't ally with them as she should on a class basis.

3. She buries herself in her home and refuses to understand the struggle of her husband on the production line. She may even complain when he goes out on strike rather than backing him up. She votes Conservative.

These are some of the reasons given by those who consider her reactionary, or at best backward, even by men who take leading roles in factory struggles and who seem to be the more able to understand the nature of the social boss because of their militant action. It comes easy to them to condemn women for what they consider to be backwardness, because that is the prevailing ideology of the society. They do not add that they have benefited from women's subordinate position by being waited on hand and foot from the moment of their birth. Some do not even know that they have been waited on, so natural is it to them for mothers and sisters and daughters to serve 'their' men. It is very difficult for us, on the other hand, to separate inbred male supremacy from men's attack, which appears to be strictly 'political,' launched only for the benefit of the class.

Let's look at the matter more closely.

Women as Consumers

Women do not make the home the center of consumption. The process of consumption is integral to the production of labor power, and if women refused to do the shopping (that is, to spend), this would be strike action. Having said that, however, we must add that that women often try to compensate for the relationships they are denied by being cut off from socially organized labor by buying things. Whether it is adjudged trivial depends on the viewpoint and sex of the judge. Intellectuals buy books, but no one calls this consumption trivial. Independent of the validity of the contents, the book in this society still represents, through a tradition older than capitalism, a male value.

We have already said that women buy things for their home because that home is the only proof that they exist. But the idea that frugal consumption is in any way a liberation is as old as capitalism and comes from the capitalists who always blame the worker's situation on the worker. For years Harlem was told by headshaking liberals that if black men would only stop driving Cadillacs (until the finance company took them back), the problem of color would be solved. Until the violence of the struggle—the only fitting reply—provided a measure of social power, that Cadillac was one of the few ways to display the potential for power. *This* and not 'practical economics' caused the liberals pain. In any case, we would not need any of the things any of us buys if we were free. Not the food they poison for us, not the clothes that identify us by class, sex, and generation, not the houses in which they imprison us.

In any case, our problem is also that we never have enough not that we have too much. And that pressure that women place on men is a *defense of the wage not an attack*. Precisely because women are the slaves of wage slaves, men divide the wage between themselves and the general family expense. If women did not make demands, the general family standard of living could drop to absorb inflation—and the woman of course is the first to do without. Thus, unless the woman makes demands, the family is functional for capital in an additional way we have not yet listed: it can absorb the fall in the price of labor power.[19] This, therefore, is the most ongoing material way in which women can defend the living standards of the class. And when they go out to political meetings, they need even more money!

Women as Rivals

As for women's 'rivalry', Frantz Fanon has clarified for the Third World what racism prevents from being generally applied to the class. The colonized, he says, when they do not organize against their oppressors, attack each other. The woman's pressure for greater consumption may at times express itself in the form of rivalry but, nevertheless, as we have said, protects the living standards of the class. This is unlike women's sexual rivalry, a rivalry that is rooted in their economic and social dependence on men. To the degree that they live for men, dress for men, work for men, they are manipulated by men through this rivalry.[20]

As for rivalry about their homes, women are trained from birth to be obsessive and possessive about clean and tidy homes. But men cannot have it both ways; they cannot continue to enjoy the privilege of having a private servant and then complain about the effects of privatization. If they continue to complain, we must conclude that their attack on us for the rivalry is really an apology for our servitude. If Fanon was not right that the strife among the colonized is an expression of their low level of organization, then the antagonism is a sign of natural incapacity. When we call a home a ghetto, we could call it a colony governed by indirect rule and be as accurate. The resolution of the antagonism of the colonized toward each other lies in autonomous struggle. Women have overcome greater obstacles than rivalry to unite in supporting men in struggles. Where women have been less successful is in transforming and deepening moments of struggle by making of them opportunities to raise their own demands. Autonomous struggle turns the question on its head: not 'will women unite to support men,' but 'will men unite to support women.'

Women as Divisive

What has prevented previous political intervention by women? Why can they be used in certain circumstances against strikes? Why, in other words, is the class not united? From the beginning of this document we have made central the exclusion of women from socialized production. That is an objective character of capitalist organization: cooperative labor in the factory and office, isolated labor in the home. This is mirrored subjectively by the way workers in industry organize separately from the community. What is the community to do? What are women to do? Act as support, be appendages to men in the home and in the struggle, even form women's auxiliaries for unions? This division and *this kind of division* are the history of the class. At every stage of the struggle those most peripheral to the productive cycle can be used against those at the center, so long as the latter ignore the former. This is the history of trade unions, for example, in the United States, where black workers were used as strikebreakers, but never, by the way, as often as white workers were led to believe. Blacks like women are immediately identifiable, and reports of strikebreaking reinforce prejudices that arise from objective divisions: the white on the assembly line, the black sweeping round his feet; or the man on the assembly line, the woman sweeping round his feet when he gets home.

When they reject work, men consider themselves militant, and when we reject our work, these same men consider us nagging wives. When some of us vote Conservative because we have been excluded from political struggle, they think we are backward, while they vote for parties that don't even think that we exist as anything but ballast, and in the process sell themselves (and all of us) down the river.

Part C: The Productivity of Discipline

The third aspect of women's role in the family is that, because of the special brand of stunting of the personality already discussed, the woman becomes a repressive figure, disciplinarian of all the members of the family, ideologically and psychologically. She may live under the tyranny of her husband and her home, the tyranny of striving to be the 'heroic mother and happy wife' while her whole existence repudiates this ideal. Those who are tyrannized and lack power are often with the new generation for the first years of their lives producing docile workers and little tyrants, in the same way the teacher does at school. (In this the woman is joined by her husband: not by chance do parent-teacher associations exist.) Women, responsible for the reproduction of labor power, on the one hand, discipline the children who will be workers tomorrow and, on the other hand, discipline their husbands to work today, for only his wage can pay for labor power to be reproduced.

Here we have only attempted to consider female domestic productivity without going into detail about the psychological implications. We have located and essentially outlined this female domestic productivity as it passes through the complexities of the role that the woman plays (in addition, that is, to the actual domestic work, the burden of which she assumes without pay). We foremost pose the need to break this role, which serves to separate women from each other, from men, and from children, each locked in her family as the chrysalis in the cocoon that imprisons itself by its own work, to die and leave silk for capital. To reject all this, as we have already said, means for housewives to also recognize themselves as a section of the class, the most degraded, because they are not paid a wage. The housewife's position in the overall struggle of women is crucial, since it undermines the very pillar supporting the capitalist organization of work, namely, the family.

So every goal that tends to affirm the individuality of women against this figure complementary to everything and everybody, that is, the housewife, is worth posing as a goal subversive to the continuation of the productivity of this role. In the same sense, all the demands that can serve to restore to the woman the integrity of her basic physical functions, starting with the sexual one that was the first to be robbed along with productive creativity, have to be posed with the greatest urgency. It is not by chance that research into birth control has developed so slowly or that abortion is forbidden almost the world over or conceded finally only for 'therapeutic' reasons. To move first on these demands is not facile reformism. Capitalist management of these matters repeatedly poses class discrimination, and discrimination against women specifically.

Why have proletarian women—Third World women—been used as guinea pigs in this research? Why does the question of birth control continue to be posed as women's problem? To begin to struggle to overthrow the capitalist management of these matters is in fact to move on a class basis, and on a specifically female basis. To link these struggles with the struggle against motherhood conceived as the responsibility of women exclusively, against domestic work understood as women's work, and ultimately against the models that capitalism offers us as examples of women's emancipation, which are nothing more than ugly copies of the male role, is a struggle against the division and organization of labor.

Women and the Struggle Not to Work

Let's sum up. The role of housewife, behind whose isolation social labor is hidden, must be destroyed. But our alternatives are strictly defined. Up to now, the myth of female incapacity, rooted in this isolated woman dependent on someone else's wages and therefore shaped by someone else's consciousness, has been broken by only one action: the woman getting her own wage—breaking the back of personal economic dependence, having her own independent experience of the world outside the home, performing social labor in a socialized structure, whether the factory or the office, and there initiating her own forms of social rebellion, alongside the traditional forms of the class. *The advent of the women's movement is a rejection of this alternative.*

Capital itself is seizing upon the same impetus that created a movement—the rejection by millions of women of women's traditional place—to recompose the workforce with increasing numbers of women. The movement can only develop in opposition to this. It poses by its very existence and must pose with increasing articulation in action that women refuse the myth of liberation through work.

For we have worked enough. We have chopped billions of tons of cotton, washed billions of dishes, scrubbed billions of floors, typed billions of words, wired billions of radio sets, and washed billions of diapers by hand and in machines. Every time they have 'let us in' to some traditionally male enclave, it was to find for us a new level of exploitation. Here again we must draw a parallel, different as they are, between underdevelopment in the Third World and underdevelopment in the metropolis—to be more precise, in the kitchens of the metropolis. Capitalist planning proposes to the Third World that it 'develop'; that in addition to its present agonies, it too must suffer the agony of an industrial counterrevolution. Women in the metropolis have been offered the same 'aid.' But those of us who have gone out of our homes to work because we had to or for extras or for economic independence have warned the rest: inflation has riveted us to this bloody typing pool or to this assembly line, and in that there is no salvation. We must refuse the development they are offering us. But the struggle of the working woman is not to return to the isolation of the home, appealing as this sometimes may be on Monday morning, any more than the housewife's struggle is to exchange being imprisoned in a house for being clinched to desks or machines, appealing as this sometimes may be compared to the loneliness of the twelfth-story flat.

Women must completely discover their own possibilities—which are neither mending socks nor becoming captains of oceangoing ships. Better still, we may wish to do these things, but right now they cannot be located anywhere but in the history of capital. The challenge to the women's movement is to find modes of struggle that, while they liberate women from the home, at the same time avoid, on the one hand, a double slavery and, on the other, prevent another degree of capitalistic control and regimentation. *This ultimately is the dividing line between reformism and revolutionary politics within the women's movement.*

It seems that there have been few women of genius. There could not have been, since, cut off from the social process, we cannot see on what matters they could have exercised their genius. Now there is a matter, the struggle itself. Freud said that from birth every woman suffers from penis envy. He forgot to add that this feeling of envy begins the moment she perceives that in some way to have a penis means to have power. Even less did he realize that the traditional power of the penis took on a whole new history at the very moment when the separation of man from woman became a capitalistic division.

And this is where our struggle begins.

December 29, 1971[21]

Notes

This text was originally published in Italian in March 1972, and the first English translation appeared in October 1972.

1   This happened as part of the massive demonstration of women celebrating International Women's Day in the U.S.

2   This is to assume a whole new meaning for 'education,' and the work now being done on the history of compulsory education—forced learning—proves this. In England teachers were conceived of as 'moral police' who could: (i) condition children against 'crime'—curb working-class reappropriation in the community; (ii) destroy 'the mob'—working-class organization based on a family that was still a productive unit or at least a viable organizational unit; (iii) make habitual the regular attendance and good timekeeping so necessary to children's later employment; and (iv) stratify the class by grading and selection. As with the family itself, the transition to this new form of social control was not smooth and direct and was the result of contradictory forces both within the class and within capital, as with every phase of the history of capitalism.

3   Wage labor is based on the subordination of all relationships to wage relationship. The worker must enter as an 'individual' into a contract with capital stripped of the protection of kinships.

4   Karl Marx, "Critique of Hegel's Philosophy of the State," in *Writings of the Young Marx on Philosophy and Society*, ed. and trans. Loyd D. Easton and Kurt H. Guddat (Garden City, NY: Doubleday, 1967), 176.

5   We are not dealing here with the narrowness of the nuclear family that prevents children from having an easy transition to forming relationships with other people; nor with what follows from this, the argument of psychologists that proper conditioning would have avoided such a crisis. We are dealing with the entire organization of the society, of which family, school, and factory are ghettoized compartments. So every passage from one to another of these compartments is a painful passage. The pain cannot be eliminated by tinkering with the relations between one ghetto and another but only by the destruction of every ghetto.

6   "Free fares, free lunches, free books" was one of the slogans of a section of the Italian student movement that aimed to connect the struggle of younger students with workers and university students.

7   In Britain and the U.S. the psychologists Eysenck and Jensen, who are 'scientifically' convinced that blacks have a lower 'intelligence' than whites, and progressive educators like Ivan Illich seem diametrically opposed. They are divided by method, but what they aim to achieve links them. In any case, the psychologists are no more racist than the rest, only more direct. 'Intelligence' is reduced to the ability to assume your enemy's case as wisdom and to shape your own logic on the basis of this. Where the whole society operates institutionally on the assumption of

white racial superiority, these psychologists propose more conscious and thorough 'conditioning' so that children who do not learn to read do not learn, instead, to make Molotov cocktails. A sensible view with which Illich, who is concerned with the 'underachievement' of children (that is, rejection by them of 'intelligence'), can agree.

8 In spite of the fact that capital manages the schools, control is never given once and for all. The working class continually and increasingly challenges the content and refuses the costs of capitalist schooling. The response of the capitalist system is to reestablish its own control, and this control tends to be more and more regimented on factory-like lines. The new policies on education that are being hammered out even as we write, however, are more complex than this. We can only indicate here the impetus for these new policies:

(a) Working-class youth reject the idea that education prepares them for anything but a factory, even if they will wear white collars and use typewriters and drawing-boards instead of riveting machines.

(b) Middle-class youth rejects the role of mediator between the classes and the repressed personality this mediating role demands.

(c) A new labor power, higher wages, and status differentiation is called for. The present egalitarian trend must be reversed.

(d) A new type of labor process may be created to attempt to interest the worker in 'participating' instead of refusing the monotony and fragmentation of the present assembly-line.

If the traditional 'road to success,' and even 'success' itself, is rejected by the young, new goals will have to be found to which they can aspire, that is, for which they will go to school and go to work. New 'experiments' in 'free' education, where the children are encouraged to participate in planning their own education and there is greater democracy between teacher and taught are springing up daily. It is an illusion to believe that this is a defeat for capital or that regimentation will be a victory. For in the creation of a labor power more creatively manipulated, capital will not in the process lose 0.1 percent of profit. "As a matter of fact," they are in effect saying, "you can be far more efficient for us if you take your own road, so long as it is through our territory." In some parts of the factory and in the social factory, capital's slogan will increasingly be: "Liberty and fraternity to guarantee and even extend equality."

9 We are not at all ignoring the attempts at this moment to make test-tube babies. But today such mechanisms belong completely to capitalist science and control. Their use would be completely against us and against the class. It is not in our interest to abdicate procreation and consign it to the hands of the enemy. It is in our interest to conquer the freedom to procreate, for which we will pay neither the price of the wage nor the price of social exclusion.

10 To the extent that only 'human care' and not technological innovation can raise children, the effective liberation from domestic work time, the qualitative change of domestic work, can derive only from a movement of women, from a struggle of women: the more the movement grows, the less men—first of all political mili-tants—can count on female baby minding. And, at the same time, the new social ambience that the movement constructs offers to children social space, with both men and women, that has nothing to do with the day care centers organized by the state. These are already victories of the struggle. Precisely because they are the

results of a movement that is by its nature a struggle, they do not aim to substitute any kind of cooperation for the struggle itself.

11 It is impossible to say for how long these tendencies will continue to drive the movement forward or when they will turn into their opposite.

12 Some English-language readers feel that this definition of women's work should be more precise. What we specifically meant is that housework as work is productive in the Marxian sense, that is, is producing surplus value. We speak immediately after about the productivity of the entire female role. A clearer discussion of the productivity of the woman, both as related to her work and as related to her entire role, will have to wait for a later text, one which we are now working on. In this text woman's place will be explained in a more articulated way from the point of view of the entire capitalistic circuit.

13 Labor power "is a strange commodity for this is not a thing. The ability to labour resides only in a human being whose life is consumed in the process of producing. . . . To describe its basic production and reproduction is to describe women's work"; Selma James, introduction to *The Power of Women and the Subversion of the Community*, by Mariarosa Dalla Costa (Bristol: Falling Wall Press, 1972).

14 This, however, is being countered by an opposing tendency to bring women into industry in specific sectors. Differing needs of capital within the same geographical sector have produced differing and even opposing propaganda and policies. Where in the past family stability has been based on a relatively standardized mythology (policy and propaganda being uniform and officially uncontested), today various sectors of capital contradict each other and undermine the very definition of family as a stable, unchanging, 'natural' unit. The classic example of this is the variety of views and financial policies on birth control. The British government has recently doubled its allocation of funds for this purpose. We must examine to what extent this policy is connected with a racist immigration policy, that is, manipulation of the sources of mature labor power, and with the increasing erosion of the work ethic, which results in movements of the unemployed and unsupported mothers, that is, controlling births that pollute the purity of capital with revolutionary children.

15 This is the policy of the Communist Party in Italy, which for some years proposed a bill to Italian parliament that would have given a pension to women at home, both housewives and single women, when they reached fifty-five years of age. This bill was never passed.

16 Today the demand of wages for housework is put forward increasingly and with less opposition in the women's movement in Italy and elsewhere. Since this document was first drafted (June 1971), the debate has become more profound and many uncertainties that were due to the relative newness of the discussion have been dispelled. But, above all, the weight of the needs of proletarian women has not only radicalized the demands of the movement, it has also given us greater strength and confidence to advance them. A year ago, at the beginning of the movement in Italy, there were those who still thought that the state could easily suffocate the female rebellion against housework by 'paying' a monthly allowance of £7 to £8 (approximately $130.00 to $150.00 U.S. dollars in 2018), as they had already done with those 'wretched of the earth' who were dependent on pensions in particular.

17 There has been some confusion over what we have said about canteens. A similar confusion expressed itself in the discussions in both Italy and other countries about

wages for housework. As we explained earlier, housework is as institutionalized as factory work and our ultimate goal is to destroy both institutions. But aside from which demand we are speaking about, there is a misunderstanding of what a demand is. It is a goal that is not only a thing but, like capital at any moment, essentially a stage of antagonism in a social relation. Whether the canteen or the wages we win will be a victory or a defeat depends on the force of our struggle. That force depends on whether the goal is an occasion for capital to more rationally command our labor or an occasion for us to weaken their hold on that command. What form the goal will take when we achieve it, whether it is wages or canteens or free birth control, is, in fact, created in the struggle and registers the degree of power that we have reached in that struggle.

18 Karl Marx, *Das Kapital, Kritik der politischen Okonomie,* vol. 1 (Berlin: Dietz Verlag, 1962), 512. "Large-scale industry makes it a question of life and death to replace that monstrosity which is a miserable available working population, kept in reserve for the changing needs of exploitation by capital, to replace this with the absolute availability of the individual for changing requisites of work; to replace the partial individual, a mere bearer of a social detail function, with the fully developed individual for whom varied social functions are modes of interplaying natural and acquired activities."

19 "But the other, more fundamental, objection, which we shall develop in the ensuing chapters, flows from our disputing the assumption that the general level of real wages is directly determined by the character of the wage bargain. . . . We shall endeavour to show that primarily it is certain other forces which determine the general level of real wages. . . . We shall argue that there has been a fundamental misunderstanding of how in this respect the economy in which we live actually works." John Maynard Keynes, *The General Theory of Employment, Interest, and Money* (New York: Harcourt, Brace and World, 1964), 13. "Certain other forces," in our view, are first of all women.

20 It has been noted that after 1917 many of the Bolsheviks found female partners among the dispossessed aristocracy. When power continues to reside in men both at the level of the state and in individual relations, women continue to be "the spoil and handmaid of communal lust"; Karl Marx, *Economic and Philosophic Manuscripts of 1844* (Progress Publishers, Moscow, 1959), 94. The breed of 'the new tsars' goes back a long way. By 1921,one can read in *Decisions of the Third Congress of the Communist International*, Part I, *Work Among Women*: "The Third Congress of the Comintern confirms the basic proposition of revolutionary Marxism, that is, that there is no 'specific woman question' and no 'specific women's movement,' and that every sort of alliance of working women with bourgeois feminism, as well as any support by the women workers of the treacherous tactics of the social compromisers and opportunists, leads to the undermining of the forces of the proletariat. . . . In order to put an end to women's slavery it is necessary to inaugurate the new Communist organisation of society." The theory being male, the practice was to 'neutralize.' Let us quote from one of the founding fathers. At the first National Conference of Communist Women of the Communist Party of Italy on March 26,1922: "Comrade Gramsci pointed out that special action must be organised among housewives, who constitute the large majority of the proletarian women. He said that they should be related in some way to our movement by our setting up special organisations. Housewives, as far as the quality of their work is

concerned, can be considered similar to the artisans and therefore they will hardly be communists; however, because they are the workers' mates, and because they share in some way the workers' life, they are attracted toward communism. Our propaganda can therefore have an influence over [sic] these housewives; it can be instrumental, if not to officer them into our organisation, to neutralise them; so that they do not stand in the way of the possible struggles by the workers." (From the Italian Communist Party organ for work among women, *Compagna* 1, no.3 [April 2, 1922]: 2.)

21 In reference to the authorship and date of this essay, see below the statement that I wrote in 2012 that clarifies for the reader my cooperation with Selma James. For further information regarding the introduction written by Selma James, see: http://www.commonnotions.org/sex-race-and-class (accessed July 28, 2018). In her recently published volume, *Sex, Race and Class: The Perspective of Winning* (PM Press, 2012) Selma James makes a number of incorrect statements relative to her collaboration with me and the authorship of *The Power of Women and the Subversion of the Community* that force me to respond, as they distort the history of our cooperation and the beginning of the Wages for Housework campaign. According to Selma James's introductory notes to the *Power of Women and the Subversion of the Community* and, in particular, her commentary concerning the essay "Women and the Subversion of the Community," I have usurped her right to be considered the author or a coauthor of this article. I reject this claim and must first point out that what has been reprinted by PM Press is a heavily edited version of the original introduction that Selma James wrote in July 1972, from which my name has now been removed eleven times. In the original introduction to *The Power of Women*, Selma James unambiguously presented "Women and the Subversion of the Community" not only as my work but as the product of the new women's movement in Italy.

Let me underline here that what is at stake is not a competition for the authorship of an essay. On the contrary, the question at stake is the historical and political origin of the campaign and struggle for wages for housework, which now appears in Selma James's account as the product of the 'inventiveness' of an individual. This could not be further from the truth.

Neither Selma James nor I 'invented' or discovered the perspective of Wages for Housework (WFH), as is claimed in the book and in the promotional material for its launching in the United States. The demand for wages for housework was promoted by feminists in Europe and in the United States since at least the beginning of the twentieth century. I discovered their analysis and demands in the late 1970s when I was working on *Famiglia welfare e stato tra progressismo e New Deal* (Milan: Franco Angeli, 1983)* and mentioned them in that book. Socialist feminists like Crystal Eastman were asking for housework to be remunerated by the state and actively working on this program by the first decade of the century. An article that appeared in 1912 in the socialist newspaper *Chicago Evening World* included an analysis of housework that was very similar to that made by activists in our campaign, pointing out that employers buy two workers for one wage and that the kind of work a man does determines the working and living conditions of his wife as well. Among male theorists, we can recall Wilhelm Reich who, in *The Sexual Revolution*, written in the 1930s, said that marriage is an institution that exploits women, that unpaid domestic work enables employers to increase their profits, and that the employers can impose low wages precisely because behind the workers there is the free work of their wives. Reich also underlined that even women who have a waged job continued to do the housework as a condition for their marriage to function. Simone de Beauvoir's *The Second Sex*, written in the 1950s, comments on the 'housework question' in a way that anticipated the analysis we produced over a decade later. Most importantly, the housework question was the central issue in the new feminism that emerged in the early 1970s in Europe and in the U.S., which marked a break with emancipationism and the demand for 'parity.' There were different positions on this question, but the problematic arising from the unwaged character of this work and the fact that housework reproduces labor power was already acknowledged by various authors, from Betsy Warrior to Peggy Morton and others, prior to the publication of *The Power of Women*.

I further want to point out that the launching of the Wages for Housework campaign was a collective process and project. Not accidentally, the launching occurred with the formation of the International Feminist Collective in July 1972, which took place in Padua, Italy, at a meeting where about twenty women, mostly from Italy but also from France, the U.S., and the UK, participated. The political perspective that shaped wages for housework theoretically and practically was a coalescing of different political currents including the Italian workerist movement, itself the product of one of the most important cycles of struggle Italy had seen in modern history. Indeed, my very first encounter with Selma James was a product of the relationship both she and I had with this movement.

By the time I met Selma James I had been involved for years in the political activity of Potere Operaio, a network of militant groups issuing from the workerist movement that later dissolved into what has become "autonomia." The political categories I was using in my analysis were those developed by workerism: the strategic character of the wage struggle, the refusal of work, and the social factory. Consequently, it is not surprising that these categories are found in the article in question. Potere Operaio made political use of the wage struggle to promote struggles for a wage by other unwaged subjects, like students, who began demanding a 'pre-wage' for the work of forming their labor power. Potere Operaio also launched the objective of a guaranteed income that is still on the table today, as part of a program where it is interwoven with the question of a minimum wage. The demand for wages for housework was clearly influenced by this political framework.

The invitation to Selma James to participate in the Padua June 1971 meeting, the first in which I presented a document discussing the question of wages for housework with a group of women activists, one year prior to the launching of the campaign, reflected my desire to connect Selma to the developing feminist movement in Italy, and it was in recognition of her merit both on the level of analysis and political practice. Selma knew very well what I would present in this meeting, because, prior to it, I read her the document I had written. From this first meeting I worked full time to make the new movement grow, and for a while my relationship with Selma was not problematic. When we decided to combine our writings in the booklet that became *The Power of Women* (published in Italian in March 1972 and in English in October of the same year), Selma James wrote an introduction that underlined the significance of the fact that my essay "Women and the Subversion of the Community" came from Italy, a country with a particularly high percentage of housewives. It is exactly this reference, along with my name and the pages that followed that have been erased in the new version of the 1972 introduction that Selma James has published in her book.

However, this is not to deny that, in the spirit of cooperation that prevailed at least for a time in the feminist movement, we fully discussed everything we published with each other and made significant contributions to each other's writings. I should add that another activist participated in our discussions about the article and contributed to it. But at the time nobody suggested that the article should have more than one signature. To be accused now of having taken advantage of this cooperation to place my name on an article predominantly written by Selma James is something I find totally unacceptable and contrary to the spirit of comradely cooperation necessary for building an international movement. I also reject vehemently and with true indignation the argument that I was "allowed to sign" "Women and the Subversion of the Community" because I needed a weapon against sexism.

I never said anything when I realized that, starting with the third edition of the book in 1975, Selma James began to add her signature to the essay, or, more outrageously, in later years, started referring to the *Power of Women* as written by her "with" Mariarosa Dalla Costa. I also never said anything about the fact that, in spite of having been a main exponent of the Padua Wages for Housework Committee, I have no record of our committee gathering to discuss the foreword to the third English edition nor of our committee deciding to add its signature to that of the Power of Women Collective. It is always very demoralizing when old sisters part ways, and I did my best over the last four decades to stay away from polemics about the authorship of this work. However, the comments made in the book that Selma James has now published force me to rectify the claims that she is making.

Last, I did not part ways with Selma James because of any split in the Wages for Housework network "on the basis of race," as her introductory notes claim. This is not the place for me to fully address this claim. I will only state that it masks what in reality were profound disagreements on political and organizational issues.

In conclusion, it saddens me to realize that Selma James decided, in presenting her work to a U.S. movement public, to both erase and degrade my contribution (as well as the contribution of other sisters) to a campaign that represented an important movement in feminist history.

In recognition of the importance of this history, we are now assembling our archives and making them public.** Thus, I hope that a more balanced view of the early history of this movement will be available to new generations of activists.

Padua, March 27, 2012

* For the English translation, see *Family, Welfare and the State: Between Progressivism and the New Deal* (Brooklyn, NY: Common Notions, 2015).
** Archivio di Lotta Femminista per il salario al lavoro domestico. Donation by Mariarosa Dalla Costa. It is located at the Civic Library, accessed July 28, 2018. http://www.padovanet.it/informazione/biblioteca-civica.

On the General Strike (1975)

Women carry signs denouncing the negative environmental impact of leather factory in the village of Santa Croce Bigolina at a May 1, 1975, demonstration in Mestre, Venice, for wages for housework.

Today the feminist movement in Italy is launching the campaign for *wages for housework*. As you have heard from the songs, as you have seen from the photography exhibition, as you have read on the placards, the issues we are raising today are many: from the barbarous conditions in which we have to face abortion through the sadism we are subjected to in obstetric and gynecological clinics to our working conditions—in jobs outside the home our conditions are always worse than men's and at home we work without wages—to the fact that social services either don't exist or are so bad that we are afraid to let our children use them, and so on.

Now at some point people might ask, what is the connection between the campaign we are launching today, the campaign for *wages for housework*, and all these things that we have raised today, that we have exposed and are fighting against? All these things that we have spoken about, that we have made songs about, that we have shown in our exhibitions and films?

We believe that the weakness of all women—the weakness that is behind our being erased from history, that is behind the fact that when we leave the home we must face the most revolting, underpaid, and insecure jobs—this weakness is based on the fact that all of us women, whatever we do, are wearied and exhausted at the very outset by the thirteen hours of housework a day that no one has ever recognized, that no one has ever paid for.

This is the basic condition that forces women to be satisfied with nurseries like the Pagliuca, Celestini, or ONMI.[1] This weakness forces us to pay half a million liras for an abortion and this, let's spell it out clearly, happens in every city and every country—and on top of that we risk death and imprisonment.

We all do housework; it is the only thing all women have in common, it is the only basis upon which we can gather our power, the power of millions of women.

It is no accident that reformists of every stripe have always carefully avoided the idea of our organizing on the basis of housework. They have always refused to recognize housework as work, precisely because it is the only work that we all have in common. It is one thing to confront two or three hundred women workers in a shoe factory and quite another to confront millions of housewives. And since all women factory workers are also housewives, it is still another matter to confront these two or three hundred factory workers united with millions of housewives.

But this is what we are putting on the agenda today in this square. This is the first moment of organization. We have decided to organize ourselves around the work that we all do, in order to have the power of millions of women.

For us, then, *the demand for Wages for Housework is a direct demand for power, because housework is what millions of women have in common.*

If we can organize ourselves in our millions around this demand—and already there are quite a lot of us in this square—we can get so much power that we need no longer be in a position of weakness when we go out of the home. We can bring about new working conditions in housework itself—if I have money of my own in my pocket I can even buy a dishwasher without feeling guilty and without having to beg my husband for it for months on end, while he, who doesn't do the washing up, considers a dishwasher unnecessary.

So if I have money of my own, paid into my own hands, I can change the conditions of housework itself. Moreover, I will *be able to choose* when I want to go out to work. If I have 120 thousand liras for housework, I'll never again sell myself for sixty thousand liras in a textile factory, as someone's secretary, as a cashier, or as an usher at the cinema. In the same way, if I already have a certain amount of money in my own hands, if I already have with me the power of millions of women, I will be able to dictate a completely new quality of services, nurseries, canteens, and all the facilities that are indispensable in reducing working hours and in enabling us to have a social life.

We want to say something else. For a long time—particularly strongly in the past ten years, but let's say always—male workers who have come out to struggle against the number of hours they work and for more money have gathered in this square. In the factories of Porto Marghera there have been many strikes and many struggles. We well remember the marches of male workers who started in Porto Marghera, then crossed the Mestre bridge and arrived here in this square.

But let's make this clear. *No strike has ever been a general strike.* When half the working population is at home in the kitchens while the others are on strike, *it's not a general strike.* We've never seen a general strike. We've only seen men, generally men from the big factories, come out into the streets, while their wives, daughters, sisters, and mothers went on cooking in the kitchens.

Today in this square, with the launch of our mobilization for *wages for housework,* we put on the agenda *our working hours, our holidays, our strikes, and our money.*

When we win a level of power that enables us to reduce our thirteen or more working hours a day to eight hours, or even less than eight, when at the same time we can put on the agenda our holidays—because it's no secret to anyone that on Sundays and during vacation time women never have a holiday—then perhaps we'll be able to talk for the first time of a 'general' strike of the working class.

Mestre, Italy, March 1974

Notes

Originally published in *All Work and No Pay: Women, Housework and the Wages Due,* ed. Wendy Edmond and Suzie Fleming (Bristol, UK: Falling Wall Press, 1975). This is the concluding part of the speech given by Dalla Costa on March 10, 1974, during the weekend of action organized by the Triveneto Committee for Wages for Housework to commemorate International Women's Day and to launch the campaign for Wages for Housework in Italy.

1   Pagliuca and Celestini were both notoriously brutal nurseries in Italy and ONMI refers to the state nurseries, which are poorly equipped.

Domestic Labor and the Feminist Movement in Italy since the 1970s (1988)

The Venice feminist collective demonstrates for wages for housework at the May 1, 1975, demonstration in Mestre, Venice.

nternationally, in both the advanced capitalist countries and elsewhere, the theme of *work* has invariably become a central focus for feminist discussion and women's movements. These discussions have highlighted the inequity common to the most diverse economic and sociopolitical systems: the woman is not only expected to do the housework for which no payment is provided but also simply to add it to her other work whether she is employed in industry, the service sector, or cultivates the land and has a market stall to sell the produce and other sundry goods, as often happens in the so-called 'Third World.'

At the same time, the other emerging theme of great importance, *female sexuality*, which is so closely intertwined with the topic of the *body*, has undergone a fundamental level of redefinition within the theme of work. In fact, the analysis of the organization of labor and, specifically, of domestic labor, has made it possible to strip the veil off of a female sexuality imposed in terms of family and social productivity. In other words, a sexuality essentially reproductive of others, rather than of oneself and one's desire. In the same vein, the negation of the woman's body by turning it into a machine for procreation is denounced.

Starting from the analysis of labor, the demand for a 'wage for housework,' whoever—man or woman—in fact supplies it, has defined an organizational sector and produced a very lively area of debate in Italy, other European countries, and North America. Since the early 1970s, when the proposal was articulated with all its various implications, the discussion of wages for housework has continued to spread in the most diverse countries, winning support and arousing polemic. It has maintained a central position in feminist debate, not least in the multiplication of initiatives for equality between men and women typical of the 1980s.

The feminist impulse has been expressed in various ways in different countries. Here, I will mention only the psychoanalytic approach, which had great weight in the French experience, and the practice of 'self-awareness' in the Italian experience, which, in certain respects, owed a debt to the 'consciousness-raising' of the United States. In discussing Italy at the national level, accepting the limits of trying to schematize a turbulent reality such as the feminist movement, the two major forms of expression in recent years of Italian feminism have been the 'wages for housework' and the 'self-awareness' sectors.

It is important to note that Italy in the 1970s represented a very specific terrain for struggles that had spread from the major factories to the universities, the schools, and the wider social context. In those years, the extra-institutional political debate developed some significant breaks with traditional Marxism. Notable examples were the rejection of work as against the ideology of work and the end of the assumption that public ownership of the means of production is the dividing line between capitalism and socialism. The state, understood as the complex articulation of capitalist strategy, emerged as the privileged target for the demands that the various movements were pursuing. In this context, the Italian feminist movement was characterized, with more emphasis than in other countries, by the *motif* of 'work/rejection of work' and, in particular, of the discovery and denunciation of femininity as labor (domestic, reproductive labor), while at the same time demanding to shift the cost to the state, reduce the work time involved, and break down the fundamental organizational cell within which the supply of this form of labor was primarily commanded, specifically, the family.

This was a novelty and a significant break both with the Catholic tradition, which imposed housework[1] on the woman as a sacrifice and mission, and with the Communist tradition, which ignored housework or stigmatized it as an expression of backwardness, urging the woman to find an outside job, if possible in a factory, as the path to emancipation, which was thus represented as the sole legitimate form of liberation.

The great workers' and students' struggles of the late 1960s laid the terrain from which the feminist movement emerged in the 1970s. The original protagonists and centers of aggregation with other women in the formation of the feminist groups were precisely those women who had experienced their own lack of representation as political subjects in the student and workers' movements and in their activism in the extraparliamentary groups. At the factories, the picket lines chanted, "More wages, fewer hours!" but on the domestic front of the unwaged working women of the home, the starting point had to be "Money of our own and no more than eight hours!"

If the students demanded a 'pre-wage' during their studies, the ten million housewives who had no wage at all could hardly be ignored. "Free transport, free meals!" the students chanted, so what could be said of the kindergartens, which had always been demanded but rarely conceded? On the rare occasion that such concessions were made they were only to let the woman take on a second, outside job, never to reduce the working hours of her first job. In this way, the terrain of struggle became a minefield where there was an increasing explosion of new contradictions.

While the debate about productive/unproductive labor flared around the factories and offices, the family was identified as the other factory, the locus for the production and reproduction of labor power within which the woman was exploited and not just oppressed as the prevalent literature claimed. Caged in a form of labor—housework—with an unlimited workday, no wage, no vacation, no pension, and no social assistance.

The productiveness of housework was debated and reiterated, although a different conclusion would have made no difference in feminist demands. It was an obligatory theme of the times that raised fewer passions in the feminist than in the male world. Productive or not, women stayed firm in their determination to free themselves of an unpaid job, as such, and from a job that also supplied an obligatory channel for their own social identity. With the emergence of the feminist movement, there was an outburst of women's determination to end the idea that you are all the more a woman, and therefore all the more accepted as a woman, the more you are available for the reproduction of others. I think one of the best definitions of a woman to emerge in those years was: "A woman is she who assumes she must interrupt whatever she is doing if there is some necessity involving the family."

In identifying the family as the other pole of production, the very questionable 'convenience' of exchanging your labor within the family against 'maintenance,' or a quota of maintenance, showed all its intolerable poverty. This analysis of the family occurred at a time when the higher levels of education, socialization, and politicization that were achieved through the processes of struggle generated an unpostponable need for women to redefine themselves as social individuals, rather than as mere appendages to family structures that were functional for plans for economic development or at moments of economic crisis. Thus, to redefine themselves as social individuals presupposed, above all, women redefining their own sexual identity, which meant a struggle against the family as the locus of an obligatory distortion of women's sexuality as a function of procreative and reproductive work. There was thus the need to launch a struggle addressing the woman's material conditions, for the conquest of elementary rights, and against her condition as a subordinate citizen. Fundamentally, though, the struggle was for the woman's right to determine her own identity and life project—and, above all, the right to change it.

In the social struggles of the late 1960s and very early 1970s, the commitment of the women defending the working-class wage (through struggles against the high cost of living and high utility tariffs and for housing, transport, etc.) reached a threshold. These were, however, still struggles in defense of a family structure, rather than to win back and redefine one's own individuality, space, and level of wealth.

It was precisely the state's response to the political struggles of the late 1960s around wages and the broader ramifications that such struggles had in society, for example, the restructuring of production, decentralization, destabilization of the market, significant increases to inflation, and growing unemployment (especially among men). In brief, the crisis management of the 1970s brought about far-reaching modifications in the family's structure and function.

Above all, the heavy attack on the stability of men's jobs and wages undermined a family pattern, both among proletarians and the middle classes, in which financial security was guaranteed primarily by the man. Thus, cracks opened in the deeply rooted hierarchy that had characterized the Italian family up until then, with the man as breadwinner and the woman as housewife—even though it is necessary to by no means ignore the contribution of women's extra-domestic work to the family income, often supplied illegally or part-time. Given this family pattern, which was typical until the start of the 1970s, the declining birth rate that, as in many other industrialized countries, saw a particularly sharp decrease from 1964 onward, should be seen, I would argue, as a decision[2] by the woman to ensure her children a higher standard of living and, hence, as a function of an improved equilibrium in the family.[3] In contrast, it was not a demand for personal identity freed of the obligation to motherhood and the role of wife, as became the case in the 1970s. "Women, let's give birth to ideas not just children" was one of the slogans that marked the change in attitude most significantly.

The 1970s, in fact, were not just the years in which the rejection of maternity was the direct expression of feminists' chosen course. They were also the years in which the rejection of marriage was a refusal to subscribe to the family as a form of life. So, as regards the rejection of work, we can say that prior to the 1970s the reduction of the number of children was a function of working less but was still contained within the horizon of the family as the general order of life. Afterwards, the further lowering of the birth rate, even the rejection of procreation tout court, formed part of a rejection of the family, as such, with a focus on feminist autonomy.

After 1972, the reorganization of production led, on the one hand, to extensive technological innovation in the factories and the progressive dismantling of certain job structures in the old industrial centers, but, on the other hand, there was also a new geographical dispersion of production. It was this so-called decentralization of production that led to more diffuse possibilities of work, and, hence, wages were often 'black market' (illegal) for a new generation of young men and women, as well as for old people. On the women's front, then, there was a convergence between the objective situation of doing without the support and guarantee of a man's wage, on the one hand, and, on the other, the women's subjectively determined course in which there was an increasingly drastic rejection of the unpaid reproductive labor, of the family itself in so far as it prescribes this way of life, and, with it, the subordination of the woman's destiny to family responsibilities. Rather, the course chosen by women led them, above all, to gain their own income, so as to pursue their journey toward constructing their own destiny. In this sense the new labor market, which was interested in more flexible and mobile labor power, provided women greater job openings.

From 1972–1979, women's formal employment grew by 1,415,000 jobs.[4] A very large number entered the service sector and a significant number also entered industry; at Fiat alone, 15,000 women were hired between 1978–1980. Elsewhere, a very large number of women were hired as undeclared 'illegal' labor. On the crest of the wave of the feminist movement's great battles, which now found a mass dimension, particularly in 1974–1976, various legislative measures were launched covering abortion, divorce, family planning clinics, reform of family law, and equality at work. These measures were designed to free women's labor power from some of the constraints and limitations that were now anachronistic in relation to the use that capital intended to make of women's labor. It was at this point that family organization became, in fact, more equal: a pattern in which, with both him and her holding precarious jobs, or with the stability of her job paralleled by the precariousness of his, everyone—including children and old people—made their contribution to the family income. This was now a family, it was argued, that was still the locus for regulating the supply of labor power and the composition of family income, but whose hierarchy was certainly less biased in favor of the man, even though the woman remained primarily responsible for reproductive work.

There was a lengthy debate and much investigation into the relationship between this new family and the new labor market. In almost all the academic research 'from the women's side,' the stress was on its function in terms of the new labor market, and there were also intensive investigations into work by women outside the home, which underscored its subordination to compatibility with work in the home. Others pointed out how this availability for wage labor, which made a growing comeback following the 'great refusal' of the late 1960s, allowed family units to maintain a reasonable standard of living in the 1970s.

I would argue, however, that this interpretation grasps only one aspect of the overall picture during those years. In fact, while both men and women were undeniably available for labor that produces goods and services, this was not so true of the labor that produces and reproduces labor power, labor for which women continued to express an increasingly marked rejection. On the one hand, the demand voiced by the feminist movement from the beginning for this labor to be paid had encountered substantial inertia on the state's part,[5] to the point that—in the second half of the 1970s—there was a further reduction in the state budget for finance and services most closely related to the reproduction of labor power. On the other hand, an increasingly extended strata of women expressed their unavailability for the labor of reproducing others. Instead, they voiced their determination to win, above all, a guarantee of their own life through their own wage labor.

It needs to be stressed that when women occupied buildings so they could be turned into kindergartens or simply took their children to work, to mention just two of the best-known examples, and these actions generated sporadic and fleeting responses from local administrations or individual employers, there was no significant motion on the part of the government to accept at least the raising of children, if not the thousands of tasks of housework, as paid working time. There was not just a growing number of employed women but also a growing number of women offering their labor power. In other words, an increasing number of women declared themselves unemployed or in search of their first job. Just as significantly, and unlike in the past, working mothers did not leave their jobs when they had children, so there was not the usual withdrawal from the labor market between the ages of twenty-five and thirty-five.[6] Rather, they used absenteeism, a strategy that in the 1970s rose to levels among women that were about double the already high levels for men.

However, there would be something mysterious in this extension of both the employment and the supply of women's labor power if, assuming, as we always have, the standard amount of housework involved in running a family totals far more than eight hours, and if we were to simply argue that an increasing number of women managed to 'double it up' with another job. While much work outside the home might induce further 'rationalization' of housework, or a new wage might make it possible to buy new household appliances, however much feminism might induce further sharing of housework chores and more equal forms of cooperation within the family (insofar as this was compatible with the man's job), if the volume of housework supplied is for the reproduction of a typical family (mother, father, and one or two children), it cannot be reduced below a certain threshold.

Thus, two types of consideration arise in explaining the extension of women's work outside the home. In the first instance, if a woman has a family of the abovementioned type and regularly works outside the home, a good part of the housework is done either by relatives (usually his or her mother) or by a third woman, a woman of color or white domestic help, and a good part of the woman's wage goes toward paying her. In fact, after a fall in paid domestic labor in the early 1970s, paid domestic work subsequently showed a clear increase once again. Families reported as using domestic help rose from 630,000 in 1974 to 1,030,000 in 1977, even though a very large proportion of those providing this help preferred to work informally and not to be declared. Above all, domestic workers find it more convenient to 'moonlight,' so they can continue having access to their husband's health insurance, something which their job does not provide, and the husband can continue to draw the family check he receives for the maintenance of his wife.[7] In the second instance, looking at the question on a higher level, an increasing number of women have rejected and continue to reject creating a family, procreating, and taking on the responsibility of reproducing men.

In my view, in political terms, the second iteration is the more significant form of behavior. This means highlighting an always neglected aspect of the relationship between family and the labor market: namely, that for an increasingly broad strata of women their new readiness for work outside the home presupposed a decision not to have children, marry, or cohabit with men, precisely to avoid being forced to use one wage for two jobs (her own and the domestic worker's). Or, alternately, work outside the home is restricted to work that is compatible with having children or a man in the house. Or else, in the hypothetical case of a husband with a high enough wage to pay domestic help without touching the wife's wage, the refusal to form a family with him was often due to a rejection of the network of mediations and complicities through social status that would very probably have annulled her political identity.

In any case, it should be stressed that while a constellation of values traceable to a moment of struggle and the exercise of power with respect to the state can always be found in the rejection of maternity, the same is not true of the 'rediscovery of maternity,' over which rivers of post-feminist ink have been spilled. The basic oversight in this latter approach is failing to note that since the conditions for maternity have increasingly deteriorated at the proletarian level, and this is true not only in Italy, the choice of maternity has in fact become a 'luxury.' Those authors who elevate maternity with first-person testimony often, in fact, perjure themselves, since, above all, they omit to mention the comfortable level of income enjoyed by themselves or their husbands and the exceptional elasticity in terms of time at some of the privileged jobs that provide the basis for their testimony.

As I have already noted, in the 1970s, there was a further fall in the birth rate, together with a rise in the number of illegitimate births. Unlike the previous period, however, this time the outcome was an expression of feminist autonomy, of women's refusal to be defined by reproduction, in order to find self-definition through a diversification of their life choices.

The rejection of procreation by these women went hand in hand with the rejection of marriage (and an increase in the number of legal separation cases), which even demographers consider the most dynamic factor of the decade. Forms of more casual cohabitation, which were fundamentally out of step with the structure of sentimental romantic relationships, less well-defined forms of being together and of relationships, women living alone (or with children or other women) became so widespread that even scholars in the Catholic area noted them, as well as of the atypical and diversified forms that the family can take, among them, the non–legally sanctioned family. Commentators even reached the point of describing reproductive situations and forms that no longer had anything to do with the traditional family as such. Alongside single people, they talked about 'family communes.' The family, or even cohabitation with a man, was rejected because within this relationship it is very difficult to free oneself of a woman's responsibilities. The rejection was not just of women's role in the family or of the material tasks of housework but also of those activities involved in the psychological, affective, and other aspects of reproduction.

Thus, for the woman in the 1970s, reproduction became the primary terrain of struggle, where achieving certain levels of rejection made it possible to store up strength for other things—to exercise different options with regards to work outside the home, to build moments of bargaining and being together, and to find a different self-definition other than that gained through men's demands and family responsibilities. Significantly, even among women who decided to have children, this choice was frequently postponed in comparison to the 'convenience of the family' that characterized earlier decades. You have a child at the age of thirty-five or forty, because in the preceding years you were pursuing one or another project; you were trying to build financial autonomy that would last.

In this connection, even though the wealth of the debate that arose must be condensed to essentials, it is once more worthwhile stressing the extent to which the great struggles on abortion, lesbianism, and, although not so obviously, prostitution fall within the same trend of a rejection of the unpaid reproductive work.

The struggle for the legalization of abortion was, in fact, a question of ending the cost not only in money but also in deaths, physical injury, and prison, as well as being the most drastic rejection of housework. There is, in fact, no doubt that the quantitative and qualitative leap in supplying this form of labor comes when children are born. So, together with the woman's self-determination regarding maternity, which was no longer accepted as a necessary passage toward self-identification nor as the necessary or casual consequence of sexual experience, stress was laid on self-determination in the explicit possibility of rejecting the quantity of housework that each extra child represents.

As for lesbianism, in the 1970s it was a practice that achieved the strength of an open political demand. Here, too, the demand was all the more urgent, not only as the right to self-determination in one's sexual choices but also as an experience in lowering the level of reproductive labor, in so far as this was supplied within the structure of relationships that tended toward greater equality. Having a relationship with a woman rather than a man required spending less energy on reaching an agreement on the division of housework, since the division was not expressed through sexual roles. It is also possible to add that since the feminist movement's construction of political work, struggles and debates were developing almost exclusively among women, so there was a greater preference to expend reproductive labor on a woman than on a man, since it was both more consistent with the type of sociality being experienced and more 'productive'—if that is the right word—in political terms. Here, in any case, the problem was not so much one of winning legalization, but rather of neutralizing criminalization by the state through blackmail at work and denial of the right to keep the children in legal separation cases.

Similarly, in the case of prostitution the problem was not legalization but, instead, as in other countries, opposition to prostitution's criminalization: to neutralize criminalization and achieve the repeal of those legislative measures that, though they did not strike at prostitution directly, supported its criminalization indirectly. Prostitution, in any case, remained a strongly criminalized activity precisely because it is a rejection of the essential terms of matrimonial exchange. In this respect, what is being rejected is the notion of unlimited labor or reproduction in exchange for maintenance, and conversely prostitution can be analyzed as the direct exchange of money for given sexual tasks. The fact that sex, the central task of domestic labor, is freed from the mystification of the marriage 'love pact' (the labor of love)[8] and achieves a direct exchange against money rather than just 'maintenance' has always attracted the highest levels of criminalization and the greatest need to isolate the women in question. Here, then, the struggle in the 1970s was extremely difficult, but it had the merit of creating a general commitment over an issue that had been largely ignored in the debate on the class struggle. It made it possible to clear the ground for the subsequent planting of a series of explicit demands.

In Italy, a Prostitute's Committee was set up at Pordenone, not far from Venice, in 1982. The prostitutes have their own newspaper, their own Charter of Rights, and have broken out of their ghetto through numerous debates in various forums. Above all, working as a prostitute also provided a more or less precarious source of income, whether adding to other wages or in the absence of other wages. During the 1970s, an increasingly large number women from more diverse social strata worked as prostitutes. In 1980, it was estimated that at least one million Italian women were working as prostitutes,[9] but the figure was considered a significant underestimate. Furthermore, it was also recognized that an increasing number of women supplied this form of labor to satisfy a trend toward increasingly high consumption, rather than for mere survival.

Today we have once more reached a significant moment for women's work and the rejection of it. On the one hand, the trend toward rejection of the unpaid reproductive labor in favor of an increasingly extensive availability for the market in wage labor has been confirmed. On the other hand, not only has there been no significant revival of the rates of either birth or marriage, the increase in the female workforce from 1977 to 1982 is almost double that of men: a rise of 872 thousand for women, compared with 469 thousand for men. It is true, however, that only two-thirds of the women's labor power on offer in fact found jobs. Analyzing the trend of the women's labor market in the same period, we find that female employment continued to fall in agriculture but was stationary in industry, where it was concentrated in small and medium-sized firms with 200–499 employees, among whom 30 percent were women, and increased in the service sector, where 58 percent of the total were women in 1982.

In 1983, women held 6,621,000 jobs in Italy, compared with 6,561,000 in the previous year.[10] At the same time, there was also an increase in the number of women declaring themselves as unemployed or in search of their first job. But a number of heavy limitations weigh on women's employment, which has already begun to show a slower growth rate.

The rapid spread of microelectronics in the 1980s and the resulting transformation of the service sector, which in previous years had been the most significant area of growth for women's employment, may have created new jobs, but it has also aroused fears of a reduction in job options. This is not only because 'further rationalization' would shift a series of tasks to microprocessors, but also because of the failure to set up training courses for women so that they might fill the new jobs that restructuring creates and, above all, cope with the change of tasks that comes with the rapid obsolescence and replacement of the machines being used. At the same time, as in all the technologically more developed countries, there is the plan, even if it is not yet a reality in Italy, to farm out work to women at home, using video terminals. Above all, especially with regards to the service sector, the policy of restricting public expenditure should not be ignored, particularly given the reduction in the number of employees on the government payroll and, more generally, a decline in employment opportunities, not least through attacks on absenteeism and the suppression of 'baby pension' rights by which some civil servants can begin drawing a pension at a relatively early age. These are all factors that place heavy limits on the further development of women's employment and annul the service sector's role in compensating for losses in other sectors of the economy.

So, for the coming years, according to forecasts that seem to be well based, the social framework will be defined by the following coordinates: a further fall in the number of births, increasing pressure on women and old people to stay in the labor market (with the latter under an ever greater obligation to do so due to the inflationary erosion of pensions and incomes), the extension of new technologies, the augmentation of education (but, in keeping with the new productive processes, for whom and for how many?), greater flexibility of labor, and a growth in part-time work. Currently, in Italy, the institutional debate is focused not so much on labor costs as on employment levels, since it is thought that the system cannot tolerate either the current levels of unemployment[11] or the levels anticipated in the immediate future, with young people, women, immigrants, and returning emigrants the hardest hit. For women, this is also because they have more difficulty in finding new jobs, and because trade union, government, and management policies seem to be united in sacrificing them.

There is a debate on reducing the workweek (to thirty-five hours) to create jobs at the same or different wage levels. But the most significant discussion is not on small reductions in the amount of time worked, which would be very problematic if accompanied by wage reductions, but rather on the creation of a totally different organization of work at the general level. By this I mean the creation of a more precarious labor market with lower wages for sectors considered less productive or functions considered less important. These conditions, which it is expected will be generally accepted, are promoted by the much trumpeted need for 'deregulation.' It is said quite openly that young people, above all, and women must be ready to accept substandard wages.

Thus, the 'microelectronic revolution' brings with it the baggage of mass poverty. Reminding us, if there was any need for it, that it too is a child of the usual capitalist mode of production, with its old vice of compressing proletarian reproduction by trusting in the 'miracles' worked by women. However, it is improbable that such miracles will eventuate. Instead, what is more likely is that the mass of working men and women, together with the old people, immigrants, and returning emigrants, will be forced into a harsh search for survival in conditions of total insecurity. With the general lowering of working hours and wages, which for most people will further reduce the possibility, if not the long vanished convenience, of procreation, how much willingness will there be left for interindividual reproduction? With the downgrading of reproduction, the 'miracle' of domestic labor laid bare, and the lover in eclipse . . . what will be the future of love?

Notes

This essay was originally published in *International Sociology* 3, no.1 (March 1988): 23–34.

1   Here, as always, I take 'housework' in the broad sense of the 'labor of production and reproduction of labor power,' not in the vulgarized sociological sense of a collection of material tasks such as cleaning, cooking, washing, etc.

2   I speak of the woman's 'decision,' which could, for the most part, only be put into effect almost entirely illegally, since at that time there was a firm prohibition against contraception and abortion.

3   In this connection, I take into account the recent processes of urbanization and the possibility of finding a job for those who came from the country and the Italian south.

4   According to ISTAT (1973), 4,881,000 women were employed in 1972, while the 1979 figure was 6,296,000 (ISTAT 1980).

5   I have dealt with this aspect and these moments of the feminist struggle in the 1970s in my article "Percorsi femminili e politica della riproduzione della forza lavoro negli anni '70," *La Critica Sociologica* 61 (Spring 1982): 50–73.

6   In this connection we should remember the incidence of a factor discussed below: the postponement of procreation.

7   Since the legislation on this form of work makes it convenient to work illegally, the women supplying domestic help build up their right to a pension through voluntary contributions.

8   Leopoldina Fortunati, *The Arcane of Reproduction: Housework, Prostitution, Labor and Capital* (New York: Autonmedia, 1995).

9   According to what emerged at the "Aspetti biologici, sociali e giuridici della prostituzione" congress organized by the Italian Academy of Moral and Biological Sciences in Rome in 1980.

10   Data from ISTAT (1984) show that 14,083,000 men were employed in 1983, compared with 14,116,000 in 1982 (ISTAT 1983).

11   According to ISTAT (1984), 2,278,000 people were unemployed in 1983, whereas the unemployment figure for 1984 (ISTAT 1985) was 2,391,000. The latter is an unemployment rate of 10.4 percent.

Reproduction and Emigration (1974)

Mariarosa Dalla Costa at an International Women's Day demonstration organized by the Triveneto WFH committee in Mestre, Venice, March 8–10, 1974.

I. Introduction

1.

Since at least the end of the nineteenth century, under the guise of the 'question' of the *optimal size of the population*, political economy has been posing the problem of state control over birth and fertility rates with an eye to the expansion or contraction of the labor market. The other side of this question was the *optimal size of the state* and the associated problem of the availability of 'cannon fodder' for imperial wars.

It is hardly surprising that this question arose precisely at the point when birth rates had begun to fall in all European countries during the nineteenth century, with the exception of France, where it had begun to drop earlier, in the last quarter of the eighteenth century.

The other side of the problem was that the *population was growing in inverse proportion to its level of well-being*, in that a rise in the standard of living was leading to a drop in the fertility rate[1] allaying Malthusian fears of overpopulation but simultaneously undermining government hopes that economic development would be secured through the adequate reproduction of labor power.

State control over birth and fertility rates means, above all else, *state control over women's fate*. It means diminished opportunities for women to be 'social individuals,' and instead casts them as mere appendages to state economic planning for growth or stagnation.

The *state only becomes concerned* about the gap between fertility and birth rates when the latter is considered to be *too low*, and it responds by abolishing all means of contraception and abortion. Both Nazism and fascism were typical in this respect, although they only enforced such policies within the national boundaries of Hitler's Germany and Mussolini's Italy and not in the colonies. However, as long as the birth rate is considered to be adequate, the state ignores any disparity between fertility and birth rates and remains indifferent to the fact that women abort or to how they abort.

We are not concerned here with listing all the independent variables that may affect the state's attitude, but it is worth noting that the state's interest in adjusting the birth rate and, to a lesser degree, the fertility rate may vary both in time and space and, most importantly, in the span of the same regime. For example, the demographic history of the USSR after 1917 (and of Eastern European countries after 1945) shows a continuous oscillation between extreme permissiveness and rigid control.[2] *Despite the provision of material incentives, the birth rate fell short* of the planner's expectations, particularly in key areas of the USSR. As will be discussed later, this was also the case in Western Europe, which will be the main focus of the analysis in this essay.

How should one interpret *women's resistance to such planning*? It can in fact be interpreted very simply as *women's lack of identification with the so-called common good.* Women could see that the 'common good' effectively meant a planned rate of economic growth that would keep them either tied to long hours of work in the factories and offices of Eastern Europe or at home and in the fields of some Western European countries.

In his excellent book *World Revolution and Family Patterns*,[3] the U.S. sociologist William J. Goode argues:

> The important change is not, therefore, that the birth rate has dropped in the last generation, for its decline had already begun in France in the last quarter of the 18th century, in the United States by the early 19th century and in England and possibly Sweden and Belgium before 1875. Rather, the change is in the general acceptance of the opinion that husband and wife may control the number of their children if they wish to do so; as a consequence, both decline and rise may occur more quickly than in the past, as rapid adjustment to alterations in the life situation, such as prosperity or war, or the particular experience of special segments of the population.[4]

We can add that this *control* over the number of offspring is a greater burden for women than for the family as a whole and *has been a growing tendency*, and not a particularly surprising one. In fact, after the war the state suffered a loss of credibility in the eyes of the average man and woman. If to this loss of credibility one adds the increasing awareness of parents that they could offer little else to their children than the prospect of a future in the factory, it is clear why women's reactions to state demographic policies were wary. Women and the state have unrelated and completely diverging interests, a divergence that is particularly visible in countries where the state wants to maintain high fertility and birth rates. It is not hard to see how the capitalist class in Italy found it had won many advantages from population growth during the years of fascism. It is also clear that women only managed to combat and evade Mussolini's demographic policies by contravening the laws of both the Church and the state. Their success in evading those laws can be measured in terms of the relatively low increase in the number of births[5] and the tens of millions of abortions that were carried out during and after the regime.

In the 1950s, the children born during the Mussolini period came of age. But where were most of that generation channeled? They went from the fields of the north and from the entire south of Italy into the *Italian industrial triangle* and to *Central Europe*. There is little doubt that the provision of labor power by the Italian governments of the time, particularly in relation to the Swiss and German governments, gave the Italian ruling class a powerful lever in bargaining with its foreign partners.

But what conclusions should women, particularly women of southern Italy, draw about a state that bargains on the basis of a flow of labor power abroad? Was this situation any different from the flow of labor power into Germany in the period between 1939 and 1942? A flow that was organized by the heads of states[6] and that people were forced to accept given the high level of unemployment in Italy. Indeed, women's *no*, their refusal to accept state coercion, had and has well-founded reasons—reasons that lie both in the past and in the future.

2.

In moving the argument to a more general level, going beyond the Italian case, one is able to see that *the formation of a multinational working class has its origins in the history of women as a section of the class.* Women, particularly *since the postwar period*, began to take their own direction in an increasingly homogeneous and diffuse way. Hence, the emergence of *a new quality of political power*, as expressed by this class, has to be both attributed to and defined in terms of the *new processes of autonomy opened up within the class by its various sections and particularly by women*. Above all by women's refusal to *procreate*.

During the second half of the 1960s, all European countries registered a dramatic fall in the birth rates[7] that cannot be wholly attributed to the increased availability of contraceptives.[8] The birth rate fell particularly steeply among those sections of the population that had previously been less successful in controlling their fertility.[9] Women were better able to reject state controls over procreation the more they resisted pressure from within the family, the elderly, their husbands, and their other children.

This rejection and resistance can be found to a greater or lesser degree in all countries irrespective of whether the number of women in wage work is high or low, whether the country is one of immigration or emigration, or whether the women are 'native' or immigrants.

Thus, *the family*, the center of unpaid work and personal dependence, has emerged as the primary terrain through which women have managed to resist and to organize themselves on a mass level. The more women succeed in freeing themselves from the constraints of the family, the more they are able to succeed in *emancipating themselves from the conditions that limit their ability to improve their lives*.

First of all in the agricultural context:

a) The process of emancipation from various family constraints that occurred with the passage from the patriarchal peasant family to the urban nuclear family has been marked by a *transformation in the way women manage the wage*,[10] even though they have overwhelmingly continued to prioritize their children's needs and not their own.

As the former authority and control by older relatives diminished, women became freer to spend their wages rather than save them, in contrast to the pressure to do so before. Women mainly spent it in order to improve their children's situations. Children began to be raised on baby food and got used to having cigarettes, tape recorders, and record players.

All of this is common in areas with a certain level of industrialization. However, this is not true in areas such as southern Italy *where women, left alone because of migration*, still have to struggle in their own interests and for improvements in the material living conditions in their neighborhoods, for water, for work, etc. But *their struggles accelerate the struggles of their children*, who use any means possible to obtain a better standard of living, and it is in this context that the higher rates of 'juvenile delinquency' and analogous phenomena found in the south should be understood.

In both instances, industrial and southern, the course of women's autonomous struggles for better living conditions for both themselves and their children has created a new generation, a new working class, and a new level of struggle.

The fact that women are less and less inclined to or interested in getting married, have fewer children, and are willing to use any means possible to improve theirs and their children's lives, *all this is reflected in the struggles in the factory*. Young male workers, immigrant or not, are less concerned about whether they marry (because women are less concerned about getting married),[11] are less likely to be the fathers of large families, and are *already used to struggling at any cost* when the family wage fails to provide a certain standard of living.

Clearly women's refusal to procreate and their attempts to improve their children's situation have met with more success in some countries than in others. In countries such as France, Germany, and Switzerland, where there tends to be a shortage of labor power and workers have higher expectations, the working class is able to earn better wages. In other areas, such as southern Italy, the Iberian Peninsula (Spain and Portugal), the Maghreb, and Turkey, women are less able to restrict the number of births and have less chance of raising their children's standard of living. But when *European capital* attempts to 'buy' the children of underdevelopment and use them against the children of development, *it finds itself increasingly faced with women's resistance, their struggle, and the value of their work.*
b) Thus *migration becomes the state's policy response to women's refusal to comply and procreate.* It represents an attempt to recuperate the working class both qualitatively and quantitatively, so as to restore adequate discipline and to achieve a population size that is functional for capital. It is also the *response to both what the refusal represents as a process of struggle and to the new relationships it establishes.* The new multinational working class is the direct expression of that process.[12]

As previously discussed, for women in Europe, the postwar years were years of struggle when they began to reject the agricultural life-style with its long hours of work in the house and the fields, to reject the patriarchal peasant family with its hierarchical power structure

74

dominated by men and elder relatives, and to reject the isolation of the small village and the power and influence of the Church. The differences in the degree of industrialization, the proportion of women in wage work, in leaving/abandoning the countryside, in immigration and emigration, and so on that one finds in various countries made no difference to the general tenor of women's struggles; everywhere they were seeking to free themselves from personal and economic dependence and from endless work schedules. It is not difficult to draw a parallel between the insubordination of mothers, wives, and daughters in the unwaged workplace—the family—and the insubordination of both men and women in the waged workplace—the factory.

In *Western Europe, emigration* was seen as the answer to struggles in both of these areas, family and factory, an *arc of struggles* that had begun to take on new qualities and that were more subversive than their predecessors.

Emigration is therefore the state's counteroffensive launched against *women's refusal to procreate* in line with state policy and against the new forms of relationships between men and women and between the waged and unwaged workplaces. Emigration not only seeks to restore the birth rate, or rather to restore the class to the required size and to the required discipline, it also seeks to break up the process of struggle that lies behind the refusal to procreate on demand.

a) *Emigration impacts* not only the individual who is separated and isolated from his/her community and its network of organization, *it also impacts the community itself, especially women* who are its main pillar and who are deprived of their links with both the younger and more independent sections of the class.

b) *Through the processes of emigration*, labor power from more 'backward' areas is pitted against labor power from 'advanced' areas. This does not only involve the use of young immigrant labor power (which is more isolated and politically disorganized) against local more organized labor power, it is also a way of hitting at the women left behind—*the women of the more backward areas*—women who have had less success in developing their own struggles. Thus, these women are effectively used against the women of the more advanced areas, against women who have gained more power.

c) *In metropolitan areas* that receive the inflow of migrants, *each new wave of migration further distances in time and space the opportunities for immigrant women of different sectors and for these women and the native women* to organize among themselves. It marks another tear in the fabric that connects work in the home to work in the factory, specifically the connection between reproductive work and productive work.

d) In addition, migration *impacts women in the waged workplace as well*, where men tend to take precedence over them.

3.

The prevalence of men taking precedence over women in the waged workplace *began to change, especially after 1968* and during the 1970s. Immigrant women began to be hired in such *sectors as mechanical engineering and the automobile and chemical industries.*

But how should this be interpreted? Did and does it mean that capital preferred to employ immigrant women rather than men in key sectors— including those mentioned above? Is it a sign of a more general shift to employing women outside the home, one that would meet with the approval of reformists who think 'women should do their best to grab this opportunity?' Broadly speaking, no. Indeed, the conclusions one can draw from this new trend are very different.

In all these sectors—the mechanics, automobile, and chemical industries—women were always employed at the lowest, most unskilled grades. Thus, one of the main reasons behind women being employed was an attempt to break the level of struggle reached by the more recent waves of male immigrants. At the same time, women's new independence had already created a tension in the relationship between them and capital and between them and the state because of the requirements of planned economic growth and the levels of reproduction (both procreation and housework) that were needed in order to meet growth goals. This has increasingly become the cornerstone of development not only in Western Europe but also in Eastern Europe and the rest of the world.[13] As previously discussed, women's refusal to procreate and to pay the price of reproduction in general affected intraclass relations and new power structures, particularly in the case of women and youth who depend on women's work.

Thus, it is in this context that the employment of women in key sectors must be examined. And the main questions are, therefore:

For how long will capital be able *to use women as a means of breaking up the struggles of the more recent immigrants* who have often already assimilated and incorporated the struggles of women in the community they come from?

How well can this policy realistically work, given that it is *based on the traditional political weakness of women in the factory* and seems to ignore the fact that *women have already opened up their struggle outside the factory?*

To what extent can women be employed in the factory at the same time as they are *being encouraged to fulfil their reproductive functions*— functions that women have shown a willingness to reject if they have to pay too high a price, given the conditions of housework and of factory and office work: given the conditions of their lives as a whole?

In addition, the context of women being employed in key sectors connects to wider issues and debates, often espoused by the many politicians who claim to be responding to the international emergence of the feminist movement: the problem of female employment. In this context it seems unrealistic to posit that the admission of women into the bastions of male employment—the mechanics, automobile, and chemical industries—represents an about-face in capital's attitude toward female employment. That is, contrary to one line of argument, it cannot be taken as an attempt on the part of capital to abolish the separation of male and female labor markets. It is no coincidence that the people who now welcome the 'mixed factory' as a means of abolishing this separation are the same people who once denied that such a separation even existed.

II. During World War II and in the postwar period the 'equilibrium' of the relationship between production and reproduction as embodied in certain geographical areas and previously existing community structures was broken.

Why start with World War II? Because World War II represented *a massive attack on the value of labor power* and the starting point for the reconstruction of capitalist power on an international level. However, because labor power has for so long been taken as male labor power, this statement cannot indicate the true complexity of the kind of attack we mean nor the complexity of the new relationships that were created during the process of forming a multinational working class.

In his very original reading of workers' struggles during the postwar resistance in Italy, Romolo Gobbi[14] cites the following important data and argues that "during this period the real wage was systematically eroded to the point where in 1945 it was only 22 percent of the real wage in 1913, thus it was only one fifth of the already low wage of thirty years before."[15] Moreover, he continues:

> During World War I, taking advantage of the growth of the workforce employed in war production, the working class had launched a powerful attack on that earlier wage level, and by 1921 had succeeded in raising the wage level to 127, taking 1913 as 100 on the index. During this cycle of struggles the workers also won other victories, such as the eight-hour day and the recognition of worker's representation in the factory at the shop floor level.[16]

By contrast, in 1945, not only had the real wage fallen to one-fifth of its 1913 level, but during the war itself the workers had clearly failed to achieve a level of power in any way comparable with that won during World War I. This indicates that World War II was based on a set of imperialist relations very different qualitatively from those of World War I.

In the USA workers were largely successful in defending their wage. Of course, no army invaded the U.S. and there was a much smaller loss of life in comparison to that in European countries.[17] There was no drastic food rationing, in that "calorie deficiency caused by inadequate diet is a problem the average American never had to face, even in wartime."[18] Women's employment in factories and offices in the U.S. did not take place in the context of a violent attack on the whole community as it did in Europe. The highest levels of violence and deprivation all took place on the other side of the Atlantic, and it was the consequent *weakening and breakdown of relationships that provided the base on which emigration was established.*

The attack on the value of labor power in Europe meant the use of forced labor—male and female prisoners in Germany and the widest possible use and employment of women in factories, offices, and services in Great Britain.

> As long as there were jobless men on the labor market they did not resort to using women in war industry. At the beginning their existence was forgotten. In December 1939, the unemployed women officially registered numbered 270,000 . . . in March 1941, the government

decided to put women to work . . . their recruiting resembled in many ways the recruiting of men for military service. The only ones exempted were the farmwomen who replaced their husbands who were called up for military service, nurses, midwives, and teachers. In May 1942, mobilization was extended to eighteen and nineteen-year-old women. In 1944, 7,650,000 women found themselves organized in industry and the auxiliary services, or in civil defense. Another 900,000 worked part-time under the control of these same services. Yet another million were unpaid volunteers in the Woman's Voluntary Service. Eventually it became necessary to incorporate the farm-women, nurses, and teachers etc. . . . and to decentralize production to the greatest possible extent. Depots and factories were hurriedly organized in residential suburban areas, where it was possible to recruit mothers. . . . Part-time work grew rapidly.[19]

On the whole, it was this *attack on the relationship between production and reproduction, on male labor power and female labor power*, that undermined any possibility of working-class defense (a defense previously maintained at women's expense) and that began the radicalization of the process of women's autonomy. Women as labor power were not only hit harder by the war but were also the ones who were made most responsible for supporting and defending themselves and the community. In the face of the state's arbitrary will, women discovered that *the community could no longer protect them from anything*, but at the same time, precisely because of the weakness and the dependency of their relationships within the community they had to pay a very high price to support it. This is why women eventually began to identify less and less with the community and also, perhaps, why they were *the unexpected force* that emerged in the aftermath of World War II.

As for Italy, let us return to Gobbi's perceptive analysis. "The nosedive taken by working-class wages and the drop in calories, which fell below the level of subsistence, were the outcome of two concomitant factors: inflation and the upsetting of the equilibrium of exchange between the city and the countryside."[20] The costs of reproduction, women's 'primary' work, rose rapidly during the war. It was not simply that work multiplied because of the difficulty of obtaining provisions and the cost of basic goods, (the echoes of the women's demonstration in Turin in 1946 "will last a long time"),[21] it was also the fact that women had to take on 'secondary' work, low-wage jobs, in order to send money and goods to the soldiers who would not have been able to survive on state pay. In order to reproduce themselves, their children, the soldiers, and the elderly, women were forced to take on every type of work possible: in the home, the fields, and the factory. But while working in a factory, in an office, or driving a bus gave women an idea of the power of having a paycheck of their own, it also revealed how low and how discriminatory their pay was in relation to that of men.[22]

In Italy it was often easier to survive in the countryside because of what could be gleaned from the land. In England, the countryside became the center for the organization of homeworking. "Villages in the peaceful English countryside began to discover the novelty of being public clearing centers for equipment and for depots of raw materials that women came to collect. In the Midlands alone, it has been calculated that the work done in the home using this kind of organization replaced more than one thousand full-time women workers. This decentralization of production was a great advantage in a country that was continuously subject to bombardments that were designed to upset its economy."[23] In countries like Italy, France, and Germany, often the only way to survive in the city was to take up prostitution. This work was often accompanied by illegitimate births, venereal diseases, and high infant mortality—the fruit of both the troops in transit and of centuries of terrorism directed against the use of contraception and abortion.

As for women's role in the resistance, there is not enough space here to go into such a complex subject. However, just to mention some of the biggest contradictions in their condition caused by the war, one point should be made, that women's role in the resistance becomes clear if one looks at it from the point of view of their work. Women, *as well as* working in the home, the fields, and the factories, often performed the *riskiest political work*, just like their Vietnamese[24] and Algerian[25] sisters. At the same time, they had almost no voice in political organization.[26]

For women, the postwar period meant redundancy, getting the sack, or relegation to the lowest paid, most insecure jobs. In Britain, though, this happened on a lesser scale than elsewhere. In December 1945, the Minister of Labour tried to control the movement of 'the return home.' Nevertheless, the men came back looking for work for themselves and expecting women to return to looking after the reunited family. The number of officially unemployed women rose quickly. In order not to lose their jobs women were forced to accept lower wages. No laws were enacted to force employers to give men and women equal pay for equal work.[27]

In Italy both the expulsion of women from waged jobs and the soaring cost of living were more extreme. In Turin, ten thousand women wanted to throw the prefect out of the window in 1946.[28] The Communist Party accepted the Lateran Agreements; meanwhile in red Puglia women were attacking religious processions with stones, and in the north there was a general air of rebellion, even in the prisons. The Italian state's response was repression, which began with attacks on the weaker sections of the class— women, youth, and others—and then moved on to attack those sectors that the Christian Democrats couldn't control.[29] *Giving the vote to women* was a mere gesture, a 'fig leaf' to cover up the discontent that the reformist parties were trying to repress by every means possible. Simultaneously, there was an attempt to relaunch the policy of demographic expansion that had been a feature of the years after 1929—this time though it went under the banner of anti-communist restoration.[30] In postwar Europe, in general, there was a concerted effort to put everyone back into their traditional roles, the places they had come from.

Not everywhere though. In some countries women were not the subject of mass sacking and redundancy. In the countries of Eastern Europe, for example, female employment in wage work rose in order to replace the millions of men who had been killed in the war. And in Western Europe, in Germany, the level of female employment remained high until 1960, after which it began to fall off.

Throughout Europe demographic policies that centered on the introduction or expansion of existing systems of family allowance were experimented with, generally coupled with other economic incentives. France began to reduce its traditionally high level of female employment and established a *salaire unique* allowance for the women who were sent back into the home.[31] This measure was not only intended to provide a small financial incentive to these women but also to encourage a rise in the birth rate. The main aim of all these demographic policies was to rebuild the relationship between women and the family. Their experiences during the war and in the postwar era had made women realize that the family structure, extended or not, was the *center of organization* of work that not only did not pay them but also *left them completely defenseless*, both when the men were absent and when they returned. Not only did the community *oblige them to procreate*, but it also exposed them to a *dual blackmail*: by the employers and by the men who expected them to return meekly to their 'household chores.'

Cutting the umbilical cord that bound them both to the 'general interest' and to the family *became an increasingly important issue for all women* in the immediate postwar years.

Above all, the rupture came with the *refusal to procreate*[32]—a function that when performed within the traditional family structure creates a high workload and restricted lifestyle. For women, the war had come to mean not only the decimation of 'the fruit of their wombs' but also a lethal attack on women's conditions, in work and toil under conditions that meant they risked their lives.

Consequently, the struggle around procreation that spread throughout Europe was and is *a struggle against the organization of the family*—which instead of protecting women condemns them to powerlessness. As a result, the rebellion that began in the family *extended beyond the confines of the family unit itself and out into the community upon which the family depends.* A community that both sustains and replicates the family: the village and the urban network of relatives and friends that help women to get by in cities and towns, where, especially in southern Italy, access to a wage is limited. In this sense, the growth, spread, and *development of a course of action led by women throughout Europe was also to determine, to some degree, the course of action followed by men.*

Women led the flight from the rural areas into the cities—from small rural landowners (sharecroppers or smallholder families), from family-owned and managed firms,[33] from the villages and smaller towns—and did so, moreover, despite the restrictions on residence imposed under fascist laws that were still in force. It was a widespread, very broad movement that revealed women's lack of identification with their social environment, their refusal to bear the costs of or accept the quality of life that their environment imposed on them. *Marriage itself was be used as an instrument for rejecting that environment.*

In countries like Italy during the 1950s and the 1960s the rejection of marriage was often used in this way.[34] The high proportion of women workers at home, and therefore unwaged, in relation to the numbers of workers working outside the home, and therefore waged, rendered the Italian situation anomalous in comparison with other European countries. Hence, the *rebellion against their situation as women* could not have been simply a refusal of marriage,[35] even if their situation within the family had been revealed to them during the war and in the postwar period.

The increase in the workload of housework during the war that was the result of the difficulty of obtaining goods and of high prices has already been discussed. Rationing continued in the postwar period until 1947,[36] and, at the same time, national income, which had been halved in the period 1938 to 1945, "never rose above the prewar level until 1949."[37] Furthermore, despite the fact that by 1948 production had reached 1938 levels again, and that by 1960 both national and individual income had almost doubled, *the national per capita income in Italy was still one of the lowest in Western Europe.*"[38]

What this meant for women in terms of work and dependence, women who were left without any wage of their own and were at best seen as appendages to their husband's wage, is succinctly revealed by the statistics, which show that it was mainly women who died of the so-called diseases of underdevelopment, vitamin deficiency and problems of blood circulation.[39] In other words, in the countryside, but not only there, women would go to bed without eating to make sure others—husbands and children—ate[40] and they would stand for too many hours and spend too much time with their hands in water.[41] Meanwhile women and youth in the city had even fewer prospects.

This is not new. However, it has not been presented in order to simply discuss what happens during and after wars; instead, these statistics, some facts, and the analysis of certain crucial aspects (ignored until now in political discussion) have been set out in order to trace and uncover the drastic break in the relationship between production and reproduction. A break that brought about the disintegration of whole social sectors, and it was on this break and the consequent social breakdown that emigration was founded. It was from here that women began definitively to separate themselves from the community that they had already wanted to leave to make their own path. Even before migration began, the community had nothing to give to women.

Before concluding this discussion, however, it is worth looking at what the *farmworkers' struggles* had meant to women. While most people would agree about the backwardness of the slogan "the land to the tiller" (with all the ambiguities of the reformist program that went with it), what is of interest is another 'backwardness,' or perhaps more correctly a weakness, whereby women still hoped to be able to use the struggles of men at a time when *the proletarian family was profoundly changed and not only for the will of capital.*

The mass emigration of men ended the cycle of insurrections wherein women occupied the land carrying red flags and barrels of water, becoming, together with men and young people, the defenseless targets of the police and taking part in actions in whose organization they were allowed no say. Angelina Mauro's death marked the end of an era.[42] With emigration, only women, children, and old people were left.

However, the migrants who now went north were able to send much less money back than their predecessors, the emigrants to America. Furthermore, they were less willing to send it home to support someone else. As a result, young women began to look for work, any work—domestic service in the cities, piecework at home, and seasonal jobs. However, one positive outcome of the farmhand struggles was that women were freed from the infamous custom of having to serve the landowner's wife for free.[43] As their husbands emigrated and became factory workers and no longer worked as farmhands, women's refusal was definitive. Simultaneously, now that there were fewer men in the agricultural labor market women's wages on the land jumped from 400 liras a day to 1,200—2,000 liras.

In addition to having some money of their own, remittances from the men began to arrive—though not all that regularly. Women also began for the first time to directly administer both money and the property left behind by the men. They were still controlled by the elder members of the family, but all the same it marked a definitive change within the southern Italian community. Women never followed the men on a large scale, although a few did, and this is why there are still so many women in the south today. If the family had been unable to offer anything to women other than dependence and work in their hometowns, what hope could they realistically have that it would be any better for them in an immigrant ghetto? Women chose another path.

III. Emigration is founded in and on this break, but it functions as a catalyst and in some areas generalizes women's paths toward autonomy that are already underway.

The Italian Case

With the advent of Italian emigration to Germany, the process of *women's autonomy radicalized* in both north and south Italy and took on many of the features of struggles in other European countries, which were also being restructured in a similar way. *Emigration is the key factor in the process of the*

European postwar reconstruction of the working class. It was used as part of a direct attack on the value of both male and female labor power: an attack that was first unleashed during the war. This use of emigration is founded on the breakdown of the organizational structures of the proletarian and on the attack on their possible reproduction. It is reproduction that had to bear the main brunt of the attack—which is why the proletariat was forced to enter the factory and become part of the multinational working class.

In 1943, women in Sicily burned down the houses assigned to their families by the fascist government, which were located far from the village, to defend the sense of community that the village offered—even if there was also a desire to leave the village itself. They did so despite their recognition of the contradictions inherent in the community. But when the men emigrated, these desires and contradictions finally exploded; the village no longer offered them anything.

Through the processes of emigration, specifically the way it revealed the precarious nature of relationships, one can trace the progress of women's tendency to refuse state policy and control. Women's refusal to submit to the state's plan for economic growth, a plan that meant having to bear innumerable children and remaining tied for interminably long hours to the house and the fields. A plan that deprived them of any personal freedom and autonomy and left them in a position of dependence on others—the family and the village, where now, in the absence of the men, the older generation held sway. In the south of Italy, administering the remittances in a family where only the elderly remained, and where women had to face the double burden of a large household and work on the land, meant paying a personal price that women would no longer accept.

This situation was common in both south and north. In the north it was particularly true in the context of small rural peasant farms. Wherever the state attempted to tie women to long hours and isolate them, they left the land and fled. In her study *Women against the Family*, Leopoldina Fortunati shows how, in the Italian context, women's struggles against the family developed through struggles against farm labor. She shows how this struggle spread and intensified as more and more women began to manage the wage (including remittances) in new ways.

The movement from the land into the towns and cities took place on a very large scale despite government attempts to control it, in that residence is only granted to those who have a job and a job is only given to those who have residence.

Among other strategies, women used marriage during this period as a way to leave the land. They were less and less willing to marry men who would not, or could not, take them to the city.[44] Moving to the city not only meant working for one person instead of for many, it also meant more opportunities to restrict and control the number of children they had, since it meant freedom from the pressures of the family and the village. "Our hypotheses are confirmed . . . the voluntary control of procreation first spread and spread faster among urban populations than among other sections of the population. Such voluntary control, coupled with a lower propensity to marry, had a considerable impact on the number of births."[45]

Concerning the fall in the birth rate in Italy between 1861 and 1961, Giorgio Mortara writes that "where birth control is practiced through celibacy or late marriage one can see a fall in the total number of married couples, particularly young married couples; where the use of contraception or the suppression of the results of conception are commonly practiced one can sometimes see a rise in the numbers of married couples."[46] He goes on to confirm our hypothesis that "the increased concentration of the population in urban centers and the suburbs has encouraged the spread of practices designed to limit births."[47]

The city meant and means *more power* for proletarian women. Not only are they *better able to control the number of children they have,* they also have *greater opportunities to improve the quality of both their own lives and those of their children.*

The French Case

The movement from the land to the city and the shift toward having a higher degree of a power and control over reproduction was a European-wide phenomenon for women. In the aftermath of World War II women throughout Europe began to fight against the demands of procreation, even in areas where the social fabric had survived better, or rather disintegrated less, than in the south of Italy. Women everywhere were finding that the price they had to pay within reproduction was too high and the dependency and isolation that it brought were unacceptable.

The situation in France is closest of all to the Italian situation.[48] The French state progressively cut female employment to a very low level. Notwithstanding this, and in part going directly against it, women deserted agriculture and small family firms in growing numbers. Moreover, French women won a degree of control over procreation earlier than women in other European countries.[49] This control created problems for capital's plans for postwar reconstruction. In 1945, the head of the Provisional Government of the French Republic, Charles de Gaulle, appealed to French women to produce "twelve million beautiful babies."[50] Simultaneously, the French government encouraged immigration from Algeria in a move that was seen explicitly as a "policy of repopulation."[51]

This is not to say that De Gaulle's grotesque appeal found any immediate solution through Algerian immigration. The real problem was not simply one of the quantitative restoration of the working class, it was rather more an attempt on the part of the state to neutralize women's struggles, which were threatening reconstruction plans. The connection between the orchestration of France's demographic policies[52] and female employment[53] after the war and the 'structure' of Algerian emigration is clear. Algerian emigration was described as a policy of repopulation, however, it would be better to call it a policy for the restoration of the working class. Algerian women came with their husbands and children and continued to produce more children,[54] children who were in the main destined to go into the factory.

It should be emphasized again that this is not a mathematical but a political relationship and should be seen in political terms. Although very few politicians recognize or even notice it,[55] the connection between an 'unacceptable' rate of population growth—uncorrected by the provision of material incentives or by the expulsion or further marginalization of women—and the use of emigration policies has a long history.

The path to autonomy taken by women in France was, as we said earlier, very similar to that in Italy. The exodus from agriculture was massive. From 1910 to 1954, one in four agricultural laborers left the land. The same percentage holds true for the period between 1954 and 1962. After 1962, the pace accelerated.[56] In 1962, there were 1,272,000 female farmers and agricultural laborers; in 1906, there had been 3,329,000.[57]

Young women tend to leave the country first, even before men. "The young peasants who want to stay on the land look in vain for a wife. The girls have all fled to the city so as not to be treated like their mothers, so as not to be treated more like servants instead of 'Queens of the Fireplace.'"[58]

The *country schools* taught boys agronomy and agricultural mechanics and taught girls home economics. The flight from the country was more than a flight from personal isolation, slavery, and backwardness. It was a flight from dual work from which not even the new agricultural nationalization could save women. The state tried once again to send women back into the house and the countryside and to demand a reproductive function that none of the well-known economic incentives could induce them to provide. In this context, it's worth noting that because the laws passed in 1920—which prohibited abortion and advertising of contraceptives—had failed to raise the birth rate significantly,[59] from 1932 on, the French government had been forced to set up *a system of family allowances*.

After the war, these allowances—the *salaire unique*—became a dangerously contradictory provision. Dangerous, that is, for a system that had traditionally managed to maintain very high levels of housework—performed by women—precisely because housework had never been exchanged for a wage. Allowances did not provide a lot of money, but they did provide a monthly subsidy given by the state to the wife. The parallel with the British family allowance program that was instituted in 1945 is evident—both seek to encourage a positive attitude toward procreation, something that had deteriorated on an international level.[60]

Although the *salaire unique* was a small amount of money, in fact, a pittance, it was money that women tried desperately to accumulate, along with any pay they might obtain from unofficial jobs. Had women declared these jobs, they would automatically have lost the right to receive this allowance payment. Thus, pieceworkers, domestic servants, and part-time workers never declared their occupation for fear of losing the allowance.[61]

Once in the city it was difficult for French women to find employment and a steady wage.[62] The underlying aim of European integration was, as we have said, to further marginalize female labor power and discriminate against it. Rather the novelty was that women began to be introduced into industrial sectors that had been exclusively reserved for male workers.

On the whole, though, female employment in industry has been falling both absolutely and relatively since the beginning of the twentieth century. However, during the postwar period important changes occurred in the distribution of this decreasing amount of female labor power. One important example of this can be found in the way in which the textile sector was restructured, creating new, more skilled, and better paid jobs that are largely given to men. The women who have been expelled from this workforce found employment in electronics and the metal working industries at low-skill and low paid levels.

In the period from 1954 to 1962, women entered the mechanical engineering industry on a large scale (the number of women employed rose from 136,646 to 194,222, an increase of 42.1 percent). After 1962 the situation remained more or less stationary. During the same period (1954–1962) the number of women employed in the electrical industries rose from 65,500 to 114,000 (up 74 percent). Again, in this period the number of women employed in the chemical sector rose from 92,196 to 104,540 (up 13.4 percent). And in the food sector the number of women rose 8.8 percent, but here thousands of seasonal workers[63] have to be added to the figures for permanent workers. A certain increase in female employment also occurred in factories producing drugs, cosmetics, and plastics.

Both in traditional female sectors like footwear and porcelain and in 'new' sectors such as mechanical engineering, female workers are always relegated to the lowest positions. The only partial exceptions are the women who supervise female workshops in the clothing sector. But these jobs are not skilled, they are merely supervisory.[64] In the electrical sector there are no skilled female workers, because skilled work is reserved for men. The number of women employed as technicians in the industry is totally insignificant.[65] As Madeleine Guibert points out, the introduction of automation seems to have had the consequence of "accentuating the confinement of women."[66]

The Algerian Case

We cannot conclude an analysis of France in the postwar period (the 1950s) without considering what this meant for Algerian women, particularly given the close relationship between demographic and employment policies, on one hand, and emigration policies, on the other. We need to examine whether the impact of emigration on areas such as the Maghreb or in Turkey is in any way similar to that in the Italian south. In Italy's case we said that emigration tended to set in motion forces that broke up the community, in particular the new experiences women gained in managing remittances and minimal wages of their own[67] gave them moments of greater autonomy and power. Is this true of areas such as Algeria?

It is first of all necessary to emphasize that the *Algerian community was not devoid of tensions or subversive ideas on the part of women.* In the Algerian community there was and still is a lot of violence toward women. The Algerian state has always been violent toward women, both before and after the revolution. Women are involved in a daily struggle against men and the state. Women's position in Algeria is revealed most clearly by the number of murders and attempted murders of women by men,[68] the number of suicides and attempted suicides by women, and the number of infanticides by mothers, especially unmarried mothers.[69] Marriage is still a bargain negotiated by the parents,[70] even among the better-off strata, although it has repeatedly been contested by women. The possibility of being renounced still exists, even though now it is called divorce, and given the condition of Algerian women it always was and still is a tragedy.[71]

In 1972, in order to maintain this situation, Boumédiène espoused De Gaulle's 1945 line about the "twelve million beautiful babies." While speaking to student volunteers for the civil service on the subject of the 'demographic explosion,' Boumédiène remarked, "I personally think that the solution does not lie in family planning but lies instead in development"[72]—development achieved in Algeria, as well as in Europe, via an unlimited supply of labor power whose *costs of reproduction must be kept as low as possible*. Thus, at least the postrevolution Algerian state has kept up tradition: the exploitation and intimidation of women in order to ensure that women procreate.[73] In this context, one that appears to be different from that of southern Italy, what changes could and did emigration bring for women?

The Algerians who emigrated during the 1950s were usually young men *who rarely had a wife with them*. It is easy to see why they were without wives if one considers that the average price of a wife, the cost of the dowry, was around 500 thousand liras, and the average annual income of an Algerian agricultural laborer was about 200 to 250 thousand liras. The women who remained behind in Algeria found themselves living in an ageing community, dominated by and the property of their husbands, fathers, and brothers and left without any control over money. The women who went to France after some migrant Algerian workers managed to save enough money for the dowry found that they had to face a new level of housework. Furthermore, the level of housework tended to increase and intensify, because for a long time each new immigrant had to join an already formed family in order to survive. Clans were formed, clans of men supported by one woman (and her small daughters), who, in reproducing this growing community of men, found that she was also having to substitute for the women who had remained behind in Algeria. When, in order to support the war of liberation, the Algerian guerrillas began to tax immigrants in France to raise funds,[74] this tax on an already meager wage meant an even greater load of housework for women. Thus, the migrant Algerian women also had a difficult role in the war, one not unlike that of women in other wars of liberation.

Hence, during the 1950s, through the use of emigration, the French government managed to solve its problem of 'development' primarily at the expense of Algerian women. In the same way, *it also managed to resolve the problem of the relationship between production and reproduction and the processes of struggle* that this implies. In short, the French state built the second great wave of Algerian immigration upon the weakness and lack of power of Algerian women both in the community and in reproduction.[75]

While in countries that had attained a certain level of industrialization—such as Italy—the war and the postwar period acted as a catalyst for the contradictions present both in the community and in reproduction, the same is not true in the case of Algeria. It could not be true because of the existing social fabric. The war of liberation could trigger certain social tensions, but because of this social fabric could not facilitate any attack by women on the organization of reproduction, or even, in more general terms, any attempt by them to win their emancipation from their conditions of confinement and isolation.

Because of the conditions from which they had migrated, as well as the conditions they met with in France, Algerian immigrant women who found themselves managing a wage for the first time were initially unable to use it as a means of gaining a new level of power within the community or outside of the community. Their conditions were far more restrictive than those of European women, even of women in Europe's 'pockets of backwardness.' Their opportunities for gaining more power were continuously being undermined, because the wage had to support a *community that increased with the arrival of every new immigrant.*

The way in which Italian women used the wage as a means of rejecting the patriarchal peasant family—or the extended family in general (also in the south, albeit with some differences)—and chose instead a smaller family that could live better on a given wage[76] was simply not possible for the Algerian women in France. They could not use the wage to improve the quality of their lives or the lives of their children, because they had to reproduce an entire community and substitute for the female labor power still in Algeria.

These comments on Algerian emigration provide a basis, a perspective, for interpreting the hierarchies of power that exist within emigration itself: both in the community of origin and in immigrant communities abroad. The Algerian case can be used to examine other flows of immigrants, for example, from the former French colonies in West and East Africa that contributed to France's development in much the same way as did the Algerians.

Lastly, the almost continuous flow of migration into France from Italy, Spain, and Portugal must also be seen in relation to both French women's early refusal to procreate and carry out reproductive work and to the state's desire to keep them in a condition of backwardness (especially on the farms). It is a flow that the French state has always more or less openly encouraged—a flow that was at first channeled toward the same French fields that French women were deserting.

The German Case

Germany, a country with a high level of industrialization, maintained an exceptionally high level of female employment in the postwar years.[77] What we have said concerning both the relation between women and the state and the difficulties women caused for capital's reconversion at all levels, from which the need for a broader use of immigration derived, applies to Germany as well. The 1950s in Germany were the years when women, finally freed from Nazi restrictions, developed their refusal of housework, as well as their refusal of agricultural labor and of work done as 'helpers' in family-run firms.[78] They also refused all the professions based on some kind of domestic economy. So great was women's refusal of housework that some German commentators proposed establishing a 'domestic service' organized like the 'military service' to fill the gap left by women.[79]

However, women's flight from the countryside was hindered by a considerable flow of immigration. This included a large 'political' flow from East Germany and, after 1957, a growing tide of Italian immigrants as well. Until the end of the 1960s these migrants (about twelve million) tended to settle in rural areas at first, areas less damaged by the war, and only later did they move into urban areas.[80] As both immigrants and Germans deserted the land and moved to the cities, rural women changed from being 'helpers' to being managers of farms in their own names. In areas such as Bavaria, it is not difficult to find families where the man works in industry and the women had to take on both housework and work in the fields, work that was formerly shared. Likewise, in the craft industries one begins to find "daughters of craftsmen who manage their father's firm alone when the son is no longer interested, and thus become the owners of bakeries, bookbinders, and decorators."[81] However, it was still more usual for women to be employed in unskilled jobs within the craft industry.

In general, the bargaining power that German women developed against *Kinder, Küche, Kirche* (children, kitchen, and church) did not translate into bargaining power in relation to working outside the home. The state saw to that by intervening with a decision to use immigrants from East Germany and Italy, thus preventing women who had rejected procreation from entering the labor market and finding employment on equal terms with German men. The fact that a flow of Italian immigrants had already been guaranteed during the 1930s,[82] and then again during the war,[83] by joint agreements made with the Italian state demonstrates that by that point the reproduction of the national working class was already inadequate.

The German state, afraid that there might be demographic gaps in a period of economic growth, continued to rigidly forbid abortion despite the fact that during the second half of the 1950s most countries in the East introduced a degree of liberalization. However, *in Germany, as in other European countries*, the dreaded '*unfortunate demographic development*' did occur, and from the mid-1960s got worse. Although German postwar development relied upon the extensive use of labor power,[84] long work hours, a lot of overtime, and the progressive depletion of agricultural labor,[85] women were heavily discriminated against with regard to industrial employment.

As in the case of France, women were eventually introduced into those industrial sectors from which they had been traditionally excluded.[86] Between 1950 and 1960, all industries increased the numbers of their female workers: the number of women employed rose by 162.3 percent in the steel and metalworking industries, and the electronics sector was not far behind. Female employment also increased both in traditional sectors, such as textiles, clothing, food, tobacco, and sweets, and in precision mechanics, optics, watchmaking, and photography,[87] areas where the consummate female skills of dexterity and precision reveal allegations of their lack of skill to be nothing more than a pretext for low wages.

IV. In the 1960s, the lines traced by the previous processes are scored more deeply. The young working class is born out of refusal, rebellion, and the struggles of the women behind it.

In the 1960s, the movement that women had started during the postwar period grew and spread. They refused to function as appendages of development plans that wanted women to be the producers and providers of numerous children, tied to long hours of work at home, in the fields, in the factory, and in the office, chained and ghettoized in conditions of personal dependence. The drastic fall in the birth rate that began in 1964 gives an almost photographic image of the amount of control women had already achieved over procreation. As was discussed earlier, on a European scale this phenomenon is not simply the consequence of the spread of contraceptives. Furthermore, the fall in the birth rate was most rapid precisely within the strata of the population that had previously been the least successful in controlling their fertility.[88]

As we have seen, this fall in the birth rate expressed the level of power that women had won but is not an 'event' that can be explained by one or another single factor. It was a level of power that had been built up through a process of struggle that tended to offset the general 'backwardness' to which every postwar or postrevolution government[89] has always tried to confine women; a *lever of power* that increasingly allows women to bargain for a new quality of life.

The restrictive policies of European planners toward women that began with European integration[90] *grew in the 1960s.* But the basic instrument of this integration—emigration—has proved to be a double-edged sword. Not only have immigrants become the spearhead of rebellion—as is fairly well known—but *emigration has also definitely radicalized the centrifugal forces* set in motion by women and youths. This is also true for the elderly, who have increasingly demanded a certain quality of life, whatever the price (though in Italy today it would be difficult to shout 'grey power').[91] One dividing line that still functions in favor of European integration (although less so during the 1960s) is that between areas where women can totally or partially manage a wage (either remittances or their own) and where they cannot. In the latter areas, survival is based on a rural income or expedients in which *women are totally dependent* either on the men of the family or on older women. In this case, the migration of some men, especially the youngest who are not responsible for supporting the community, does not undermine the community itself. The case of Algeria is typical in this respect but different from that of the Italian south, which has areas of industrialization and is part of an industrial country. Not by chance is it possible for young women in the south of Italy to flee from the countryside, a type of behavior that is unthinkable in Algeria.[92] If some southern Italian women come to the conclusion that they had better find a dowry on their own, because no more money is likely to come from Germany, whatever they decide, they have options that are not available to Algerian women.

Another phenomenon connected to women's growing independence that needs to be analyzed in order to understand the wave of working-class struggles in the late 1960s is the fact that women have been able to impose a different use of the wage *within* the family—either when the elderly were not present or when they failed to subordinate women. Increasingly, the wives of Italian men who left for Germany and the wives of workers in Naples and Gela were expected to administer the remittances and paychecks their husbands sent home, or even their own wage. *These women chose to invest in their children the money that the elderly would have traditionally saved or invested in land.* The young proletarians from the south who went to work at FIAT in the 1960s *assimilated this new form of investment* and with it the expectation of a higher standard of living.

We do not wish to downplay or minimize the innovative aspects of the rebellion of each new generation of workers and students. However, we want to emphasize that this rebellion involves more than a direct confrontation outside of the family context. It also involves a certain level of disintegration of the family itself. *We need a new perspective on the family.*[93] *We must consider the erosion of authority that emerged in the 1960s, even in the proletarian family, and relate this phenomenon to women's management of the male wage.* This management has taken hold among increasingly wider sectors of proletarian women as European integration (based on migration) has progressed in the postwar period and as the process of urbanization initiated by women has spread throughout Europe. In addition to the woman's own occasional wage (often earned in the underground economy, cottage industry, piecework, or part-time work, and in many cases the only source of support for the entire family), *managing the man's wage gives women more power in relation to men and leads to a different relationship between the children and their mothers and fathers, giving rise to a certain crisis of authority.*

In countries like Italy, during the 1940s and 1950s, certain sectors of *proletarian women first experienced the management of a wage.* Emigration did not affect these women in the same way it affected women in countries such as Algeria. In Italy, emigration catalyzed women's first steps toward independence. While in countries like Algeria, at least in the short term, it worsened women's position. In countries with high levels of female employment *the breakdown of the family* associated with increasing insubordination among youth inside and outside the factories was the result of the tensions stemming from the fact that women were working both at home and outside the home.[94]

However, in both cases the young working class set in motion an entirely new cycle of struggles: in Italy (Turin, Piazza Statuto, 1962) and in

Europe in general. This new cycle of struggle was born from the increasing refusal and rebellion of proletarian women who created and sustained the conditions for the struggle to develop in.[95] As we have already said, the attack on women, present since the beginning of European integration, became more intense during the 1960s. Furthermore, this tendency was heightened by the wave of workers struggles at the end of the decade.

Although the left has ignored it, in Italy the expulsion of women from the factory that began in 1962 is not over yet: another million women have joined the unemployed.[96] In Germany, after 1960, capital-intensive development and rationalization in the processes of production gave rise to a further worsening of the situation of female work outside the home.[97] Women were increasingly expelled from the factories and forced to resort to part-time work, piecework, and temporary jobs: from 1961 to 1971, part-time female workers increased by 83 percent, reaching 2.3 million.[98] Immigrant women were employed either as unskilled (60 percent) or semiskilled (33 percent) workers.[99]

In France the percentage of women employed in the new industrial sectors from 1962 to 1968 increased: in the electrical industry it rose 11.1 percent, from 114,000 to 126,660; in the chemical industry it rose 14.2 percent, from 104,500 to 119,440; in the food industry it rose 8.6 percent, from 126,100 to 137,000; in the mechanical engineering industry it rose 4 percent, from 194,220 to 202,160. However, these changes did not significantly alter the sexual composition of the sectors.[100]

In 1970, speaking at the Fourth National Congress of the CGT on female labor, Christine Gilles said, "*The second figure* I mentioned, *that of 33 percent*, represents the difference between the real wages of men and women. . . . In 1945, the ratio of a female machine operator in the clothing industry were equal to P1 and P2 in metallurgy. They are far from being equal today. Last May, minimum hourly wages were 3.93 francs and 4.10 francs."[101]

As for *immigrant women*, and Algerian women in particular, it should be remembered that between 1962 and 1963, fiscal policy forbade any Algerian to leave Algeria with more than ten francs. This provided one more reason to have someone already established in France and for the structure of a group of men supported by a few women. Since 1967, there have been further restrictions forbidding Algerian immigrants sending francs back to Algeria, and this has worsened the already bad situation of the women there, because, without remittances, they can't buy certain goods that can only be bought with francs.

After the war of liberation, *Algerian emigration* changed. Small family groups or *single women* also began to emigrate. In that, it was single women who rejected rural life or impositions of city life, like eating in a kitchenette separate from men, as expected by the leaders of 'Islamic socialism.' Most of the women who emigrated alone to France were not proletarians. In fact, most managed to enter the country by means of a tourist or student visa. Once in France, however, *these single women—unlike single men—could not and cannot integrate into the Algerian community, because the community does not accept women unless they are under the control of a man.* Therefore, they end up at best as waitresses but also often as prostitutes. Proletarian migrant women in general—from Algeria, Tunisia, Morocco, Turkey, Yugoslavia, and Portugal—either become waitresses or unskilled workers in the mechanical engineering sector.

V. After 1968, the 1970s. Women began to bargain about reproduction. The immigrant community no longer needs to reproduce itself.

After 1968, the investment that women in Europe made in their children, by improving their children's lives as well as trying to improve their own, *has been revealed by the potential for and level of struggle* expressed by the working class on a European-wide scale. Following these struggles there was a further reduction in the flow of Italian migration,[102] and Italians moved up in the hierarchy of the immigrant labor market. Now, the flow of immigration from other areas of the Mediterranean has increased; Turks, Greeks, Algerians, Tunisians, Spanish, and Portuguese have moved in to take over the lower skilled and unskilled jobs.

Although one should not be too optimistic, it is clear that over the last few years migration has, as the *Financial Times* openly admitted, brought the *"spectre of revolution,"* rather than social peace.[103] Because of this there has been an attempt, though fairly limited, to discover a source of labor power, a sector, that no matter where it comes from, is weaker and more easily black-mailed than male immigrants: *women*. Here lies the problem of the 1970s, for in these years, the path trodden by women has reached a decisive turning point. In Europe, as well as in the United States, it has become a mass movement that expresses women's need for independence and autonomy—a life no longer paid for at the price of the factory or of the home.

If men are less and less willing to submit to factory discipline it is unlikely that migrant women will prove any more pliable. In this instance, too, the power difference that exists between men and women, particularly among immigrants, must not be forgotten. But given the direction in which women are moving—both in more 'developed' and in 'less developed' areas—it does not seem very likely that the use of women will or can provide a long-term solution for the problems of European capital. In the midst of other better-known images of 'paper tigers' and 'white elephants,' perhaps the best image of this particular capitalist game is of 'a cat chasing its own tail.'

European planners are now faced with a problem that appears to be as difficult as that of 'squaring a circle.' In Germany, France, and Italy (in FIAT after 1969) there have been further attempts to introduce women, particularly migrant women, into the workforce to replace male migrant workers who have proved disinclined to accept factory discipline. In Sweden, at Saab's Scania's of Sodertalje, comparable only with FIAT at Cassino, one finds "star like"[104] ways of organizing labor—especially adapted to be suitable for housewives, including older women. At the same time, however, European women are themselves less amenable to accepting unwaged housework along with factory work and are becoming more and more determined to make their reproductive work cost. Thus, on the one hand, capitalist development is founded upon determinate levels of reproduction that must be continually guaranteed and that so far have cost the state very little, and, on the other hand, women have begun their attack precisely from this base: reproduction.

While it is true that the state is often successful in blackmailing the politically weaker strata of women into working in the factory and working in the home, in Europe at least, the state is being forced to respond to women's demands for payment of the costs of reproduction. Among the most important examples of this are: the proposal presented in France by the Union National des Associations Familiales for a wage for housework that would be the equivalent of 50 percent of the minimum wage, which would be subject to taxation and considered to be a wage in every respect.[105] The proposal already has some support in government circles. Another example is that of Italy, where women receive a monthly check of fifty thousand liras to pay for the extra housework involved when they look after a disabled relative at home instead of leaving him or her in an institution.[106] In Italy laws are also being proposed to raise the amount of the family allowance. While family allowances do not constitute a 'wage' for housework, they are nonetheless a clear indication that reproduction is already a bargaining area.

Before concluding, we should look briefly at the case of Britain, a country that has only recently joined the European Community. Britain remains closely tied to U.S. capital, which explains some of the similarities found between the two countries' policies and strategies concerning both population and female employment. The traditionally high level of female employment in Britain has already been mentioned. During the 1970s, the government encouraged and financed broad studies on the condition of women and their levels of employment. The commissions set up for this purpose continually ended up recommending maximum flexibility in the organization of work so that "women could choose between part-time and full-time jobs." They recommended a "rapid expansion of day care centers and nursery schools, with flexible schedules adjustable to the mother's needs" (mothers who should then go to work), they also recommended setting up cafeterias that would provide "meals to youngsters and children whose mothers work, *even during the school holidays*" (emphasis added). Furthermore, they recommended that the "Minister of Education should stay *in regular contact with women's organizations*," and that an "adequate investigation be made into the proportions and conditions of home-working" (which apparently is not only a Mediterranean problem).[107]

Yet despite all this it has still proved impossible for the British government to persuade British women to take factory jobs and replace West Indians, Africans, Indians, and Pakistanis. British women have already shown resistance to accepting the discriminatory jobs they are constantly being offered. Thus, it seems unlikely that they will quietly accept jobs such as secretary or typist[108] that are the roles offered as a result of the talk about the need for more widespread employment of women at a certain skill level. Also, the struggle around the costs of reproduction and for a wage for housework has already begun in Britain and has reached a national level in the campaign around family allowances.[109] Not only was the government forced to abandon its plan of abolishing the family allowance (the only money that women receive directly), it also had to face the growth of a movement that has irreversibly opened up a struggle and begun bargaining about reproduction.

At the same time, *the migrant men and women's community has reached a level of subversion that is already too high to permit the state to use women against men.* Indeed, the *numbers of migrant women in wage work is very high*, remarkably high in the context of a labor market where the *division between the sexes is very rigid*. The degree of subversion of the migrant working class has been raised by the new generation of workers, the sons and daughters of the original migrants. These young men and women, particularly women, who were either born or have grown up in Britain, are freer from the innate constraints of their parents, who came from social areas where any wage was already a conquest, and have no illusions that they will be able to move more easily up the social and labor strata.

Crucially, the *stability* of a waged job has allowed the second generation to achieve a new level of power strong enough to break that very stability itself. These young workers have the same attitude to wage labor as any of their peers internationally, although their struggle is sharpened by the struggle against racism within the labor market. It is also sharpened by the fact that a supervisor is often seen in terms of the slave master of old. Specific to women is the struggle against and refusal of the limitations imposed by family life, a family life that the parents' wages both sets up and requires. Women's protest in the factory and at school has not yet reached the levels of that of the young men, however, the force with which they confront their mothers and fathers, a struggle they often have to carry out alone and isolated within the family, is a sign of their preparedness to struggle. Since these young women are rarely to be found in the streets in battle with the police, their struggle for independence is often not even seen.

The black movement in Britain has also completely neglected women's condition within its programs and aims. However, the results of their efforts can be surmised from the way in which the parents of these young people are increasingly more willing to become involved and help youth in clashes with the police and in dealings with the authorities in general. But while young men remain the visible protagonists, the young women's struggles, although hidden, are often as effective.

Sometimes, a black West Indian, realizing he was unable to support his family at home would escape to Britain, leaving his wife and children behind. Women had to go very far from home in order to achieve any independence of their own either with or without a man. Often it is the women who send money back so that their children can join them when they settle. It did not take long for this situation to generate a crisis of authority. The British government, while long promoting *limitations on immigration*, now in the 1970s has promoted the exclusion of these children by attempting to stop West Indian women from procreating; it *attacked the black birth rate* by encouraging doctors to sterilize black women. This is *in line with U.S. policies of the 1960s*, both toward its own black population and toward the

Third World in general. When migration ceases to work well, it is better to export capital, to take the factories to the workers. But Third World men and women do not seem ready to accept them peacefully.

Notes

This article first appeared in Alessandro Serafini, ed. *L'operaio multinazionale in Europa* (Milan: Feltrinelli, 1974). This English translation by Silvia Federici and Harry Cleaver, and revised by the author, is from the second Italian edition (1977).

1   See: Michael T. Sadler, *The Law of Population* (London: C.J.G. and F. Rivington, 1830); Thomas Doubleday, *The True Law of Population* (London: Effingham Wilson, Royal Exchange, 1842). These two authors observed that population growth proceeds in inverse proportion to its well-being, and that a rise in the standard of living causes a fall in the fertility rate, removing the danger of overpopulation feared by Malthus.

2   Until 1936, there were no restrictions concerning abortion in the USSR; from 1936 to 1955, abortion was strictly controlled. Starting in 1956, the state again allowed a certain degree of liberalization. The popular democracies, after substantial incentives for population growth in the postwar period, introduced a number of very permissive measures between 1956 and 1958, but they abolished them in the 1960s: e.g., Romania in 1966. Czechoslovakia, Hungary, and Bulgaria tried to stimulate population growth by means of material incentives, such as increases in family allowances, services for children, and special maternity leave for waged and salaried women.

3   William J. Goode, *World Revolution and Family Patterns* (New York: The Free Press, 1970).

4   Ibid., 53.

5   The Italian Statistical Yearbook (ISTAT) for 1943 gives the following figures for the birth rate: 139.2 for the period 1920–1922; 110.2 for the period 1930–1932; 104.8 for the period 1935–1937; 106.0 for the period 1939–1940. As we can see, the period in which the index of fertility rose—but only from 104.8 to 106.0—coincided with the provision of economic incentives.

6   Edward L. Homze, *Foreign Labor in Nazi Germany* (Princeton, NJ: University of Princeton Press, 1967).

7   Professor Roland Pressat, a well-known expert in demography who teaches at the National Institute for Demographic Studies in Paris and the author of an interesting work, "Analyse demographique," in his book *Population* (London: Penguin Books, 1973), 96, shows in a very clear graph the fall of the birth rate after 1964 in Holland, Italy, Great Britain, West Germany, France, Belgium, and Luxembourg. In any case, this is a phenomenon that is widely recognized by all demographers.

8   "Further, the degree of diffusion of the latest contraceptives, at least in Europe, has not been such as to account for the recent reduction in the fertility rate"; ibid., 97. We add that in those European countries dominated by the Catholic Church, up to this day it is difficult for the overwhelming majority of women to gain access not only to the latest contraceptives but to any contraceptives at all. In this respect, Irish history has a new hero. Mrs. Mary McGee, aged twenty-eight, the wife of a fisherman and the mother of four children, who has already had cerebral thrombosis twice, was arrested last year at customs by an officer, who, searching in the woman's handbag, discovered an intrauterine device. Exasperated, Mary McGee appealed to

the High Court, which, in December 1973, issued the first liberalizing sentence on the matter: "It does not pertain to the State," the court decreed, "to interfere in such intimate and delicate matters"; *La Stampa*, March 22, 1973, 3.

9   See Roland Pressat, *Population*.

10 This is one of the main theses developed by Leopoldina Fortunati in *Le donne contro la famiglia* (Woman against the Family), which analyzes women's relation to capital over the last thirty years in Italy. In addition, her work that focuses on an analysis relevant to the war period and early postwar period can be found in Leopoldina Fortunati, "La famiglia verso la ricostruzione," in Mariarosa Dalla Costa and Leopoldina Fortunati, *Brutto ciao: direzioni di marcia delle donne negli ultimi 30 anni* (Rome: Edizioni delle donne, 1976), 71–147.

11 Bennett Kremen, "Lordstown—Searching for a Better Way of Work," *New York Times*, September 9, 1973.

12 The general manager of General Motors' Assembly Line Division said, "Yes, our workers are less keen than they used to be to commit themselves. . . . There is a lot of restlessness, and we feel this on the assembly line—war, youth, rebellion, drugs, race, inflation, moral crisis. Marriage is no longer what it used to be. We feel that their minds are elsewhere!"

13 On a worldwide scale this refusal leads to rather contradictory policies, as demonstrated by the World Population Conference held in Bucharest in 1974.

14 Romolo Gobbi, *Operai e resistenza* (Turin: Musolini, 1973).

15 Ibid., 3.

16 Ibid., 3–4.

17 David Thomson, *Europe since Napoleon*, (New York: Alfred A. Knopf, 1957). Concerning the war losses, Thomson gives the following figures: 500,000 in France, 445,000 in the Commonwealth, 2,250,000 in Germany (just on the battlefield), 7,000,000 officially dead in Russia (but there are other figures), compared with 325,000 from the United States. See also F. Roy Willis, *Europe in the Global Era: 1939 to Present* (New York: Dodd, Mead & Co., 1968), 180; Nicholas Valentine Riasanovsky, *A History of Russia* (New York: Oxford University Press, 1963); Denna Frank Fleming, *The Cold War and Its Origins* (New York: Doubleday, 1961).

18 Romolo Gobbi, *Operai e resistenza*, 8. For a more detailed analysis, see Shepard Bancroft Clough, *The Economic History of Modern Italy* (New York: Columbia University Press, 1964); Rosario Romeo, *Breve storia della grande industria in Italia* (Bologna: Cappelli, 1973).

19 Evelyne Sullerot, *La donna e il lavoro* (Milan: Etas-Kompass, 1973), 166–67.

20 Romolo Gobbi, *Operai e resistenza*, 11.

21 Liliana Lanzardo, *Classe operaia e partito comunista alla Fiat: la strategia della collaborazione, 1945–1949* (Turin: G. Einaudi, 1971), 332.

22 While this phenomenon is usually ignored by current political literature, we find it acknowledged and stressed in the earliest feminist literature. See, among others, in France, Evelyne Sullerot, *La donna e il lavoro*, in Italy Luisa Abbà et al., *La coscienza di sfruttata* (Milan: Mazzotta Editore, 1972).

23 Sullerot, *La donna e il lavoro*, 167.

24 "The man would join the army to participate in the resistance and the woman would replace him working in the fields and in the management of the household. Besides this she participated in the guerrilla struggle and gathered supplies for the front"; *Aperçus sur les institutions de la République Démocratique du Vietnam (Nord)*,

Hanoi and from *Nuova Rivista Internazionale*, 6, quoted in "Vietnam, la famiglia nel diritto vietnamita," *Donne e politica* 4, no. 19 (October 1973): 30.

25 What we described in the footnote above holds true also for Algerian women. It is well-known that the bombs that exploded in the bars and the stadiums during the terrorist phase were all placed by women. But all over the world, wars of liberation have always put women in a position that the literature of liberation or resistance has only mystified. What can we say about the classic example of the shaven woman, who is exposed to the ridicule of the population, when the war forces women into prostitution as the only form of survival? We can say that the war is also a celebration of male sadism and highlights in a less mystified manner the relationship of men with women. Women are not only forced to guarantee reproduction at a very high price, but they are also forced to defend themselves once more from men: from 'the enemy' who rapes them, the 'partisan' who shaves them, and the neighbor who despises them because they prostitute themselves.

26 The case of Vietnamese women may seem the 'most advanced.' But the political power they had access to was always very 'sectorial.' It is no accident that up to this day Vietnamese women who want to abort must ask permission from a special judicial commission. It is a sad analogy with 'advanced European situations.'

27 Sullerot, *La donna e il lavoro*, 169–70.

28 Liliana Lanzardo, *Classe operaia e partito comunista alla Fiat*, 332.

29 The biographies of two women summarize the situation (the biography of 'Margitt' and the last in the book: 'Girl'), see Danilo Montaldi, *Militanti politici di base* (Turin: Einaudi, 1971).

30 Not the least of the means adopted for the restoration were the campaigns connected with the Holy Year and the sanctification of Maria Goretti and Domenico Savio.

31 Sullerot, *La donna e il lavoro*, 207.

32 Pressat, *Populations*. See also Giorgio Mortara, "L'Italia nella rivoluzione demografica 1861–1961," *Annuali di Statistica*, anno 94, serie VIII, vol. 17 (1965); Massimo Livi Bacci, "Il declino della fecondità della popolazione italiana nell ultimo secolo," in *Statistica* 25, no. 3 (1965).

33 This is the topic of a number of ongoing studies whose results will, hopefully, soon be available.

34 See Livi Bacci, "Il declino della fecondità della popolazione italiana nell ultimo secolo."

35 See Fortunati, *Le donne contro la famiglia*.

36 Clough, *The Economic History of Modern Italy*, 370.

37 Ibid., 378.

38 Ibid., 388.

39 See Annuari Statistici Italiani, ISTAT. The fact, however, that science takes no account of the harmfulness of housework makes necessary a logical interpretation of every statistic.

40 "Those who are waged or destined to be waged eat better," no matter who works more. From this point of view, we don't believe that urbanization made much of a difference.

41 In this respect it is striking to discover that in that period electric household appliances were among the most important exports; see Clough, *The Economic History of Modern Italy*, 407.

42 Angelina Mauro, wounded in the insurrection of Melissa, died after eight days at the hospital in Crotone, on the November 9, 1949.

43 It was not just a matter of 'customs and habits.' This practice was also ratified on paper. Examples of contracts between landowners and 'those who work the land,' including a clause concerning women's unpaid work, are included in Vincenzo Mauro, *Lotte dei contadini in Calabria* (Milan: Sapere, 1973). Moreover, *Il Giorno*, September 2, 1973 reports—via a letter to the editor—that during the assembly of fishermen being held in Trapani and attended by women as well as men, someone cried out, "We will no longer put up with ship owners only choosing fishermen whose wives will go work in their houses for free!"

44 This is a well-known fact. Today the men who remain on the farms in the north increasingly resort to the good services of some women or men in the south who 'deal in marriages.' Thus, through an exchange of pictures they find (in some isolated village of Campania, Lucania, or Sicily) the women who did not manage to leave by themselves. But it is not just agricultural laborers who look for these women; it is also those workers who are far from obtaining an 'eight-hour' workday.

45 Livi Bacci, "Il declino della fecondità della popolazione italiana nell'ultimo secolo," 410; see also graph no. 3 for the proportion of married women versus single women and graphs 1, 2, and 12 for the rate of wedlock fertility, general fertility rates, and out of wedlock fertility.

46 Mortara, "L'Italia nella rivoluzione demografica 1861–1961," 6.

47 Ibid., 6.

48 Before the twentieth century France was comparable to the USA and Great Britain for its long tradition of female employment. By the beginning of the century, however, this employment had already declined. The 1962 census registered 6,585,000 active women, compared to 7,694,000 in 1906.

49 See Goode, *World Revolution and Family Patterns*, 53.

50 Marie-Françoise Mouriaux, *L'emploi en France depuis 1945* (Paris: Librairie Armand Colin, 1972), 35.

51 "Cet accroissement de la population en France entre 1958 et 1965 est dû pour 52.4% à un excédent de naissance sur les décés et pour 47.6% à l'immigration" [This population increase in France was 52.4% the result the birth rate exceeding the rate of death and 47.6% the result of immigration]; "Les travailleurs immigrés parlent," *Les Cahiers du Centre d'Études Socialistes* 94–98 (September–December 1969): 19.

52 Besides the 'salaire unique,' there was a complete reorganization of the system of family allowances. "After World War II, a new organization, the High Consultative Committee on Population and the Family, was established by decree on 12 April 1945"; The Population Council, "Country Profiles: France," New York, May 1972, 8. This commission brought about many changes in the family allowance system in line with what was happening in all the European countries; see 9–10.

53 From the McCloy plan of 1949 to the Schuman plan of 1950, European economic integration postulated the profitability of a "political project . . . based on a non-downward rigid wage, that is on a widening of the downward stratification of labor power, obtained through the maintenance and expansion of highly labor-intensive sectors. This project implied a massive introduction into factory production of quotas of new and politically weak labor power . . . female labor power fitted only partially into this project. . . . Women resisted being deskilled"; Franca Cipriani,

"Proletariato del Maghreb e capitale europeo," in Alessandro Serafini et al., *L'operaio multinazionale in Europa* (Milan: Feltrinelli, 1974), 79.

54 At present Algerian women are also urged to perform this function through 'courses of home economics' taught by 'social workers.'

55 But with respect to the trends in French employment, Marie-François Mouriaux writes, "Par suite d'une natalité très faible, la nation recourt de manière très large a l'immigration." [Following a very low birth rate, the nation made a significant turn to immigration.] Mouriaux, *L'emploi en France depuis 1945*, 29.

56 "Les travailleurs immigrés parlent," 20.

57 Sullerot, *La donna e il lavoro*, 206.

58 Ibid.

59 A further step in this attempt was taken with the approval of the Code de Famille in 1942.

60 More specifically, the family allowance was given directly to the mother (it was not included in the father's paycheck, as in Italy), whether married or not, who 'would certainly spend it on her children,' thus assuring that qualitative improvement of labor power that those in the Labour Party (which was back in power) aspired to and promoted with a general policy of social assistance.

61 We know, on the other hand, the whole series of reasons, from the loss of pensions to the loss of family allowances, etc., that in each country rendered these works essentially undeclared. This is why, also in the case of France, the extent of these markets can hardly be measured by statistics, but we can easily presume a rather wide range, especially when we consider both the low percentage of waged women and the heavy discrimination the state managed to impose since the postwar period against women's efforts to gain an autonomous income.

62 There is, however, a substantial level of employment in the service sector. This too is a European-wide phenomenon. With respect to France, see François Lantier, "Le travail et la formation des femmes en Europe: incidences de la planification de l'éducation et du changement technologique sur l'accès aux emplois et aux carrières," *La Documentation Française, Bibliothèque du Centre d'Etudes et de Recherches sur les Qualifications* 4 (October 1972): 44. In particular, see graph XIII, 45.

63 Lantier, "Le travail et la formation des femmes en Europe," graph XIII, 45. Sullerot, *La donna e il lavoro*, 208.

64 Lantier, "Le travail et la formation des femmes en Europe," 54.

65 Ibid., 54.

66 Ibid., 55.

67 Besides the case of agricultural laborers we previously mentioned, see "Il lavoro a domicilio," *Quaderni di rassegna sindacale* 11, no. 44–45 (September–December 1973) for the much greater proportion of cottage industry (as well as seasonal, temporary work) in the south compared to the north.

68 On Arab women, see in general (at least the women of the Maghreb are not subject to clitoridectomy), Yussef El Masry, *Il dramma sessuale della donna araba* (Milan: Edizioni di Comunità, 1964).

69 Fadéla M'Rabet, *Les Algériennes* (Paris: Maspero, 1969)—a book whose import and sale is forbidden in Algeria—gives evidence of a very high suicide rate among women. Moreover, when we evaluate these percentages, we must keep in mind that women are undercounted, both at birth and death, and neither their suicides nor suicide attempts, e.g., jumping out of a window but failing to die, are counted.

Suicides in general are recorded as 'accidental' deaths. Infanticide is also wide-spread among single women and is, along with abortion (169), the only available means of birth control.

70 The Algerian woman is forced to get married when and to whom her parents choose. This is also true for the small educated minority that takes a few university courses. But we must remember that as a rule women are withdrawn from schools—those who go to begin with—after the second year of elementary school. Today, the small minority who, besides university courses, has also discovered the birth control pill, has found a very specific use of the pill in marriage. Since they do not have the power to resist the imposition of marriage, these women get married, then with the pill they can pretend they are sterile; this in a short time leads them to repudiation-divorce, which in this case is what they want.

71 But the mass of Algerian women has little chance of making use of the divorce they obtain through their initiative, first because of the material conditions in which they live, and furthermore because many of them have not been registered at birth. In fact, Algerian 'civilization,' while considering women very precious as a good also considers them nonexistent as persons.

72 From a speech by Boumédiène to the students volunteering for the civil service, in *Moudjahid*, July 22, 1972.

73 Concerning the condition of the hospitals and the cases of obstetric lesions, see Ministère de la Sante, *Tableaux de l'economie algerienne* (Algeria: 1970), 82–83.

74 Yves Courrière, *La guerre d'Algérie, Tome II: Le temps des léopards* (Paris: Fayard, 1969).

75 The first wave should be calculated from 1935 to World War II.

76 Fortunati points out in *Le donne contro la famiglia*, with respect to Italy, that the transition from the peasant patriarchal family to the urban nuclear family was the product of the disintegration of a certain kind of family operated not only by capital but by the women themselves.

77 Sullerot, *La donna e il lavoro*, 231.

78 See Organisation for Economic Cooperation and Development, *Labour Force Statistics* (Paris: 1970), 96–97.

79 Sullerot, *La donna e il lavoro*, 230.

80 Bruno Groppo, *Sviluppo economico e ciclo dell'emigrazione in Germania occidentale*, in Serafini, *L'operaio multinazionale in Europa*.

81 Sullerot, *La donna e il lavoro*, 231.

82 On this subject, see Homze, *Foreign Labor in Nazi Germany*.

83 During the war they resorted to the forced labor of women sent from the East and, as is well known, of Jewish, gypsy, and political women.

84 Groppo, *Sviluppo economico e ciclo dell'emigrazione in Germania occidentale*.

85 Ibid., graph no. 4.

86 In this respect we always speak of novelties in a relative sense. When we go to the roots we always discover that every industrial sector has been based on a very large use of female and youth labor power. For the Italian situation, see Stefano Merli, *Proletariato di fabbrica e capitalismo industrial: il caso italiano, 1880–1900* (Florence: La Nuova Italia, 1973).

87 Sullerot, *La donna e il lavoro*, 231.

88 See note 9 above.

89 We refer here specifically to the Algerian situation, to which we will return.

90 See note 53 above.

91 Fortunati, *Le donne contro la famiglia*.

92 This 'evasion' also takes place in Algeria, both as an escape from the fields and as an escape from their husbands. These are desperate escapes in the attempt to disappear into the homes of Europeans in Algiers, working as maids. But under the rule of Ta'a, the police regularly take the woman back home. See the last chapter in El Masry, *Il dramma sessuale della donna araba*.

93 We say "develop a new perspective," because the perspective implicit in this analysis began in the late 1960s in the USA and in the early 1970s in Europe with the rise of feminist movement on an international level. In these years, sociologists and politicians only further confused the topic. See also Mariarosa Dalla Costa, "Quartiere, scuola e fabbrica dal punto di vista della donna," in *L'Offensiva* (Turin: Musolini, 1972).

94 Mariarosa Dalla Costa, *Quartiere, scuola e fabbrica dal punto di vista della donna*, 27.

95 Mariarosa Dalla Costa and Selma James, *The Power of Women and the Subversion of the Community* (Bristol, UK: Falling Wall Press, 1972), 26–27. "In the factories youth refuse the leadership of older workers, and in the social revolts they are the diamond point. In the metropolis generations of the nuclear family have produced youth and student movements that have initiated the process of shaking the framework of constituted power: in the Third World the unemployed youth are often in the streets before the working class organized in trade unions" (8).

96 From the March 1972 ISTAT monthly bulletin it appears that at the time of the inquiry 21,754,000 people over thirteen years of age were included in the workforce, of which 16,168,000 were women and 5,586,000 were men. Among the women 10,701,000, that is 49.1 percent, were housewives. More precisely, in 1970, among employed women, 22 percent worked in agriculture, and almost all of them were married and were not young. Among the others, 45 percent work in the service sector (married or not, young or not) and 33 percent in industry. For a comparison with the situation in England, see M. Pia May, "Mercato del lavoro femminile: espulsione o occupazione nascosta femminile," *Inchiesta* 3, no. 9, (January–March 1973): 27–37.

97 In general, see Organisation for Economic Cooperation and Development, *Labour Force Statistics*.

98 Bruno Groppo, *Sviluppo economico e ciclo dell'emigrazione in Germania occidentale*.

99 Ibid.

100 Lantier, "Le travail et la formation des femmes en Europe," graph 13, 45. In general, see Organisation for Economic Cooperation Development, *Labour Force Statistics*.

101 Mouriaux, *L'emploi en France depuis 1945*, 150.

102 The first slowdown of emigration took place after 1962.

103 "Europe Keeps Revolution at Bay," *Financial Times*, February 28, 1973: "The spectre of revolution, this ghost moves about from place to place, visiting even the Netherlands, but is fondest of all of Italy. . . . What is important is that it is quite apparent that a great many of our leaders in industry, the trade unions and the government itself are aware, some consciously, others only vaguely, that Western society is in a more fragile state than it has been at any time since the war."

104 We refer to the arrangement of workers on the line. We read in "Car Plants without Mass Disaffection," *Financial Times*, March 12, 1973: "The assemblers, all housewives

with no previous factory experience, work in groups of three." This example, however, is an isolated case.

105 "Les femmes au foyer," *Le Nouvel Observateur*, April 10, 1973.

106 This check, issued by the provincial administration in some Emilia centers, is officially in the name of the disabled relative, for whom it is supposed to play a therapeutic role, so that he or she not feel 'dependent' or like 'a burden' on their family. The fact that the person staying at home means an immediate intensification of housework for the woman, which the fifty thousand liras do not come close to 'paying for,' is officially ignored.

107 See Her Majesty's Stationary Office, Sixth Report from the Expenditure Committee, session 1972–73: The Employment of Women.

108 It is enough to take a look at the 1973 *Financial Times* and *Le Monde*.

109 For a brief history of the family allowance system in Great Britain, see Suzie Fleming, *The Family Allowance Under Attack* (Bristol, UK: Falling Wall Press, 1973); *Hands Off Our Family Allowances, What We Need Is Money* (London: Crest Press, 1973). As for the perspective behind the struggle over wages for housework and its relationship with the struggle of women who clean at night, see *Radical America* 7, no. 4–5 (July–October 1973): 131–92. The whole issue deals comprehensively with the debate over wages for housework that has been going on in Italy, Britain, and the United States.

Emigration, Immigration, and Class Composition in Italy in the 1970s (1980)

Translated by Richard Braude

The Padua WFH committee's musical group performs at a May 1, 1976, demonstration for wages for housework in Naples. The slogan on the banner reads: "Love too is housework."

1.

The purpose of one of my earlier research projects[1] was to provide an analysis—from a female standpoint—of European emigration policies from World War II onward, interpreting the period as a moment of serious attack on conditions of reproduction, one that shattered the relationship between production and reproduction.

Emigration—as is now generally recognized—is above all an attempt to quantitatively and qualitatively reconfigure the workforce. But if the most obvious element in this reconfiguration has been the competition established in relation to the workforce originally on the site of production, the element that is of greater interest for our current investigation is the attack on the conditions of the labor of reproducing the workforce; the attack, that is, on the work performed by women—both in the areas where people arrive as well as those from which they depart—and the parallel attack on the levels of autonomy that women had been able to experiment with in relation to such work.

Our focus is, in other words, the politics of emigration as seen in terms of the use of labor power produced in the areas where women have less power, pitted against the labor power in those areas were women have greater power.

But—and this is the central axis—through the struggle that they express within the process of the reproduction of the labor power, women not only transmit 'greater training' but also greater political power.

The creation of a struggling, multinational working class seen in the 1960s, is thus reflected in the history of women as a section of the class that, especially from the war onward, began to indicate its own autonomous route in ever more similar ways.

The refusal to procreate, whether totally or through a drastic reduction in the number of children, has been the primary axis around which this process of autonomy has developed. The struggle against the family and against regressive living situations more generally—in which women are required to guarantee a large number of offspring, are subordinate to a hierarchy of family orders, and are anchored to burdensome working hours in the home and on the land—failed to translate into a refusal of marriage. In countries like Italy, marriage was also used as a way to make one's way to the city, and consequently the guarantee of a male wage—or even one's own wage—as well as greater equality between women and less isolation. It was, after all, young women who abandoned the land, even before men did so.

The importing of labor power can thus be understood as a response to women's refusal to reproduce an adequately large and disciplined class— and, alongside this, of being mere appendices to plans either of economic development or stagnation. In the wake of the wave of struggle that the multinational working class waged in the 1960s, in the first years of the 1970s we noticed the intake of women into traditionally male strongholds of industry, especially (though not only) immigrant women. This was a pattern that repeated itself across Europe.

On the one hand, while the immigrant community had already reached overly high levels of subversion, it was fairly difficult to imagine a consistent use of a female migrant workforce to oppose that composed of male migrants. The main alternative, that of exporting capital, was thus already clear enough. The young women and men of the Third World, however, did not seem particularly disposed to accept this without opposition, as we used to say. On the other hand, what guarantee could the employment of native women provide at the very moment when they were increasingly developing their own struggle against the conditions of reproduction? That is, could they be relied upon to combine a certain quantity and quality of domestic work with factory work?

To consider the modifications that characterized the state's response in the 1970s, this essay provides a case study of the Italian situation.

2.

During the 1950s and 1960s, Italy—as has been noted—provided the process of European formation with a vast reservoir of labor power. In effect, Europe's entire model of development structurally relied on immigrant labor power.[2] Previously, I have argued that this involved a regime of terrorism toward women by both state and Church, not only in the banning of every kind of contraception and pre- or extramarital sexual practice, but above all in the exhausting, immiserating conditions imposed upon the raising of this workforce. From the war till the 1960s, around 6,880,000 people left Italy. Up until 1958,[3] 41 percent of them crossed the Atlantic. After 1958, there was a prevailing tendency to move to Switzerland and Germany. It should also be noted that between 1961 and 1971 a large part of the workforce left the Italian south for the 'industrial triangle' of the north, that is, Milan, Turin, and Genoa.

In the early 1960s, Italy was in crisis. From the statistics provided by ISTAT—which only began its investigations into the Italian workforce in 1959—it can be seen that between 1959 and 1972 female employment decreased by 1,360,000 units. A hasty reading might connect the crisis to the expulsion of women from the factories. In reality the critical moment of this was neither this crisis nor the one immediately following it. From 1959 to 1964, in fact, though there was a reduction of female employment by 772,000 units. This reduction ought to be considered alongside the flight from agriculture, where women were counted as employees in family businesses or as farmhands (including cases when the wage was paid directly to their fathers or husbands). The critical moment for women in the factories came in the years immediately following this—the so-called period of 'development without employment,' from 1964 onward.[4]

From 1964 to 1972, female employment dropped by 587,000 units, this time effectively representing an expulsion of many women from the factories, above all because they could not compete with young men from the south. An analogous situation took place in the same period in Switzerland and Germany, where foreigners replaced Swiss and German female factory workers. In the Italian case it was only in 1963 that employers were legally banned from including a clause in work contracts stating that women could be sacked upon marriage. But we should also grasp the fact that rather than the cause of these firings being a surplus of employed workers, women lost their jobs because they did not have sufficient contractual power to stand up against the competition represented by the new migrant workforce from the south (nor did the workers' movement or the unions). It was not only that they were not able to oppose the trend; they could not even make sense of it. We should also take into account the fact that, supported by the more secure and consistent male wage that accompanied this moment of development, some women decided to leave the factory of their own accord. However, I do not believe that this can fully explain the exodus of women from the factory in that period.

The end of the 1960s, as is well known, were years of worker and student insurrections. In the immediate wake of these movements, from the end of 1970 through 1971, there was nonetheless still no particularly large feminist movement. The emergence of 'the woman' as a political subject came later. This was a subject, who on a mass level—and for the first time in Italy—would emerge with the potential to upset the traditional relation of the dependence of the social context on the factory, uncovering the heart of a social location and site of production in itself: the organization and supply of domestic labor.

The roaring years of the feminist movement between 1974 and 1976 represented a period of mass rebellion against such work, against its material and immaterial tasks,[5] against its entire premise as a work of love. With all the goodwill toward those who are currently 'discovering' that domestic work is also sexual, affective work and involves the labor of reproducing interpersonal relations,[6] all of the struggles and new forms of female reproduction that were experimented with in those years lead to this conclusion, if interpreted correctly. This includes a range of activities, from the refusal to procreate to the struggle for abortion (which, it seems, still attracts all of the Church's fury) to the innumerable acts of refusing a whole range of tasks both in the home and outside of it, from the practice of lesbianism to the women's communes and women living on their own—to cite just some of the more well-known moments.

From around 1973 onward the crisis—with its 'austerity' program and the pressure of its restructuring of production, a process that unfolded both throughout the big factories (having begun in 1972),[7] as well as through the decentralization of production and the expansion of unemployment (around 1,700,000 unemployed in 1979), with runaway inflation[8] and, along with this, a frightening increase in the cost of living—had become the most severe response to the struggles of the 1960s and the early 1970s. Along with it came the fracturing of the class composition that had to be overcome, that is, the end of the hegemony of the mass worker and consequently the end of its influence over the wage. Within the reorganization of production as determined by the crisis, the class became increasingly stratified. Unemployment, domestic work, precarious work, out work, uncontracted work: there was a whole *mare magnum* in motion around the mainstays of production that were themselves restructured (one example would be the automation of FIAT, though robots were also introduced into various jobs at Zanussi, Alfa Romeo, Ansaldo, and Olivetti).[9] The dividing lines of sex and age stratified workers' conditions even more. The very young, the unskilled, and women suffered the worst fates. The slice of the new, more highly qualified work from home, such as that assisted by a computer-programmed machine (to cite but one example), was destined for the qualified male worker. It is easy enough to imagine how all of this aided the hierarchical position of the male in the family. I recall a reflection that an audience member offered me in Italy during a conference in Padua organized by the Italian Communist Party[10] on "*Operaismo* and the Centrality of the Worker": that the central worker was perhaps precisely the one performing decentralized work, in the home, and not necessarily or exclusively in the large factory: that is to say, a new hegemony of the male worker within the family, thanks to the new kind of working from home.

The new layers that emerged were produced by the crisis. The struggle burst open into the social sphere—the struggle over housing[11] and the autoreduction of bills, to mention the most famous examples. But above all there was a huge individual and widely felt pressure regarding income. And some matters ought to be specified here, from the standpoint of women. Attentive analysis of the relation of income to consumption has shown that, despite the serious attack on real wages, consumption did not in fact decrease. Equally, there was no fall in proletarian savings.[12] Rather, unemployment and depressed real wages were simply the most immediate and formally evident aspect of the crisis. The decentralization of production, which essentially meant working without contracts, became the underlying method for reconfiguring a hidden employment, along with a generalized industriousness that nevertheless guaranteed a certain quality of life at the level of the family. There can be no doubt as to the importance of industriousness in decentralization. And this means that during the 1970s the family, including women, children, and young people, produced ever more commodities. And, even if we are not in a position to evaluate this in percentage terms, the elderly also contributed to this production. It was precisely this new familial operation, due to its characteristics and the breadth of its diffusion (by now recognized on a quite general level) that has allowed some to define the family in the crisis as the 'nucleus of survival' or even a 'family firm.'[13]

Now, if the explanation of the maintenance of the level of consumption essentially relies on the nuclear family—and consumer durables (household appliances, the car), goods that we know all too well are typical to family consumption—then we must at the same time show that a large section of this informal workforce sought out possibilities for 'autonomous' survival. That is, groups of young women and men, when allowed a certain level of consumption, focused on music, travelling, clothing, etc. These were new generations who, on one hand, did not want to depend on their original family and, on the other hand, did not tend to try to form themselves around a new family.[14]

The level of official female employment rose once again in the 1970s: 1,415,000 between 1972 and 1979. A very large percentage entered the tertiary education sector (a sector that, however, in comparison to other industrialized Western countries, was neither particularly large nor feminized in Italy), and a significant proportion went into industry. FIAT was exceptional in that fifteen thousand women entered its workforce between the end of 1977 and 1980.[15] What was new about the women who became officially employed between 1972 and 1979, however, in comparison with those of the preceding years, is worth noting to better understand the situation. These were women of all ages, no longer either very young or over thirty-five, as had been traditional for the official female workforce. They were both married and unmarried and did not abandon their first workplace immediately after having children, as had been the case previously. They registered levels of absenteeism almost twice as high as those of men, which had also notably increased. Many opposed part-time work, because they were single and wanted a full wage adequate for supporting themselves, especially those women living in big cities. As a worker from FIAT said: "On my line there are at least four unmarried pregnant women."[16]

After the brisk awakening in 1968, the refusal of work represented an awareness of the only possible praxis that could confront the current relationship between work and capital, an awareness that followed the sudden awakening of the Italian proletariat after 1968. Alongside this, capital was faced with the demand for a wage income for each person, man or woman, to meet his or her needs. In response, capital broadened out its productive base. But it did it in a precarious, underground, and thus not immediately evident way. Fundamentally it was informal work. And simultaneously, for women there was a significant offer of regular employment. The refusal of work that women had previously expressed, a refusal that was built, as we have already said, on a journey begun before 1968, but which had been provided with a mass character through the great tide of that year, had above all been a refusal of reproductive labor, that is, of domestic labor as we have defined it.

The stakes in this refusal were the shortening of the total workday,[17] whether paid or unpaid, the extent of dependence on men, and social isolation. In our opinion, the explosion of the subject of the body that has dominated certain sections of the feminist movement in Italy and the feminist movement in France more generally did not derive from a struggle over health and safety by the mass worker,[18] but was instead the historically necessary transformation, by the female subject, of a body conceived of as a reproductive machine into a desiring body. This was something that only women could achieve, since the body of the male worker has never been mechanized for production to the same extent. There is a character to this discourse on the body as developed by feminists that could not arise from any discussion of the body conducted by men. As far as this theme is concerned, the feminist discourse can only radicalize the male version. Indeed, it was this very discourse—one that women alone were able to develop, through the abstraction of their bodies into laboring machines—that allowed a discussion to begin to move to the field of 'needs,' most of all of sexuality against the work of procreation and reproduction, of sociality against isolation, from the body to relations. For this reason, women did not derive anything whatsoever from 'male innovations' relating to social relations, or 'emotional' relations in particular. Historically, the initiatives for these innovations were necessarily taken by feminism. Because what was at stake was women and their work not men.

Capital responded to women's refusal by proposing different work and different discipline. This did not mean an alternative to domestic work, but rather, in place of the old division of labor within the family, another kind of familial cooperation. This cooperation was soon backed up by a series of legislative provisions[19] that tended to favor some modifications in the division of the domestic tasks necessary to women's twofold work and to an overall different mobility of the workforce. At the same time, however, a mass of young people, male and female, entered the scene who tended not to organize their lives into nuclear families, but instead took turns cooperating and otherwise, sometimes living together, sometimes not—that is, they engaged in extremely fluid and flexible forms of aggregation. The women often lived alone or with other women, rather than with men, and they often renounced having children.[20]

Such choices make the tendency among women that we have already cited quite obvious: paid rather than unpaid work and a reduction of the total workday, above all through certain radical choices that left them time for themselves instead. They moved away from being materially and psychically available to others on an uninterrupted basis. In other words, they established a *threshold of unavailability*. This was a tendency that was expressed through fairly homogenous behavior by groups of young women, and that we nonetheless find was also expressed by large groups of slightly older women, particularly in major metropolitan areas. This was fundamentally the basis of a new form of female reproduction. It was the way that women had decided to reproduce themselves first and foremost, as opposed to simply serving the function of the unpaid reproduction of an entire nuclear family.

In Italy, of course, research and energy continue to be spent on measuring women's productivity in market-directed production. But in our opinion this risks leading to disheartening conclusions if not correctly accompanied by a broad and perceptive inquiry into how much reproductive work women managed to shake off, how much time they freed up, and how much psychophysical energy they conquered for themselves, replacing the time spent working for others.[21]

3.

It is within this discourse, one that begins with the centrality of domestic work and focuses attention on the rupture—both central and, at the same time, neglected—not only of the supply of material chores but of being psychically 'available' that I want to raise some points relating to the labor of the domestic worker.[22] On the one hand, such labor leads us back to the *mare magnum* of uncontracted and precarious work, because, despite quite precise legislation, such labor is all too frequently (if not predominantly) organized in contravention of this legislation. On the other hand, as well as leading us to considerations regarding alternate kinds of work, it helps to reveal the use to which the foreign workforce present in Italy in the 1970s was put.

We could even say that in Italy the refusal of unremunerated domestic work for the reproduction of one's own family went hand in hand with the refusal to reproduce other people's families for very little payment. What was at stake was not only the exhaustion involved and the length of the workday but, in keeping with the amount domestic work going on in one's own family, also the isolation, control, and pressure to engage on a personal level the endless tasks and—especially for the 'live-in domestic'—the unavailability of one's own reproductive space and time. That is, the reality of life was determined twenty-four hours a day by the family for whom one was working. In other words, the reality of always being 'available.' If the live-in domestic worker's situation was paradoxical, a good deal of this control and personal involvement was also experienced by the 'morning to evening' domestic worker, even if she did not sleep under the same roof as the bosses; and again, in a smaller way, it was also experienced by the domestic worker who was paid by the hour.

It is precisely for these reasons that women preferred factory work or the production of commodities in jobs without contracts. Even if legislation was making the pay comparable to that of many other jobs, in the 1970s, it was almost impossible to find an Italian woman who would accept being a 'live-in domestic.'[23]

Even 'hourly' domestic work was increasingly refused, due to the blackmail involved, and the de facto low salaries. In recent years, Italian women have once again begun to take 'hourly' domestic work, while maintaining a near total refusal of employment as live-in domestic workers. At the same time, however, the range of women of different social backgrounds, levels of education, places of origin, etc. ready to accept this latter form of employment has vastly increased. It has become one of the many precarious jobs undertaken by extremely diverse subjects. It is frequently a way for female university students to pay for their studies and a room in a shared flat. But this also means that third-party domestic work is no longer work 'for life' for the latest caste of subjects who perform it. The range of subjects who regularly participated in the struggle in recent years and the possible connections and circulation of information has at least led to an ability to slow down the rhythm, an important limitation on the tasks involved, and, above all, the capacity to refuse certain levels of physical strain. For this reason, domestic workers paid by the hour often refuse to work in houses that do not own electrical appliances. Thus, there have been some gains in this area. And even with the widespread industriousness induced by the crisis, there has also been a certain level of quantitative and qualitative refusal of work. In other words, just as had occurred in the arena of domestic work as labor 'done out of love,'[24] a threshold of unavailability was established, one which is being gradually pulled back to ever more advantageous levels.

If these are the basic modifications that intervened in the ways of performing third-party domestic labor in general, a different discussion ought to be had about domestic work performed as a live-in domestic worker. As I have said, it was almost impossible in the 1970s to find Italian women who would take on this work, even though a new law had limited working hours of a live-in domestic worker to eight hours a day. But, quite clearly, it was the lack of any real detachment of one's own life from that of the boss that made such work unacceptable. It was precisely this sector that in the 1970s became the reserve of work for women from Asia and Africa, deriving from an influx of foreign labor power that began to arrive in Italy at the end of the 1960s, together with an influx of labor power from poorer European countries. The domestic workers of color would grow to a total of 100 thousand, from a total immigrant workforce that in 1977 was estimated at 300 to 400 thousand people.[25] As has been demonstrated in recent and detailed research,[26] these workers would come to play the role of a true vanguard of immigrants of color in Italy.

What was the general situation of this workforce? The overwhelming majority (300 thousand if we refer to an estimated 400 thousand) of the immigrants of color in Italy were not only without documents, having arrived due to the Italian government's general *laissez-faire* policy, but, above all, one could not claim that they functioned as a 'reserve army' for the Italian workforce. Indeed, even though there was very high unemployment in Italy in the 1970s, many young people preferred not to accept various kinds of work on offer or the accompanying wage levels, instead turning to other, clearly more acceptable kinds of uncontracted work, or simply putting themselves on employment agency waiting lists. It was the immigrants of color who accepted and continue to accept the positions and wage levels refused by the local workforce. The nearly half a million workers estimated to be present in 1980 eventually ended up in domestic work (above all in the big cities), the private sector (hotels, restaurants, cleaning), agriculture and fishing (Sicily), the building industry (Friuli), and the mines and steelworks (Emilia-Romagna).[27] These jobs were for the most part concentrated in the large metropolitan areas (Milan and Rome) and, above all, paid famine wages.[28]

Obviously, due to the limited space available here, only the briefest of discussions on the composition of the migrant workforce in Italy can be provided. Nonetheless it seems important to note the following evaluation:

> From the beginning of the 1970s, when the Italian working class, involved in the most noxious kinds of work and with endless working hours, proved itself ready to demand wage levels equal to those of workers in the leading sectors, the reaction was quite clearly the

importing of a migrant workforce. This concerned first of all waged domestic work, which in turn brought about poorly paid work in the food sector. As well, there was the worst kind of industrial work, monetizing health conditions, effectively removed from contracts. Finally, this included the most exhausting aspects of the transport, agriculture, and building sectors. These are the ghettoized worlds where we find illegal immigrant workers today. And this represents another lost opportunity for Italian society to take a step forward and to leave behind a solid employment structure that it might otherwise have given up. 'Decrepit' is the mildest judgement one could make of the whole situation.[29]

4.

One could say, therefore, that in the atypical situation that Italy represented—first as a land of emigration, then as a land characterized by migration from a less developed zone to a more developed one within the country itself, and, finally, from the end of the 1960s onward, a land of immigration for a new flow of labor power not only from poorer European countries but, more consistently, from Africa and Asia—the relationship between reproduction and emigration has functioned in the following way. The flow from Italy to Central European countries and from the Italian south to the industrial triangle meant an attack on the 'stronger' section of the class (including its female component); and at the same time an attack on the level of struggle over reproduction that had been established by women in the most developed areas, drawing on the relatively lower level of power women held in less developed areas (in the south, in particular). But the political use of this flow has in the end been contradictory both at the site of production and in the reproductive sphere. The cycle of struggle manifested by the working class at the end of the 1960s, both in Italy and elsewhere, represented a zenith of power. And, as far as the reproductive front is concerned, the journey toward female autonomy that began with postwar emigration generalized and deepened in the 1950s–1960s, eventually exploding as a movement at the start of the 1970s. This represented a limit that eventually clashed with emigration policy, both on the productive and reproductive fronts, as the Italian state was no longer able to guarantee, domestically or externally, a low-cost, available supply of labor power from less developed zones.

Control over class composition in the 1970s within Italy itself was thus based not so much on a polarized south-north stratification around the great productive centers, but rather on the reorganization of production. This concerned not only the important centers of production but also, and more importantly, decentralized production, enacted broadly and with damaging effects through dividing lines of sex and age. The productive base expanded and, at the same time, partly transformed the division of labor within the family itself. This also functioned as a response to the levels of the refusal of reproductive work that women had demonstrated.

This new stratification meant that the Italian proletariat became tied to certain seemingly irreversible levels of consumption and income. We have already seen how a widespread industriousness had become the means of ensuring all of this. What relationship did this industriousness have with the refusal of work that, in our view, had been irreversibly impressed into the consciousness of the Italian proletariat from 1968 onward?

Despite the general industriousness that capital managed to impose in a new situation of growing unemployment and increasing precarity of living conditions, the refusal of work continued to expand. Proletarian youth completely rejected certain kinds of work and pay levels, instead exercising other options: they privileged work that did not entrap them too soon or compromise their lives, as well as the capacity for change.[30] Of the 1,700,000 people unemployed in 1979, young men and women looking for a first job, who for the most part had nonetheless rejected the majority of jobs they had been offered, accounted for 852,000 of them. Clearly the kinds of work and the pay levels offered were not appealing.

As we have seen, primary among the paid jobs rejected by women in Italy was live-in domestic work. It was exactly in this sector that the largest proportion of migrant workers, almost all of them women, were employed. Along with this kind of work there were others that the Italian proletariat were not disposed to undertake, jobs that were accepted instead by the 200 to 300 thousand immigrants of color.

Given the way in which this workforce entered Italy, apparently without any planning by the Italian state, and due to its size and sites of work, it is difficult to assess its current impact or what influence it is destined to have in Italy over the coming period. What seems clear for now, however, is that yet again this workforce, confronted with a labor market that had already been profoundly restructured around divisions of both sex and age is being split up along the classic imperialist division of labor, according to a color line imposed on the 'blacks' who accept the jobs that no one else in Italy is any longer willing to perform at the wages offered in compensation.

Even within the limits of what we can assess today, it is difficult to imagine that the Italian state will eventually be able to rely on an immigration policy to undermine the results of the power attained by women, and the young generation more generally, in both the north and the south. It seems improbable that these immigrants, both male and female, will accept the ossification of weakness and ghettoization that apparently awaits them, either on the industrial margins or in the living conditions reserved for them. I think it is much more likely that there will be a mixing with and weaving into the local proletariat, rather than a radical separation, especially in the large metropolitan areas.

Notes

This essay was originally presented by Mariarosa Dalla Costa at the conference Le tiers-monde dans la division internationale du travail, Université du Québec, Montréal, October 23–25, 1980.

1   Mariarosa Dalla Costa, "Riproduzione e emigrazione," in Alessandro Serafini et al., *L'operaio multinazionale in Europa* (Milan, Feltrinelli, 1974); republished in this edition as "Reproduction and Emigration."

2   To provide some basic background, beyond Serafini, *L'operaio multinazionale in Europa*, see also Stephen Castels and Godula Kosack, *Immigrant Workers and Class Structure in Western Europe* (London: Oxford University Press, 1973); Issoco, abstract for the conference Emigrazione nell'Europa del Mec, Rome, July 10, 1973; Charles P. Kindleberger, *Lo sviluppo economico europeo ed il mercato del lavoro* (Milan: Etas Kompass, 1968); "Studi emigrazione," *Regioni e migrazioni* 22 (1971); *Il mercato del laboro comunitario e la politica migratoria italiana* 23–24 (1971); *Cause della emigrazione* 30 (1973); *Sociologie du travail* (monograph), July–September 1972; for the role of the Italian south, in particular, see Luciano Ferrari Bravo and Alesandro Serafini, *Stato e sottosviluppo* (Milan: Feltrinelli, 1972). Finally, there is the recently published volume by Eleanora Petroli and Micaela Trucco, *Emigrazione e mercato del lavoro in Europa occidentale* (Milan: Franco Angeli, 1981), which contains a full and commendable bibliography.

3   At the risk of stating the obvious, in 1958, the Treaty of Rome constituted the European Economic Community (EEC). In relation to this, Serafini, "L'operaio multinazional," in the essay collection of the same name observes: "In reality the effect of such regularization [alluding to the regularization that came with the establishment of the EEC] has been that it is more difficult for workers in the EEC to find work abroad. Along with showing a diminished availability to work, the migration flow—especially from Italy—has been hit by regularization. Under the guise of free movement and equal treatment, the rules of the EEC have ended up discouraging businesses from taking on EEC workers" (12).

4   Cf. the presentation by Mara Gasbarrone, "Lavoro donna/donna lavoro," *Il Manifesto*, June 1980. The phrase "development without employment" is taken from D. Del Boca and M. Turvani, *Famiglia e mercato del lavoro* (Bologna: Il Mulino, 1979), which shows how this kind of development threw the nuclear family into crisis, even in areas where all the conditions for it existed (85).

5   For this discussion, I refer back to my own considerations in "Emergenza fem-
    minista negli anni '70 e percorsi di rifiuto sottesi," presented at the conference La
    società italiana: crisi di un sistema, Faculty of Political Science, Padua, May 29–30,
    1980; available in Gustavo Guizzardi and Severino Sterpi, *La società italiana, crisi di
    un sistema* (Milan: Franco Angeli, 1981), 363–75.

6   This new categorization can be found with more precision in numerous articles in
    the review *Inchiesta*, as well as elsewhere, that define domestic labor as only one
    of three spheres that constitute family work. A second sphere is constituted by the
    labor of sexual, affective reproduction, the reproduction of interpersonal relations,
    etc. We have already had a chance to express our disagreement with this categoriza-
    tion in that it totally denaturalizes domestic work: the extraordinary long working
    hours and the infinite tasks that it comprises without a wage cannot be explained
    without considering the 'amorous' content of the marriage contract. For this dis-
    cussion, I refer you to Giovanna Franca Dalla Costa, *Un lavoro d'amore*, (Rome:
    Edizioni delle Donne, 1978). [Available in English as *The Work of Love* (Brooklyn,
    NY: Autonomedia, 2008).]

7   Andrea Graziosi, *La ristrutturazione nelle grandi fabbriche, 1973–1976* (Milan:
    Feltrinelli, 1979). The literature is obviously vast; see also "Fiat: robotizzazione ris-
    trutturazione e riformismo," *Magazzino* 2 (May 1979). On the relationship between
    the restructuring of the large productive sites and decentralization, see *Quaderni
    del territorio* 1–5; more specifically on the theme of class composition, see Primo
    Maggio, *La tribù delle talpe*, ed. Sergio Bologna (Milan: Feltrinelli, 1978); Toni Negri,
    Dall'operaio massa all'operaio sociale (Milan: Multhipla edizioni, 1979).

8   From 1970 to 1979 the percentage variations in the consumer price index for families
    of workers and employees are: 5.1; 5.0; 5.6; 10.4; 19.4; 17.2; 16.5; 18.1; 12.4; 15.7; in
    October 1980 there is a variation of 20.5 compared to October 1979 (ISTAT data).

9   Italy was then ranked third in Europe for utilization of robots in factories, after West
    Germany and Sweden.

10 The papers from this conference are collected in F. D'Agostino, ed., *Operaismo e
    centralità operaia* (Rome: Editori Riuniti, 1978).

11 For a text that brings together interviews with women who were involved in squat-
    ting houses in Falchera (a working-class neighborhood in Turin), see Gigliola Re
    and Graziella De Rossi, *L'occupazione fu bellissima* (Rome: Edizioni delle donne,
    1976).

12 The social situation in 1978 can be seen from the twelfth CENSIS report, among
    other sources. Changes from this situation can be seen already in the first months
    of 1980; CENSIS, *Quindicinale di note e commenti* 348 (1980): 1141.

13 This is an expression widely used in contemporary literature on the relationship
    between the family and the labor market: there is the large report by IRER, *Lavoro
    femminile e condizione famigliare* (Milan: Franco Angeli, 1980). From our standpoint,
    however, the risk remains of believing that the new cooperation for the production
    of commodities will cause sexual hierarchy to fade, whereas frequently it deepens
    rather than weakens it.

14 "After peaking during the economic boom, the number of marriages began to fall
    again. After a brief rise in the early 1970s, there was a new and intense decrease, so
    much so that there were just over 325,000 weddings in 1979, compared with 419,000
    in 1973. The marriage rate thus went down by more than 8 percent in 1963–1964
    to less than 6 percent in 1978–1979. This does not exclude the fact that, alongside

the legal routes for forming families, there were also other routes being more frequently used, as has been happening for years in various countries. The rise in
illegitimate births went from 20,000 in 1964–1965 to 26,000 in 1978–1979, while the
legitimate birth rate dropped from around a million to 650,000 in the same period,
confirming the same hypothesis. It would be useful to research what kinds of
transformations are triggering these tendencies. In conclusion, the most dynamic
aspect of recent demographic evolution seems to be the decrease in marriage, with
obvious reflections related to the decreased birth rate, the probable creation of
forms of non-sanctioned cohabitation, and an increase in illegitimate children";
CENSIS, *Quindicinale di note e commenti*, 801–2.

15 On the new class composition at FIAT, see Silvia Belforte and Martino Ciatti, *Il fondo
del barile*, (Milan: La salamandra, 1980); "FIAT 1980," *Quaderno di Controinformazione*
3, supplement in *Controinformazione* 19, 1980. See also "Dossier Lavoro," supplement in *Il Manifesto* 248, and *Lavoro donna/donna lavoro*.

16 E. Bouchard, "Le 15,000 che prima non erano in FIAT," in *Lavoro donna/donna
lavoro*.

17 It seems important to emphasize here that when we say the total workday, we
mean both domestic work and extra-domestic work. Other scholars, when using
the same term, mean the workday given by the total labor power expended in the
production of commodities, which we prefer to call the social workday, and which
is thus only a *part* of the 'total.'

18 Cf. Sergio Bologna, "La tribù delle talpe," in Primo Maggio, *La tribù delle talpe*, 33–34.

19 Maria Vittoria Ballestrero, *Dalla tutela alla parità: la legislazione italiana sul lavoro
delle donne* (Bologna: Il Mulino, 1979); Laura Remiddi, *I nostri diritti* (Milan:
Feltrinelli, 1976); AA. VV, *Donne e diritto* (Milan: Gulliver, 1978); Carla Porta, *Senza
distinzione di sesso, guida pratica al nuovo diritto di famiglia* (Milan: Sonzogno, 1975).

20 There were around 350 thousand fewer births in 1979 than in 1964, a drop of one-
third. Another drop can be outlined for 1980. This is a strong change that is having
and will continue to have direct consequences on many aspects of social life. Every
year there are fewer students in nursery schools and elementary schools; in a sector
once considered to lack of infrastructure and staff, there is now an surfeit. There is
now a growing excess of nursery schools and elementary schools; the productive
industry of edible and other goods for children is having to convert itself to other
uses due to the significant drop in demand; CENSIS, *Quindicinale di note e commenti*
339 (1980): 270–71.

21 A sociopolitical research project at the Institute for Political and Social Sciences, in
the Comparative Politics course, at the Faculty of Political Science of the University
of Padua is currently investigating this matter.

22 The more recent regulations (collective contract, December 14, 1978), along with the
new provisions for *migrant domestic workers*, are included in N. Latilla, *Il lavoro
domestico* (Rome: Buffetti, 1981). This volume also provides pay rates for migrant
domestic workers up to October 1, 1979.

23 Live-in domestic workers, as cohabitating domestic workers were called, was
already disappearing in Italy in the 1960s.

24 Borrowing an expression from Giovanna Dalla Costa, *Un lavoro d'amore*, we are
referring to domestic work within a family relationship defined by a formal marriage contract or otherwise.

25 CENSIS, *La presenza dei lavoratori stranieri in Italia* (Rome: 1978); the study was conducted in 1977. It shows that the places of origin in Africa are mainly Morocco, Tunisia, Algeria, Egypt, Somalia, and Eritrea; for Europe, they are Greece, Yugoslavia, Spain, Portugal, and countries within the EEC. There is no more up-to-date data. It is nonetheless worth underlining that of around half a million foreign workers estimated to be present, in Italy the largest proportion, around 350 thousand, arrived between 1974 and 1977. As CENSIS again tells us in *Quindicinale di note e commenti* 345–346 (1980): "The Italian government is about to ratify the BIT agreement 'on migration in illegal conditions and on the promotion of equal opportunities and on the treatment of working migrants.' Furthermore, in January 1980, bill no. 694 on 'Norms integrating the current rules for the control of foreigners' was presented. This bill only deals with the problem of police checks and leave to remain, not tackling problems related to social security or equal treatment as contained in the BIT accord" (1047–48). Many associations of foreign workers and students have spoken against this version of the bill, including the Camera del Lavoro in Milan. Furthermore: "According to the employment agencies, only 9,507 foreign citizens began to work in 1976 (of whom 2,887 were seasonal workers). The position of foreign workers in relation to tax contributions is also irregular: the majority of employers 'save' on this part of the work costs—which constitute around one third of the total cost—because foreign workers from non-European countries ensured by INAM [the national insurance office] in 1976 counted only 2,013, of whom 1,179 were clerical workers and manual laborers"; CENSIS, *Quindicinale di note e commenti* 344, (1980): 1016.

26 D. Bacchet, "Indagine sul lavoro degli stranieri in Italia con particolare riferimento alla Lombardia e al Veneto," (PhD diss., University of Padua, 1978–1979); Ferruccio Gambino, *Alcuni aspetti della erosione della contrattazione collectiva in Italia*, in Guizzardi and Sterpo, 129–41.

27 CENSIS, *Quindicinale di note e commenti* 344, 345–46 (1980).

28 Bacchet, "Indagine sul lavoro degli stranieri in Italia con particolare riferimento alla Lombardia e al Veneto."

29 Ferruccio Gambino, "Alcuni aspetti della erosione della contrattazione collectiva in Italia," in Guizzardi and Sterpi, *La società italiana, crisi di un sistema*.

30 Cf. Bologna, *Irrompe la quinta generazione operaia*, in "Dossier Lavoro," 15.

Family and Welfare in the New Deal (1985)

Translated by Richard Braude

The Padua WFH committee's musical group performs at a March 8, 1974, demonstration for wages for housework in Mestre, Venice.

"**W**as the New Deal a success or a failure?" Regarding this much debated question, I maintain that there was no doubt a crucially positive aspect to the New Deal in the United States. I see the New Deal as an important test case for the functioning of the modern family in times of crisis. One in which the woman—as housewife and administrator of the wage, primarily responsible for the good running of the family, but also as an external laborer, and as a laborer involved in unregulated work—must provide the family with sustenance in a context of overarching male unemployment, market instability, and the establishment of social security/assistance procedures.[1]

In the 1930s, female labor power—via processes that had unfolded over the preceding decades and involved a radical transformation in the family structure—was asked to serve a new function, a function that was central to the emergence of a new system of reproduction of the labor force. This emerged, on the one hand, through the establishment of 'collective bargaining' and the state's new role in relation to the economy in order to ensure the size and increase of the wage and, on the other hand, through the establishment of social security to guarantee the reintegration of labor power during periods when it is not directly involved in the productive cycle—including policies for the elderly and the unemployed—or when it could not, in any case, be employed, for example, sick pay and, in a different way, aid to families with dependent children.

The spread of unemployment, which increasingly appeared to be connected with the new forms of the cycle of accumulation, gradually made the political establishment aware of the necessity to invest in human capital in order to regulate the market and raise labor productivity. The new role demanded of public funding and the acceptance of budget deficit were the political establishment's response to the necessity to support the reproduction of labor power and a closer connection of its forms to those of the production of commodities. In this sense, we can say that in the 1930s the most progressive nineteenth-century recommendations advanced by many authors matured, especially Marshall's proposed investment in the working class, finding concrete expression in the attempt to create a plan on both productive and social levels. By 1914, Ford's "Five-Dollar Day" wage policy[2] already guaranteed workers in the most advanced sectors the possibility to support a wife and have a house.

After the crisis of 1929, this 'reproductive form' of labor power had to be guaranteed on a much wider social basis, effectively a 'general' one, and the necessity to invest in human capital so as to raise and sustain its reproduction beyond the cyclical oscillation of employment opportunities became increasingly clear. The new social security/assistance measures formed the basic response. Yet within this framework of radically transformed social reproduction (the new role taken on by public spending in relation to the development of production and the system of welfare), entrusting human capital to female labor to secure a final product from the investment itself remained. In the nineteenth century, Marshall had claimed: "The most valuable of all capital is that invested in human beings; and of that capital the most precious part is the result of the care and influence of the mother, so long as she retains her tender and unselfish instincts."[3] The emphasis on domestic work as a labor of love, which already set the 1920s apart from the two preceding decades,[4] was then proposed in the 1930s as the key to a well-functioning modern family, inasmuch as it formed the location for connecting the attempt to relaunch production with the new welfare system.

The wage increase, in fact, could not be translated into an adequate level of consumption if the woman did not also—through the free domestic work imposed on her as the loving duty of a wife and mother—continuously intensify the range of tasks required for the choice, purchase, maintenance, and transformation of the acquired products. Inasmuch as the role of the wife is made increasingly complex and professionalized,[5] she is obliged to acquire a new level of information in a series of areas that the reproduction of labor power is now obliged to include, for example, diet, health, sexuality, leisure, education, and entertainment.

If there was a renewed insistence on knowing how to spend the wage, one which had already characterized the discourse of some economists at the dawn of the twentieth century, significantly the emphasis was no longer placed on being thrifty, but rather on *spending* in a careful and purposeful manner. In this context, it is worth recalling Keynes's own recommenda-tions—even if these were, in this instance, directed at English housewives:

> Therefore, oh patriotic housewives of Britain, sally out tomorrow early into the streets and go to the wonderful sales that are everywhere advertised. You will do yourself good—for never were things so cheap, cheap beyond your dreams. Lay in stock of household linen, sheets and blankets to supply all your needs. And have the added joy that you are increasing employment, adding to the wealth of our country, because you are setting on foot useful activities, bringing a chance and hope to Lancashire, Yorkshire and Belfast.[6]

On the other hand, the welfare system, even if with a series of selective criteria, took care of the older, unemployed, and disabled sections of the population—but not of the workforce still in the phase of growing up, or the workforce in training.[7] These sections of the population remained reliant on the male wage, as did the woman. Beyond this, it ought to be noted how these same forms of assistance and welfare policies can only work if the old person, the unemployed, or the invalid is able to rely on a family structure.

Furthermore, the relation between the development of production and the market, that is, the new market regulation, is based not only on the woman's ability to produce and raise the new workforce but also to main-tain the existing workforce via the administration and spending of the wage and, broadly speaking, through domestic work in its entirety, while also contributing to keeping the unemployed workforce 'in reserve.'

This centrality and novelty of the functions demanded of women in the initial attempt to construct a plan also explains how the New Deal funda-mentally contained within itself a tendency to consolidate the family, pur-posefully undervaluing—and even condemning, according to the words of its most authoritative exponents, as we will see—women's extra-domestic work.

In the meantime, female employment outside the home, while not reaching the same mass dimensions that it would during World War II, was becoming an indisputable fact, specifically in relation to the kinds of jobs involved. Nevertheless, women's waged employment faced strong ideo-logical and practical opposition during the 1930s. A woman who worked outside of the home was typically accused of being a *pin money worker*, that is, someone who worked only to satisfy superfluous needs. Frances Perkins, the Secretary of the Labor Department frequently advanced this criticism, a theory that the Women's Bureau complained was one of the most serious obstacles faced in its effort to protect female employment.[8]

At the same time, neither the AFL nor the CIO were truly concerned about keeping accurate records of their female members.[9] Various sections of society raised the alarm that women were taking men's jobs and that their mass entrance into the active workforce in the preceding years was responsible for male unemployment. In 1936, the National Industrial Conference Bureau published a response in the form of a study called "Women Workers and Labor Supply," to demonstrate the lack of grounds for any such alarmism.[10] Paradoxically, the married woman with an external job—who was at the same time under increasing pressure to find remunerative work, even on the black market, to maintain the family due to the unemployment suffered in the male sectors—became the most penalized figure. In many states laws were reactivated that allowed the sacking of teachers and women employed in public services once they married.[11] In addition, the leadership of the AFL ended up maintaining their support for the discrimination against the employment of women who had husbands with stable work.[12] These discriminatory measures against married women were not only enacted in public employment but also in the private sector.

Despite all this, the percentage increase in married, employed women remains one of the more revealing facts of the Depression. Married women's employment increased from 11.7 percent in 1930 to 15.4 percent in 1940. Nevertheless, after an initial increase in the first decade of the century, from 5 percent to 10.7 percent, it dropped to 9 percent in 1920, and then immediately increased to the levels indicated above in 1930.[13]

This trend indicates that in the 1930s the stability of the family, beyond the deprecating words of politicians and trade unionists, was supported by the fact that women shouldered the burden of free domestic work along with whatever kind of external work or piecework at home, independent of the length of the workday or the decline in wages. Indeed, inasmuch as women were fundamentally the administrators of the household finances, as has been noted,[14] even earning their own wage reconfirmed their role as a domestic administrator. This judgement seems sound if we take into account the overall social conditions in which this external work unfolded and, above all, the fact that this was still not mass employment.

The New Deal included discrimination against women in welfare policies that set out the direct delivery of funds or work plans. As the Women's

Trade Union League frequently pointed out, women had great difficulty in accessing these projects if they were not perceived as having dependents.[15]

We can conclude by saying that, in a very modern way, the New Deal, in combining production and the establishment of a welfare system, relied upon and developed through the double availability of female labor. The woman and mother were praised, while obscuring the fact that to provide for the family this woman was also a factory worker, an employee, or a worker without a contract, who also maintained the pride of the absent *breadwinner* and negotiated with the welfare agencies.

It seems to me that the new social and economic reconfiguration had to have applied Keynes's own judgement when analyzing the vitality of the English economic system. Also, he included "the greater economic output of women" among the contributing factors to the serious state of crisis.[16] Indeed, the very fact that unemployment affected everyone, including women, means this judgement cannot be understood as referring only to the greater scale of female employment, which had been historically determined, but rather to the different structural role of female labor, both in the family and beyond. The woman, whether employed in extra-domestic work or unemployed, was by then a stable element in the labor market and, along with the changing methods of performing housework, had a significant influence on the production of social wealth.

Notes

Originally published in *Economia e Lavoro* 19, no. 3 (1985): 149–52.

1   In this essay I maintain the main argument—which here I sum up in a brief way—published in *Family, Welfare and the State* (Brooklyn, NY: Common Notions, 2015). I refer the reader to this volume for all of the bibliographical references.

2   This wage level represented the most striking aspect of what Ford himself announced as "a general wage agreement"; cf. Huw Beynon, *Working for Ford* (Harmondsworth: Penguin Books, 1973); Allan Nevins, *Ford: The Time, the Man, the Company* (New York: Charles Scribner's Sons, 1954).

3   Alfred Marshall, *Principles of Economics* (London: Macmillan & Co., 1920).

4   From the turn of the twentieth century onward, more or less until World War I, emphasis was placed on being a 'spendthrift,' while also insisting on the possibility of a greater rationalization of domestic work via better organization helped along by recent technological innovations. Domestic work was openly treated as work that encumbered proletarian women—almost always black or migrant women—who, as well as working in their own homes, were employed as domestic workers for better off families. After World War I, however, given an increasing shortage of domestic workers (whose salaries, like others, increased), the middle-class housewife would be increasingly directly involved in housework. It was in this period

that the 'working' quality of this labor was removed on an ideological level, with the 'loving' character emphasized instead.

5   It is enough to note the diffusion of training courses for parents, with those teaching people the art of parenting presumed to have professional diplomas from universities and social work colleges.

6   John Maynard Keynes, "Saving and Spending," in *Essays in Persuasion* (New York: W.W. Norton & Co., 1963).

7   While the Aid to Families with Dependent Children marked an important turn in establishing federal responsibility toward children of single parents in need, by definition this constituted a rather narrow remit.

8   Cf. Winifred D. Wandersee, *Women's Work and Family Values, 1920–1940* (Cambridge, MA: Harvard University Press, 1981), 68, a text that is rich in data on the trend of female unemployment in the period.

9   This fact was strangely not dealt with in the trade union's New Deal literature. Cf. Dale Yoder, *Labor Economics and Labor Problems* (New York: McGraw-Hill Book Company, 1933), 364. The estimate of 700 to 800 thousand female members in the union in 1938 was judged very approximate by the author and quite low in relation to the overall number of female workers.

10 Wandersee, *Women's Work and Family Values*, 97.

11 R.W. Smuts, *Women and Work in America* (New York: Schoken Books, 1959), 145; William Henry Chafe, *The American Woman: Her Changing Social, Economic and Political Roles, 1920–1970*, 2nd edition (New York: Oxford University Press, 1974), 107–9.

12 Chafe, *The American Woman*, 108.

13 Cf. Wandersee, *Women's Work and Family Values*, 91; Yoder, *Labor Economics and Labor Problems*, esp. 347.

14 Wandersee, *Women's Work and Family Values*, 27.

15 I provide some information relating to this in *Famiglia, welfare e Stato tra progressismo e New Deal*, 110–13; cf. Wandersee, *Women's Work and Family Values*; Gladys Boone, *The Women's Trade Union Leagues in Great Britain and in the United States of America* (New York: AMS Press, 1968 [1942]), 195–96.

16 Keynes, *Essays in Persuasion*, 231.

On Welfare (1977–1978)

Translated by Richard Braude

Mariarosa Dalla Costa speaking in Piazza Ferretto during a WFH demonstration on March 8, 1974.

thought I would use my reading of the editorial that appeared in *Primo Maggio* 6, along with an article titled "From March to November: A Critical Update," to briefly outline some ideas on the theme of *welfare* that have been introduced into Italy within the remit of the debate on public spending. While the following article is only meant to flag some important points, it is nonetheless more urgent than ever to clear up some matters. Indeed, an incorrect interpretation of welfare means an incorrect interpretation of class and of the relationship between class and capital today, including the infamous risk of arriving at conclusions that are substantially defeatist, in relation to which even scrap metal collecting, refused by the working class for many years now, might seem justified.

The first thing to say is that we continue to talk about welfare without seeing that those receiving it are, on a mass level, *women*. The figures speak clearly enough: in the USA, 85 percent of recipients are women, generally mothers with dependent children (Aid for Dependent Children). As concerns Supplemental Security Income (SSI), which is designed for the sick and elderly, and which up to 1975 was part of the welfare system, before being subsumed within Social Security (SS), the largest percentage is again constituted by women, comprised of housewives who have no pensions because 'they have never worked,' that is, they have never had a wage for a long enough period to allow them to access a social pension.

On the other hand, as to the processes of struggle that led to the current situation, so misunderstood by historians here in Italy, it should be enough to simply take a glance at the photos from the welfare movement that exploded in the USA in the 1960s, essentially a movement of women—black women—who knew how to provide a strategic outlet for the subversive energies of the youth. Young people burned the cities and carried out acts of mass appropriation—an outlet capable of establishing lasting power: a mass request for money that, inasmuch as it was made by those without wages, constituted a new mass power of the class. Spearheaded by women, the welfare movement was at the same time a wage demand and a rejection of the intensification of work, as they refused to take on a second job, instead demanding 'wages for housework.'

The perspective of the women who led these struggles is clearly expressed by statements like:

> "The mother of a family already works full time at home, she doesn't need a second job."
> "When there's a war the state suddenly remembers that they own our sons [it was the era of the Vietnam War]. Okay, so now they should pay us for how much it cost to raise them."
> "Welfare isn't charity like the state wants us to think, it's our right, because we've already worked for this money."[1]

However, in the editorial and article mentioned at the outset, the focus is laid not so much on women but on unemployed whites or, more usually, black and Puerto Rican youth. In the author's mind, this is clearly a male proletariat, a fact that can be noted from the definition of welfare as 'income without work':

> The politics of welfare derives from an idea of generalized public assistance, from an explicit assumption of the necessity for a certain level of unemployment in order to be able to effectively control social processes (marginalization, ghettoization, urban conflict, etc.). What brought this about was the continuous restructuring of the productive apparatus and, therefore, of class composition.[2]

On the one hand, there was the strength of blacks and Puerto Ricans that Nixon was trying so hard to break, as well as attempting to undermine the direct relationship between the increase in factory struggles and the possibility of earning outside of the productive relation.[3]

In a version similar to the one already cited, those allusions to "the *welfare mothers* who Gisela Bock speaks about" are simply grotesques.[4] The women are rendered invisible, as is their labor and their struggle against it—and so is their first mass victory regarding wages for housework.

As well as this lack of recognition of welfare's 'political subjects,' there is also a distorted reading of the 'crisis,' one that is irrevocably bound to the discourse on welfare as the most significant sector in public spending.

The problem is that the popular interpretation of the crisis in general (and the bankrupting of New York in particular), as one that is derived from the imbalance between productive and nonproductive sectors, says nothing about the basis that determined this crisis and the actual processes of class recomposition.

To be blind to the women on welfare is to be blind to the struggle over reproductive work as the determinative struggle regarding the very processes behind the crisis itself. The striking events of their indiscipline and refusal of work derived directly from the refusal of domestic work in the home, the office, the school, the nursery, and the factory. Furthermore, in relation to the elephantiasis of the public purse, it is nothing other than the state's desperate attempt—in the context of a *scaling up of refusal*—to continually *reconstruct and scale up* the *collective wife and mother*, who might once again discipline the workforce and persuade it to work. To be blind to all this is to fail to interpret the *necessity of growing imbalances* in state investment in public spending and to fixate on a void, providing a definition of the crisis that remains no more than descriptive, such as:

> The available information tells us that the New York bankruptcy, as in many American cities, resulted from the huge increase in public spending, above all on welfare and on the growing bank debt.... From these two pieces of information one can agree with what so many have been saying, that is, that the current crisis everywhere is the result of an imbalance between the 'productive' and 'nonproductive' sectors.[5]

From 1965 onward, the welfare sector began to explode, both in terms of the number of recipients and of the kind of voices[6] through which the state forced the struggle to be expressed. That this was a women's struggle can be seen from the fact that it was precisely the category of the Aid for Dependent Children (AFDC) that exploded, while other categories[7] remained, on the whole, stagnant.[8] The other fact that has escaped Italian historians is that for the first time in the history of welfare the increase in the number of people receiving it was inversely proportional to unemployment. In fact, as Moynihan has already shown with some concern in his *The Politics of a Guaranteed Income*, the explosion in welfare was triggered in a period of mass economic expansion in the USA. For the first time, the relation between unemployment and welfare was completely broken.[9] This breakdown continued from 1966 until 1970, the year in which all American newspapers were in agreement that welfare was the 'national crisis' and that the situation 'was only getting worse.'

But what really was this national crisis that from 1970 onward became the thorn in the side of the American state?

The symbol of welfare dependence was the family with a mother at its head. Their continually growing number, to the point that in 1969 the *New York Daily News* reported—with neither anger nor disapproval but simply as a fact—"There is a quiet social revolution establishing itself in the country's slums, especially here in New York: the number of cases of absent fathers and illegitimate children is exploding, at the cost of the traditional family itself."[10]

Furthermore, Moynihan writes:

> The social fabric here in New York is falling to pieces. . . . For an ever-larger part of the population, the sense of discipline, of doing it oneself, of industry is slipping away. . . . The number of illegitimate children is growing; the family is ever more atomized and in the hands of women alone; crime and disorder are starkly increasing. . . . In short, we are seeing a growing disintegration of society.[11]

Ever since his famous report on the black family, Moynihan has claimed that the origins of the ghetto revolts lay in the fact that the majority of black families are led by women: having no other authority over themselves, they rejected their function of disciplining their children. In the article "America," again from 1965, Moynihan writes:

> From the wilds of Irish slums of the Eastern seaboard, to the riot-torn suburbs of Los Angeles, there is one unmistakable lesson in American history: a community that allows a large number of young men to grow up in broken families, dominated by women, never acquiring any stable relationship to male authority, never acquiring any set of rational expectations about the future—that community asks for and gets chaos. Crime, violence, unrest, disorder—most particularly the furious, unrestrained lashing out at the whole social structure—that is not only to be expected; it is very near to inevitable. And it is richly deserved.

Even in today's debates about restructuring welfare, Moynihan continues to repeat the fact that giving money to women means undermining the family structure, and thus the entire structure of work. That welfare might function "not so much to bring stability but *independence* and consequentially the possibility of creating entirely different family relations"[12]—and this, we must understand, begins above all with women—is a fact about which we have no doubts whatsoever. As all of the government documents from 1965 up till today verify, the explosion in welfare was concurrent with drastic increases in: 1) the number of so-called illegitimate children (this year in Washington, for the first time the number of illegitimate children overtook the number of legitimate ones); 2) the number of divorces, a figure that breaks new records every year. Furthermore, it is no longer the case that women who get divorced are childless.[13] All of this means a continual increase in the number of families with women at the head: between 1960 and 1970, an increase of 16 percent.

The *scaling up* of public spending, as I have already briefly mentioned above, was an act *forced on the American state by women's refusal of* reproductive work. The victory of the women over welfare—and in this sense, welfare is indeed the most important sector—has allowed for the generalization of this refusal. This is a refusal that has had the ability to move ever larger and more articulated investments into the sector of the social reproduction of the workforce. One really needs to be very blinkered in order not to see that the creation of the so-called 'third sector' is simultaneously a process of socialization of domestic work. Psychologists, sociologists, sexologists, teachers, social workers, therapists, doctors and nurses, etc. all have to perform the tasks that women increasingly refuse to undertake; all of them, to be precise, have to become the *collective wife and mother*. It is only in the light of this fact that one can understand why "service workers have had the lion's share."[14]

It was exactly in order to move toward a socialization of domestic work that the famous Title 20 (an amendment of the Social Security Act) was passed in 1975. It ensured the organization of a system of social services planned by the various states but, in the end, financed for the most part by the federal government, which created a new and mobile institution across the country that was destined to furnish domestic work, with the quite clear aim of controlling it. This included home services for the elderly and husbands with wives who were unable to perform domestic work and the provision of 'care' and 'alternative arrangements' for children growing up in 'inappropriate' housing, etc.

However, not even provisions like Title 20 managed to deal with the situation. Instead, the refusal only increased, taking on a mass character, producing a striking indiscipline from the home to the factory, a refusal of production and of being governed in any way, rendering the problem of public spending increasingly dramatic—not only for its fiscal aspect, though this was increasingly relevant, but also for its substantial endurance. By now, as capital knows all too well—even if some of its scholars are a little less clear—there is a quite precise connection between the *kitchen blues* and the *blue-collar blues*. In other words: the refusal in the kitchen means in turn an immediate refusal at the conveyor belt and in the army.[15] It is no accident that in mainstream newspapers like *Business Week* and *Magazine* women are blamed more and more for the explosion of struggles in schools, for the lack of victories in Vietnam, and for the clear lack of interest in working in general, as well as for the ever rising 'delinquency.'

However, the state knows it does not have adequate political instruments to deal with this problem. Investment in public spending is increasingly 'disproportionate' and 'expansive,' without there being any way to put the brakes on the situation, which has recently worsened because the new kind of human capital (social workers, etc.) in whom a large part of the public funds has been invested (and *had to be* invested), with no particular guarantee that this investment will not simply spiral out of control. The new agents who have to discipline those who have already refused the discipline are themselves undisciplined. As Peppino Ortoleva shows: "As far as the public service sector itself is concerned, those who administer the wide-ranging assistance, there are many recent examples of joint mobilizations that have included not only these workers but also 'their' recipients."[16] More specifically, focusing on the ambit of welfare, which always remains the most significant, this unity in struggle between women recipients and women social workers, who increasingly refuse to act as police officers, is the most evident outcome of the refusal of domestic work by both parties. It is precisely due to the wave of this refusal that American capital has been forced to attempt the path of a growing computerization of welfare.[17]

The Nixon administration's counterattack began with the apparent 'failure' of Johnson's 'Great Society' plan (the realization of Kennedy's 'war on poverty'). This counterattack took many forms, from the attempt to stop the reproduction of the proletariat on welfare *tout court* (from 1970 to today the sterilization of black and Puerto Rican women, and those supported by welfare more generally, has increased threefold) to the cutting of welfare, primarily through the elimination of the 'special needs' category, and the introduction of the 'flat grant.' Overall, there has been an attempt to reconnect welfare to the male wage. Moynihan, always ahead of his times in this regard, had by 1965 grasped that only the consolidation of the economic position of the black male would solve this spiral of indiscipline by the black proletariat. In this sense the Nixon administration's Family Assistance Plan (FAP) is the first program destined to explicitly reconstruct the family, work, and masculine authority. Money will no longer be directed to women but is to be attached to the wage of the male worker to whom the woman and her children are once again to bind themselves.[18] The FAP has still not passed Senate, but it nonetheless shows the general direction of all the proposed reforms that have been and are currently being debated. This general direction remains the imperative of the discourse among the more intelligent section of capital:

> The question isn't just about welfare but whether we'll give whole families the same economic help which we give to 'broken' ones today. Governor Car[e]y [of the State of New York] has said that a system of welfare is necessary to keep the family intact. But that's not what we've got today. The current system provides a huge incentive for families to break up. So that's the basic issue: whether to give to the working poor [read: the poor man] the same economic support which we give to poor people on welfare. Everything else is simply administrative detail.[19]

There are others, however, who think instead that the solution might lie in federalization, to the extent that federalization represents first and foremost a wage cut[20] but would also lead, with the centralization of welfare management, to the elimination of local contracting and therefore to the possibility for both the assisted and the assistants to organize on a local level.[21]

In any case, even if everyone is in agreement on the need for structural reform of welfare, this still hasn't affected the process, precisely due to the 'difficulty' that this presents.[22] A series of policies have been enacted, however, that tend toward stabilizing masculine authority within the family and, above all, to granting responsibility to the man for the maintenance of the children. It will suffice to cite merely the most important of these measures: the attempt to blackmail women by offering economic compensation for officially providing the name and address of their children's father;[23] macroscopically, this attempt has failed—women know all too well that to reconnect their children to the father also means to submit to his command—so more drastic means have been tried. In April 1976, the federal government opened the way to a kind of manhunt by allowing the Department for Health, Education and Welfare (HEW) access to Social Security numbers, thus granting them the ability to trace fathers across state boundaries.[24] New York City went further still: on February 16, 1977, it was decreed that every woman who makes a welfare claim—the policy is also retroactive—must declare who the father of the child is, providing an address and any information that might allow him to be traced, as well as declaring "if at the time of conception she had relations with other men," as it is written in the new form that women have to fill out.

From the above it can be understood, therefore, that there is currently (and not only in the USA) an unprecedented *renewed interest by economists* in the *family* and that the *consolidation* of the family is today at the *center of the American government's politics*. It is no accident that the recent elections have brought Moynihan and Mondale to power (the latter the current vice president), the first being an expert on women and the second on children, and that Carter himself put praising the family at the center of his electoral campaign. We have already spoken about Moynihan at length. As far as Mondale is concerned, he introduced the Child and Family Services Act in 1975, which stated the *government's deep responsibility for the rearing of children*. There was hope that this Act would mean the allocation of federal funds for a vast range of projects for children in a range of states.[25] More recently, Mondale also asserted that every government plan ought be accompanied by a Family Impact Statement, so as to assess the influence that programs might have on family stability.

I have only spoken about the USA here. But insofar as the USA represents the country that leads capitalist reactions, we hope that this clarification might also provide some important indications about the dynamics of the 'world state' and of the class struggle over reproduction. We do so in the hope, as always, that those who are studying in order to contribute to the working-class debate do not, thereafter, in the great tradition of both the 'revolutionary' and the 'reformist' left, take an interest in simply rendering capital more intelligent.

Padua, April 1977

Notes

Originally published in *Primo Maggio: saggi e documenti per una storia di classe* 9–10 (1977–1978): 76–80.

1   Milwaukee County Welfare Rights Organization, *Welfare Mothers Speak Out: We Ain't Gonna Shuffle Anymore* (New York: W.W. Norton & Co., 1972).

2   *Primo Maggio* 6 (Winter 1975–1976): 8.

3   Ibid., 18.

4   Ibid., 19.

5   Ibid., 3.

6   Beyond the monthly allowance (calculated on the basis of the number of family members), the principal expression of welfare lies in the category of 'special needs,' which allows access to money for 'emergency cases,' among other things, and which is to be used for acquiring new furniture, clothing, and books for children, etc. It was on this basis that women were able to wage an ongoing struggle for more money. And, not by accident, it is this category that will be the first victim of all the welfare reforms introduced since the early 1960s. It was also in this period that welfare came to be presented as a 'flat grant,' that is, as a fixed sum that is meant to cover all of the family's needs.

7   Cf. Daniel Moynihan, *The Politics of a Guaranteed Income* (New York: Vintage Books, 1973).

8   None of which removes the fact that in the last two years the number of recipients of Home Relief, who used to represent a minority, has exploded. In fact, it is only due to the great wave of unemployment that struck the East Coast in particular that New York City was forced to concede Home Relief to all of the unemployed whose support had run out. Home Relief, to be precise, is a non-federal category of welfare and exists at the discretion of local authorities. In fact, it exists only in New York City and a few other cities. It consists of money provided to those who can demonstrate that they have no income and cannot find work.

9   Moynihan, *The Politics of a Guaranteed Income*, 82–83.

10   Ibid., 29.

11   Ibid., 66.

12   Cf. Heather Ross, *Poverty: Women and Children Last* (Washington, DC: Urban Institute, 1976), 11.

13   Ibid., 5. In relation to this, also see: Joint Economic Committee, *Studies in Public Welfare*, Paper no. 12, part 1, "The Family, Poverty and Welfare Programs: Factors Influencing Family Instability" (Washington, DC: U.S. Government Printing Office, 1973), esp. 154. One can not only calculate that today the number of divorces has increased by 60 percent since 1965, but that one in three marriages end in divorce.

14   *Primo Maggio* 6, 3.

15   It was exactly because of the refusal of the young to 'serve their country' that the American government has been forced to turn into a voluntary army for some years now.

16   *Primo Maggio* 6, 19.

17   "City Opens Computer Center to Check on Eligibility of Welfare Recipients," *New York Times*, February 28, 1975.

18   Cf. Moynihan, *The Politics of a Guaranteed Income*, which centers on an analysis of the FAP.

19   "Welfare," *Robert MacNeil Report*, July 7, 1976.

20   On the federalization of welfare projects, cf. "The Welfare State and the Public Welfare," *Fortune*, June 1976. The proposal for the federalization of welfare paves the way for the homogenization of quotas on a national level (the quantitative quota

currently varies from state to state). This 'homogenization' will of course not be achieved on the basis of areas where the cost of living is the highest but where it is lowest, as has already been shown in the case of SSI.

21 In fact, centralization means the reduction of offices—welfare centers—that have until now always been the nerve centers of daily conflict.

22 It is telling that Carter's economists, who made this reform the flagship policy of his electoral campaign, recently announced that a full reform would not be possible before 1980.

23 Beginning on February 16, 1977, a new form had to be filled out by women on welfare declaring where the father of their children resided, so that the state could track him down. They also had to divulge whether they had had any other sexual relationships at the time of conception. A "wise" about-turn from the days when it was necessary to hide any trace of a man at home in order to maintain welfare support.

24 "Social Security Numbers Will Track Runaway Fathers," *New York Times*, April 7, 1976.

25 This proposal has been subject to a vast amount of criticism from American parents, who have seen it as an attempt at 'Sovietization' of child rearing; see "A Twisted Attack on Day Care," *Newsday*, January 30, 1976, which, despite the sensationalist title, highlights its merits.

Excesses in the Relationship of Women to Medicine: Some History (2005)

Translated by Richard Braude

Mariarosa Dalla Costa uses a megaphone to address a January 24, 1976, demonstration for abortion rights in Piazza dei Signori, Padua.

Over the years, I have occasionally focused my attention on the excess of hysterectomies and their affect upon women, operations that compromise the completeness of the body and cause unnecessary hormonal and psychophysical imbalance. Alongside other scholars, I contributed to a volume on this subject to which I refer the reader for a more exhaustive treatment of this theme, including historical references, as it is impossible to provide a detailed explanation here.[1] It is enough to simply recall that the numerical excess of such operations is characteristic to a range of advanced countries. The USA constitutes the leading country for unnecessary hysterectomies, with figures that have shown that one in three women can expect to be subject to this intervention by the time they are sixty, and 40 percent of women by the time they are sixty-four years old. Moreover, in half of cases there are complications during the operation, and it is a given that in all countries, including Italy, there is also a mortality rate of around one woman for every five hundred who undergo an abdominal hysterectomy, and one in a thousand for those who undergo a vaginal hysterectomy. According to the U.S. Agency for Health Care Policy and Research (1996), there are notable differences between regions (the South has a higher rate of 78 percent undergoing the operation), between races (non-white women undergo hysterectomies at a rate 39 percent higher than white women), and between different social classes (women from the poorer and less educated stratum are operated on more), all differences which cannot but raise some questions.

In southern Australia the frequency of the intervention is one woman in every three before the age of sixty, as in the USA. In Europe the overall rate is lower, but with notable difference between countries. France and Holland have a relatively low average. On a national level one woman in every twenty in France can expect to undergo the intervention, and one in every twenty-five in Paris and the surrounding area (around 12 million people), and in France, as in many other countries, there is a downward trend. Italy is distinguished, on the other hand, by a relatively high average and a rising trend. In Italy, the number of hysterectomies rose from thirty-eight thousand a year in 1994 to sixty-eight thousand in 1997, meaning that one woman in five can expect to undergo the operation, and in some regions, like the Veneto, one in four. In 1998 and 1999, on a national level, hysterectomies rose still further, up to seventy thousand a year.

The Italian data, compared with that from France, and Paris in particular, indicates that around 80 percent of hysterectomies in Italy are unnecessary. However, similar conclusions can also be drawn by observing the relationship between the reasons hysterectomies are performed and plausible reasons for the intervention. In the lion's share of cases the reasons given are dysfunctional metrorrhagia (35 percent) and fibroma (30 percent), conditions that should almost never result in a hysterectomy.[2] Research undertaken by Gianfranco Domenighetti, professor of economics at the University of Lausanne and Geneva and long-time director of the Department of Health in the Canton of Ticino, and the economist A. Casabianca has shown that in Italy the women least subjected to hysterectomies are the wives of lawyers and female doctors, and those subjected to it the most are the women with the highest levels of health insurance and the lowest levels of education. While launching a media campaign addressing these figures on hysterectomies and the correct indications for such interventions, Professor Domenighetti maintained that the number of operations was decreasing but less so in the teaching hospitals. The two scholars concluded that "the idea could no longer be excluded that gynecologists exploit women for personal gain or in order to receive some hidden pleasure from such interventions."[3]

Dr. Stanley West, specialist in sterility and head of the Department for Reproductive Endocrinology at the St. Vincent Hospital in New York and author (with Paula Dranov) of *The Hysterectomy Hoax* (1994) claims that in the USA more than 90 percent of hysterectomies are unnecessary, an opinion that appears to be shared by many authorities on the subject. Furthermore, he emphasizes the physical, psychological, and sexual consequences of the operation can seriously compromise a woman's health and well-being.[4] Thus, even at first glance, at an international level the number hysterectomies displays a frequency of occurrence that departs from the indications alone. The frequency of this surgical procedure exploded in the twentieth century, almost as if the ready availability of anesthesia, antibiotics, and antisepsis finally allowed the practice of a previously desired act of aggression on the female body. An act of aggression that was perhaps latent in a gynecological profession that until a short while ago was largely in the hands of male doctors, just as the chief positions are even today almost entirely occupied by men. This anxiety of aggressive conquest of the female body has, as we will see, the story of gynecology written all over it, ever since it was transformed into an official science and a masculine medical profession.

There are two particularly significant moments in this history. Firstly, all across Europe from the fifteenth to seventeenth centuries, there was the period that saw the beginning of gynecology as a medical science and masculine profession in opposition to the obstetric and gynecological knowledge that had always been in the hands of women, healers, and midwives. Secondly, in the USA, during the period from the second half of the nineteenth century up to the beginning of the twentieth, in which—in an analogous manner—we can observe the confirmation of official medical science, including gynecology, provided by universities opposing popular knowledge drawn from different schools.

The first moment was manifest through a long and ferocious experience of aggression against women's bodies and knowledge. It is thanks to the work of feminist scholars that this series of events has been brought out from the shadows and analyzed within the historical context of medicine as an official science and its function in repressing women. The feminist research published in the 1970s and 1980s constituted an important stepping-stone insofar as it laid the basis for a body of knowledge that would become the initial instrument in the feminist movement's confrontation with health care systems and the medical profession. First and foremost, *Witches, Midwives and Nurses* (1973) by Barbara Ehrenreich and Deirdre English must be mentioned, along with *Il Grande Calibano* (1984) by Silvia Federici and Leopoldina Fortunati and *Caliban and the Witch* by Silvia Federici (2004). All of these authors dedicated a great deal of space to the subject, analyzing the macroscopic operations that unfolded with capitalism's origins, forging the kind of society and figure of the woman that suited it the most.

During the thirteenth and fourteenth centuries the first target of the newborn official medicine in Europe was not so much the popular knowledge of female healers among the poor but the knowledge of educated female healers in the cities, with whom the medical profession competed for the wealthy customers who already provided consistent demand. The educated urban healers were unseated from their profession not only through the ban on women entering almost any university but, more fundamentally, by laws that forbade anyone without university instruction from practicing medicine. A noteworthy example is that of Jacoba Felicie, an educated woman who had taken 'special courses' in medicine and was more of an expert, as her patients recognized, than any other doctor or surgeon in Paris, and who was taken to court in 1322 by the Faculty of Medicine in the city's university and accused of illegal practice. The strategy, combining 'access forbidden' and 'outlawing,' was so effective that by the end of the fourteenth century the professional male doctors' campaign against the educated female urban healers was practically complete in Europe. The male doctors had achieved a monopoly over the practice of medicine for the wealthy classes. Obstetrics, however, remained beyond their abilities, even for wealthy clients, and was a field that women continued to dominate for three more centuries.

Obstetrics was reconstituted much later, through an alliance of state, Church, and the (male) medical profession, to also transfer this sector to the 'regular' medical profession, now under the control of state and Church, at the price of massacring the so-called 'witches,' who were for the most part healers and midwives. However, the persecution of the 'witches' constituted only a part of the macroscopic social operations that were executed in different periods, some as early as the fourteenth century, others only in their fullness from the end of the fifteenth up to the eighteenth century, of which the most famous was the *expropriation and enclosure of common land*. If these social operations created the misery necessary for the beginning of the capitalist mode of production, making an immense quantity of labor power available, then the *witch hunts* served to *expropriate women's bodies*. Depriving them, first of all, of the knowledge of and power to make decisions about their own reproductive powers or about their sexuality and procreation, because the reproduction of individuals, which was by now the reproduction of labor power as far as it concerned an expropriated and impoverished population, had to be under the control of the state, through the mediation of the medical profession.

Silvia Federici in particular has observed how the European witch hunt extended from the fourteenth to seventeenth centuries, with the peak period falling between 1550 to 1650, with around a hundred thousand women being atrociously tortured, and then burned alive. The victims, she has written, were for the most part country midwives who were guilty of not only knowing about birth but also about abortion and methods of contraception. There were also healers and women accused of having loose morals. However, it was much easier for women to be accused if they were alone, unmarried, old, and, above all, among the leaders of urban and peasant revolts caused by price hikes, the continual imposition of new and heavy taxes, and the expropriation of the land. Virgins and pregnant women were, as a rule, not sent to the stake.

This made for the greatest femicide in recorded history, representing a fundamental moment in the history of the struggles between classes and between sexes, eliminating not only the condemned women themselves but also popular medicine, especially the obstetric and gynecological knowledge that had exclusively been in their hands. This knowledge was replaced by an official medicine under the control of state and Church that required centuries to fill the void left behind by the extermination of healers and midwives able to provide any real form of therapy. It also is worth noting that while witches had a deep knowledge of bones and muscles and of herbs and drugs, the male doctors of the period still derived their prognoses from astrology. So vast was the witches' knowledge that Paracelsus, considered the 'father of modern medicine,' threw his own text on pharmaceuticals into the flames in 1527, confessing that he "had learned from the Sorceress all he knew."[5] The new capitalistic states now took over that knowledge and, more importantly, the control of human reproduction via a science that would pass through the universities, and therefore through the heads of men from the dominant classes, given that the universities, with few exceptions, forbade women. This murderous expropriation of the popular legacy that women had constructed and handed down excluded, among other things, the possibility of curing the poorest classes in the population. But above all the stake served, along with the midwives and other condemned women, to burn that figure of the medieval woman who had rebelled against the feminine model required by the family in the newborn capitalism.

This medieval woman was present in many professions and crafts, not only medicine. She was extremely social, living in an environment in which her sexuality was not subordinated exclusively to the needs of procreation. However, if enjoying a 'bad reputation' had already proved sufficient to send someone to the stake, we ought to bear in mind that exactly during this passage to a new mode of production, women—excluded both from accessing the earth due to the continued expropriations and enclosures, and from the old crafts, as well as forbidden from entering new ones[6]—were for the first time in history forced to turn to prostitution on a mass level.[7] In this context, the stake and the politics of terror it represented served above all to redefine the women's social function. In order to be transformed into a 'mechanical reproducer of labor power,' she had to be increasingly isolated, sexually repressed, subjected to marital authority, a breeder of children deprived of her own economic independence and her knowledge of and power over decisions relating to her sexuality and of procreation. But the stake was also there to destroy equal cooperative relations between women in the area of obstetrics and gynecology and between the female midwife and the woman giving birth or otherwise in need of care or advice. This relationship had to be replaced by one of authority and hierarchy between the male doctor and female patient. During the witch trials the doctor was the expert who had to provide a scientific stamp to the whole process, testifying to which women could be judged as witches and what diseases could be produced by witchcraft. The witch hunts thus provided an easy cover for the daily incompetence of male doctors: anything that he could not cure was attributed to sorcery. The distinction between 'female superstition' and 'masculine medicine' was codified in the roles assumed by the male doctor and the witch during the trials.[8]

The first male midwives appeared in the seventeenth century, and within a hundred years obstetrics had passed into male hands.[9] In the first instance through the barber-surgeons who boasted of their technical superiority because they used forceps, which were legally classified as surgical instruments, while women, who had already noted the instrument's dangers, were excluded from surgery by law. This was despite the fact that women were experts in surgical practice, because, among other factors, they knew how to amputate prolapsed uteri.[10] As such, obstetrics passed into the hands of official (male) doctors and became—initially for the wealthy English classes—a lucrative practice rather than a local service.

The USA during the nineteenth century represents another extremely important moment in this history. At this point, popular medical knowledge—embodied for the most part by a large number of female medical healers, as well as men of various ethnicities, including African and Native American men—confronted an aspiring official medical science. However, the confrontation rewarded the former and gave life to the Popular Health

Movement, which reached its apex between 1830 and 1850, coinciding with the dawn of an organized feminist movement (with which it is generally confused). This feminism had a conception of health care that differed significantly from that of official doctors, above all considering it not as a commodity but as a common good and fundamental right to guarantee collectivity. While the 'regular' doctors (as they were called once they left university) held to the official medical science, they never managed to monopolize medicine during that period, a transformation that was only later made possible by the interventions of the Rockefeller and Carnegie Foundations in the early twentieth century.

The philanthropic programs of these foundations were bound to the plans of the class that dominated the social, cultural, and political life of the USA, a central focus of which was *medical reform*. They funded the financially secure regulated medical schools and were prepared to begin the necessary changes to bring them in line with the directives adopted by John Hopkins University, founded in 1893. The other schools, where the majority of women, blacks, and poor whites studied, were not only denied this funding but were also forced to close. Thus, the population lacking wealth remained less protected in terms of their health care, inasmuch as it then became difficult to pay for official medical care. A little later, new laws excluded midwives from what had always been their field of expertise. Obstetrics now fell under the control of professional doctors, who were far too inclined to use surgical techniques that damaged the mother, the child, or both. The consequence was that poor women remained without any assistance, with predictably negative—sometimes documented—effects on both mothers and their children.

It is within the *'regular' medical profession* that took hold in the U.S. during the nineteenth century that we find a *kind of medicine* directed toward women that functioned, in reality, as a *powerful instrument of control* over their behavior and eventually led to *aberrant castration practices* such as *clitoral removal*, because female sexual stimulation was considered a pathological state, and *ovarian removal* for varied and inconsistent problems. This is why I think it is high time to write a 'history of female genital mutilation in Western civilization.' In relation to clitoral removal, Ehrenreich and English address the last of these operations in the USA, which was on a five-year-old girl who masturbated, and which took place around twenty years prior to the publishing of their text in 1973. However, in nineteenth-century Europe clitoridectomy found its supporters, including exponents from the world of official medicine, among them Dr. Isaac Baker Brown of St. Mary's Hospital, in Paddington, London, who was also recognized for developing safer surgical techniques. In 1865, he published an article on the possibility of curing some forms of madness, epilepsy, and hysteria by clitoridectomy, and even managed to publicize the success of such a practice. He was, fortunately, expelled from the Obstetrical Society of London for this practice.[11] However, it begs the question of how many other doctors on both sides of the ocean continued with this medical crime against women without the least concern? What is clear is that from the beginning of the nineteenth century to the 1960s, in psychiatric hospitals (though there have been cases in nonpsychiatric hospitals as well) across Europe and the USA clitoridectomies were performed for unfounded medical reasons, essentially as a form of punishment against a woman and her sexuality.[12]

Taking up Ehrenreich and English's observations about the nineteenth century in the USA, we have to point out how the medical profession identified middle- and upper-class bourgeois women as ideal clients, continually emphasizing that their illnesses were caused by, if not directly identified with, biological characteristics and flaws of the female body, while also underlining the importance of continual visits and therapeutic methods, essentially represented by the patient's tranquillization, isolation, and 'bed rest.' Beneath this was the 'theory of energy conservation,' according to which any energy spent on functions other than reproduction worked to the latter's detriment, meaning that the woman was also dissuaded from engaging in intellectual activity or other pursuits. However, the cruel assault on the female body that led to *widespread* practice of ovariectomies, accompanied by a disavowal of women's medical knowledge in the American case, led to the construction of a professional male science that eventually formulated a theory that Ehrenreich and English define as a "psychology of the ovary."[13] According to this theory the uterus and ovaries were the dominant parts of the female organism, and as such it was claimed that the ovaries influenced the entirety of a woman's personality. For this reason, any alteration of what were held to be a woman's 'natural characteristics'—alterations that ranged from irritability through madness to the manifestation of sexual desire—could be reduced to an ovarian illness. I omit mentioning the range of abuses committed at that time by gynecologists against the female body on the basis of the assumption, common to men of that epoch, that female sexuality can only be pathological, with a focus on the operation 'for personality problems' that was the most brutal and widely used of gynecological surgeries, the ovariectomy. Thousands of these interventions took place between 1860 and 1890.

A specific theory relating to this was the so-called 'normal ovariectomy,' or the removal of the ovaries for illnesses unrelated to them, a theory developed by Dr. Robert Battey of Rome, Georgia, in 1872. This is referred to by Dr. Ben Barker-Benfield, who describes the illnesses considered for this kind of intervention:

> Among the indications were troublesomeness, eating like a ploughman, masturbation, attempted suicide, erotic tendencies, persecution mania, simple 'cussedness,' and dysmenorrhea. Most apparent in the enormous variety of symptoms doctors took to indicate castration was a strong current of sexual want on the part of women.[14]

Generally, the patients were brought for surgery by their husbands, who complained of their wives undisciplined behavior, which, after the operation, according to Dr. Battey, then became more "manageable, ordered, industrious and clean." Given the conditions in which surgery was performed at that time, it is legitimate to ask *for how many women this punitive therapy actually constituted capital punishment*. Obviously, sometimes the threat of the operation alone would have been enough to keep women in line. Some doctors claimed to have removed between 1,500–2,000 ovaries. In the words of Dr. Barker-Benfield, "They brought them round on plates, like trophies, at medical conferences."[15]

During this time, the *hysterectomy* also underwent medical theorizations that called for its implementation for more varied problems, including hysteria and 'menstrual melancholia,' which today we might call 'premenstrual syndrome.'[16] It ought to be noted that doctors' pride in demonstrating their abilities meant that they performed the hysterectomies as social events, inviting not only other doctors but also friends and numerous strangers to assist in the operation—and given the lack of knowledge of the times, they did not usually wash their hands or put on gloves and masks before the operation. They were indifferent to the trauma experienced by the woman, who had to pass alone through a nightmare of pain without anesthetic, feeling the scalpel go in from the sternum to the pubic symphysis. However, even after the first kinds of general anesthetic had been developed, such as chloroform, some doctors claimed that they preferred to not use it, as the tension induced in the patient by the intervention was said to help with the postoperative recovery. Among these doctors was Dr. Charles Clay, who gave the name 'ovariectomy' to the surgical removal of the ovaries. Dr. Clay had the greatest reputation for such operations. He carried out 395, of which 25 were fatal, and conducted the first abdominal hysterectomy, in Manchester, England, in 1843, which unfortunately resulted in the patient's death by hemorrhage. Clay claimed to prefer not to use anesthetic because the determination that a woman demonstrated in order to endure the intervention without anesthetic would, according to him, guarantee her ability to recover.[17] Are we here perhaps dealing simply with the long-held assumption, well received by gynecological-obstetrical science of the time (and not only back then), that a woman must suffer? In his article, "Hysterectomy: A Historical Perspective," Sutton is amazed that, despite the high mortality rate, especially in relation to abdominal hysterectomy, so many women accepted the operation. However, it has to be asked, as we have already in relation to ovariectomies, how much coercion and how much violence did these women endure from their husbands, brothers, fathers, and doctors for the sake of punishment and sadism in some cases and for sadism and professional interest in others? How much male complicity has caused entirely useless and equally terrifying suffering upon women's bodies? Which begs the question: What relationship exists between those abuses and the abuses of today?

Notes

This essay is drawn from a talk given at the conference "La salute della donna," Vicenza, March 3, 2004; originally published in *La rivista della Società Medico Chirurgica Vicentina* 15, no. 1–2 (December 2005).

1   Mariarosa Dalla Costa, ed., *Gynocide: Hysterectomy, Capitalist Patriarchy, and the Medical Abuse of Women* (Brooklyn, NY: Autonomedia, 2007).

2   Ibid. For the incidence of these and other pathologies, and the appropriateness of the indication as a method of evaluating the percentage of hysterectomies that might be difficult to justify, see Dr. Samaritani's intervention.

3   G. Domenighetti, "Effect of Information Campaign by the Mass Media on Hysterectomy Rates," *Lancet*, December 24–31, 1988; G. Domenighetti and A. Casabianca, "Rate of Hysterectomy Is Lower among Female Doctors and Lawyers' Wives," *Lancet*, December 24–31, 1988.

4   Stanley West and Paula Dranov, *The Hysterectomy Hoax* (New York: Doubleday, 1994).

5   Barbara Ehrenreich and Deirdre English, *Complaints and Disorders: The Sexual Politics of Sickness* (New York: The Feminist Press, 1973).

6   Evelyne Sullerot, *Histoire et sociologie du travail féminin* (Paris: Editions Gonthier, 1968).

7   Leopoldina Fortunati, *The Arcane of Reproduction: Housework, Prostitution, Labor and Capital* (Brooklyn, NY: Autonomedia, 1995).

8   Barbara Ehrenreich and Deirdre English, *Le streghe siamo noi: Il ruolo della medicina nella repressione della donna* (Milan: Celuc Libri, 1975).

9   Alice Clark, *Working Life of Women in Seventeenth Century England* (London: Frank Cass Co., 1968); Jean Donnison, *Midwives and Medical Men* (New York: Schocken Books, 1977).

10 C. Sutton, "Hysterectomy: A Historical Perspective," in *Baillière's Clinical Obstetrics and Gynaecology* (London: Baillière Tindall, 1997).

11 Sutton, "Hysterectomy," 10.

12 Mariarosa Dalla Costa, *Isterectomia: il problema sociale di un abuso contro le donne*, 3rd edition (Milan: Franco Angeli, 2002), 185; Bernard de Fréminville, *La ragione del più forte* (Milan: Feltrinelli, 1979).

13 Ehrenreich and English, *Complaints and Disorders*.

14 Ibid., 119.

15 Ibid., 120.

16 Sutton, "Hysterectomy." 16.

17 Sutton, "Hysterectomy," 4, 6.

Women's Autonomy and Remuneration of Care Work in the New Emergencies of Eldercare (2007)

Translated by Silvia Federici

A musical performance by women from the Padua WFH committee at the May 1, 1975, demonstration in Mestre, Venice.

Every construction of autonomy has its own history, one that evolves within a specific context and must face specific obstacles and battles. With regards to women's autonomy, some of the first stages of this history can be located in the initiatives of the feminist movement—a movement in which I directly participated—initiatives that were necessary for women to regain sovereignty over their bodies. This struggle for autonomy on a planetary level is a battle that is far from over. In this essay, I would like to consider other aspects of this history, starting again from the initial moments of that political experience, and in doing so assess what the relation between women and autonomy is today with respect to some emergent problems, as well as to ask, in relation to the latter, what has happened to both the demand that housework (or care work) be remunerated and to women's economic autonomy.

First Act

Today there is a great celebration of difference. But I always feel the need to specify what difference we are talking about—from whose point of view, for whom it constitutes a problem, and to whose benefit or disadvantage it is. This is the only way to focus on the question of difference and find any solutions.

At the time of the feminist movement we thought it was enough to identify one *difference insofar as it produced a crucial hierarchy*: the difference of being, as reproducers of labor power, unwaged workers in a wage economy where men, as producers of commodities, would be destined in the capitalist sexual division of labor to be wageworkers. We worked on this question, and it kept us busy for about ten years. The rest followed from this fundamental fact. By demanding *wages for housework* we wanted to attack *the capitalist stratification of labor* starting from *its deepest division*:

the division between the male work of production of commodities and the female work of production and reproduction of labor power. Insofar as *this work was vital for capitalism,* producing its most precious commodity, labor power itself, we had in our hands a *formidable lever of power,* in that we *could refuse to produce.* Starting from this fact, we could demand a new type of development centered on different conditions for the care of human beings, beginning with *women's economic autonomy* and a more equitable sharing of care work with men. For this reason, we also demanded a *generalized and drastic reduction* of worktime outside the home, so that both women and men could share the burden but also the pleasure of reproduction. Thus *time, money, and services* were in those years the basic elements of our demands.

The *high point of the movements* in Italy at the end of the 1960s and beginning of the 1970s was the *training ground for our militancy,* the arena where many of us learned to struggle and analyze that perverse thing that is capitalist development. I, too, at the beginning of my work at the university in 1967 was holding seminars for students on *Capital,* vol. 1, but first I would go to leaflet in Porto Marghera, in a pale dawn full of mosquitoes, discovering what a factory is, its rhythms, its health hazards, and its history. Because factories, as I wrote in a leaflet trying to explain the concept, are not like trees that have always existed. I do not by any means remember that period as a time of convivial living, as others claim to. It was rather a period of great learning, of very austere living, of much sacrifice and commitment, and of much determination. Perhaps the most beautiful thing was the immediacy of relations, finding ourselves active in the same cause, and the blooming of this great community to which we belonged. It was not necessary to fix appointments in order to meet, we all knew where the others were, it was a life in common. Seen from a woman's viewpoint, that experience undoubtedly represented a *decisive emancipation from one's family* of origin and its expectations. It meant finding a *free and friendly territory* from which to discover the world, without being forced to marry soon, a territory *for learning things other than* those necessary to be a good wife. Yes, like for the *insurgents* of the EZLN, the question "When are you going to marry?" remained more and more unanswered.

But precisely the capacity that we had elaborated to recognize a problem and analyze it meant that at a certain point we discerned that for us as women there was still some *suffering and uneasiness* in those relationships. For all relations are *power relations,* and even in the *sexual revolution*, which certainly took place, everything that we represented and did as women continued nonetheless to count for very little or to go unrecognized. We felt *split* between the imperative to be like men, to be capable of being and acting like them, and the feeling that we belonged to another world, one where men would also ask different things of us and expect us to be different. But then the window would close again over that world that remained without a name. It was a sort of *clandestine femininity*. But it was not long before we would come out of this clandestine world and pass from resistance to attack.

By 1970, I had begun to elaborate a new course, the feminist analysis and path that I would undertake, although I usually point to 1971 as the turning point, because in June of that year, in Padua, by inviting some women activists to discuss a document I had drafted, I held the first feminist meeting. I gave birth to the organization that would be called Lotta Femminista, which was later transformed into the Wages for Housework network of committees and groups that were active at the national and international level.

The *separation* from the male comrades was *not without pain*. Our hypothesis that they would be happy because by engaging in new struggles we broadened the anti-capitalist front was not borne out. Because they thought that certain struggles were crucial, the fact that we privileged other struggles meant for them that we withdrew militant power from their struggles. The price we paid for no longer working under their watchful eyes or engaging in the same actions was to be perceived by them as 'doing nothing.' Just as they had not seen our housework, now they did not see our autonomous political work. We were accused, especially at the beginning, of risking taking part in struggles that did not promote a class viewpoint and were interclassist, including, for example, the struggles around abortion and the violence that affected all women. Moreover, as women 'in movement' we changed, and consequently relationships, even personal ones, broke down.

When we began to speak of housework, the first reaction from the male front was a mocking smile. What were we bothering with? After all it was not a big thing, not even real work to be sure, and with day care centers all problems would be resolved. The strange idea that a few hours of childcare would resolve all the problems of housework lasted for a long time. There was not even a basic understanding of the number of material and immaterial tasks, predictable and unpredictable, that constitute the daily allotment of reproductive work. We were also charged with being separatists, with wanting to divide the movement. In contrast, actually I think that it was no longer possible to speak of an anti-capitalist struggle without seeing how much unpaid labor the wage commands, starting with women's labor, and without therefore taking into account women's 'insurgency.'

In Rome, on July 7, 1972, we organized a workshop on female employment at the university. We decided that it should only be open to women. This was an absolute novelty; it had never before happened at the university. The reaction of a group of men—generically self-identified as comrades—was to prevent the workshop from taking place. They launched condoms full of water from outside the room that broke the windows. What followed was an intense debate in the pages of *Il Manifesto* and *Lotta Continua*[1] that gives an idea of what the times were like—just the fact that women chose to meet by themselves provoked a violent reaction. It would not be right to overstate these kind of reactions. There were indeed some male comrades who understood the centrality of our discourse and the importance of the work we carried out and behaved accordingly. But that episode is indicative of how hysterical the male response could be when faced with the new fact: women analyzing and discussing autonomously without the presence of men.

Concerning the charge of separatism, I want to make it clear that we never theorized *separatism*, but instead theorized autonomy. However, there were at least *three good reasons* why we, like many others, had to work separately. First, precisely because of the power relations between men and women, their presence would have limited our ability to speak and would have prevented the emergence and thorough analysis of the issues that most directly concerned us, and for some of them it would have undoubtedly have created some uneasiness. Second, these issues were so big that they absorbed all our energy. Therefore, as I have said on other occasions, the idea of a dual militancy (as feminists and in some extraparliamentary group) was never an option, because we would not have had the time for it. Finally, if the behavior of the comrades was also a reason for our separation, they had to confront the problem and figure out how to address it. Reversing the charge, we could say that it was their male chauvinist behavior that divided the movement.

From what I have learned, the same charge is now being made against Mayan women. I believe that only the women who experience a certain situation can decide with how much separation or how much togetherness they can conduct a cycle of struggle. It is true, however, that how much we can struggle 'together' is a question that must also be confronted by the other side, that is, by men, in support of the issues raised by women, because generally support is given only by one side, the women.

Today in Italy, young women who are active around issues such as the precariousness of work and the transformations taking place in the university consider it unacceptable to work separately from their male companions; they do not feel the need for it. It must be stressed that they obviously benefit from the victories won by their mothers and by the feminist movement of the 1970s. Their relationships with their male partners are more egalitarian, and the hard struggle to regain control over our bodies was fought by those who preceded them. Although there are still political forces that try to take away the freedoms that women have won,[2] women today have the means to live their sexuality with fewer risks than a quarter of a century ago. At a very basic level, even if a woman becomes pregnant, it is not likely that she will be thrown out of her family home. On the contrary, many women decide to become pregnant independent of a relationship with a man. They are determined to have a child but are less eager to embark on the type of life in which it is necessary to negotiate your decisions with a partner on a daily basis. They are also determined to break up a relationship, even a marriage, if it is not satisfactory. In contrast, on other issues, various associations made up only of women or predominantly of women have been formed, first among them the anti-violence centers.[3]

Thus, today we have a complex situation where women feel the need to work only with women in some instances and not in others, depending on the issue. The context, however, is not comparable to that of the movement of the 1970s. Today, organizing in associations that have a relationship with formal institutions *has taken the place of the action of the spontaneous groups of previous decades. Those previous groups functioned as a battering ram and demolished the doors of the many prisons* in which the rights of women were enclosed. Today, these associations try to monitor the situation and offer a first point of reference and aid to those who continue to have their rights violated.

It was immediately clear to us that *building our autonomy* required a *great battle*. We had to equip ourselves. Immediately maternity emerged as a *difficult knot to untangle,* for it is an irreversible choice that conditions the entire life of a woman, and it is not, as we were told it would be, resolved by taking children to a day care center. But, above all, it became clear to us that the *refusal of work* strategy, which was a strategy that we still approved of as a form of struggle, *was not applicable in all cases* to reproductive work or care work. We could extend our refusal to marriage and even to cohabitation with men, so as not to see our energies absorbed by having to respond to male expectations (a woman at home is always on call, we used to say). However, we could never have had children and then refused to take care of them. Care work, insofar as it is work that concerns human beings, put precise limits on our options for action and presented a situation where the strategy of refusal of work appears as impractical, a utopia. In our hearts we had to decide. Those of us more engaged in organizational work renounced having children, because it was incompatible not only with the amount of political work that we planned to do to make the world more moonlike (to recall the ancient Mayan divinity, half sun, half moon) but, above all, with our *mental availability* to organize and deal with the deadlines and contingencies of our activity. This too was in perfect accord with the decision of many Chiapas *insurgents*, given the impossibility of combining motherhood with that type of militancy.

However, maternity became a cardinal point of our discourse. If the *productivity* of the capitalist family and the female body was centered on the production of children, then women's liberation required that we break with this imposition, with being condemned to this sole function and on the fixation of this role. Hence the slogan: "Women let's procreate ideas not just children!" This was a cry of liberation from biological determinism, an invitation to a different creation, to procreate ideas that could generate another world in which the mother-wife function would no longer constitute our only possible identity or be paid for at the cost of so much toil, isolation, subordination, and lack of economic autonomy. This is why we put forward *the demand for wages for housework*, to reject its gratuitous attribution exclusively to womankind and so that women's economic autonomy might be constructed starting from the recognition of that first work. In the refusal of maternity we read a behavior that would become increasingly widespread not only in Italy but also in most other developed countries, and more recently in countries not particularly developed,[4] leading in the case of Italy to a birth rate of 1.2, which is considered very negative by politicians.[5] *Not only the demand but, above all, the perspective of making the work of reproduction cost* in all the places supported by this work brought our struggle—a type of struggle very different from those that had been waged so far—to the neighborhoods, the schools, the universities, the factories, and the hospitals. It would be impossible here to deal with all of them, however, everything has been fully documented in the materials we used on our militant front: leaflets, pamphlets, journals, and small books.[6]

What was the *response of the state* to all this? Specifically, to the autonomy that women had begun to build by reappropriating their own bodies, which nonetheless still needed to be rooted in an economic autonomy starting from the recognition of their reproductive work? The response was fundamentally *a bit more emancipation*. However, at the end of the 1970s, this was accompanied by the repression of all movements. From 1972 to 1979, female employment in Italy increased by 1.5 million. The new Family Code[7] was approved, and at its center was the parity of the partners (this also had to do with the necessity that the decisions of wives who were increasingly looking for and finding work outside the home not be subordinated to their husbands' will). However, real wages diminished, and during the 1970s the buying power of families was guaranteed by the broader involvement of various members of the family in the labor market. Often this was through under-the-table jobs in the new context offered by the decentralization of production.[8] With the passage from Fordism to post-Fordism the family would need to be supported by at least two incomes.

The state managed to evade the demand that the women's movement had put forward on an economic level, so women accepted the only kind of autonomy that was being offered, emancipation via wage work. However, *they did not manage the miracle of coupling, cost what it may*, their unpaid work in the family, including childcare, with work outside the home. Many never married, many decided to live alone, the number of divorces and separations increased,[9] and the birth rate continued to collapse. Women's refusal of procreation triggered a significant *crisis of social reproduction* that was later reflected in the imbalance between young and old; at the time, however, there was no great cause for alarm.

The prevailing *sociological literature* spoke of the women's *double presence* as a female capacity to combine the two spheres of work, domestic and extra-domestic, and described the many strategies women used to achieve this. In my opinion, *there were only two strategies:* the first, a drastic reduction of the number of children; the second, the use of unpaid work of women relatives or the employment by the hour of other women as domestic workers. But in the past the sociological literature did not speak of this side of the story. While, in Italy, the permanent live-in domestic worker was a figure heading to extinction, domestic workers by the hour provided very important support for women's outside employment. *Thus, salaries for housework proceeded in indirect ways.*

More and more women consistently refused unpaid domestic work, changing the modalities of its condition, 'rationalizing' it to the extreme, and reducing it, including by making life choices different from those of their mothers. They chose as their priority the construction of their own economic autonomy, an autonomy that state policies allowed them only through extra-domestic work. They held more money than they had in the days before the movement. With that money they paid other women to do a significant amount of housework, while other aspects of housework left the home to be transformed into goods and services offered by the market. To give one example, it is enough to think of the restaurant and catering sectors. Thus, unpaid housework shrank, while paid work expanded inside and outside of the family. Although the employment of a domestic and/or babysitter often consumed a large part of the female wage, women increasingly refused work that was unpaid.

In Italy during the 1970s, a migratory flow was growing, one that had already brought to the country hundreds of thousands of people. As part of this, by 1977, it was calculated that domestic workers of color made up 100 thousand of a total immigrant workforce estimated to be 300 to 400 thousand people. This female labor force tended to take jobs as live-in maids, which Italian women no longer wanted. It was the beginning of a type of immigration of men and women, mostly from Africa and Asia, of whom many would be destined to domestic work, a flow that in the following decades would become more robust and would be restructured as immigrants came from a broader range of countries. The *question of the relationship between immigrant women and care work*, the so-called question of the *globalization of care*, was to become in time increasingly important.

At the end of the 1970s, in Italy and other developed countries, women's autonomy has made great steps forward with respect to the reappropriation of their bodies and themselves as people. Laws that are fundamental to women's autonomy had been approved, like that on the voluntary interruption of pregnancy and the law instituting the *consultori* (clinics for family counselling). The referendum on divorce was won, and there was a new family law code. However, this autonomy remained in a precarious state as far as domestic work or care work was concerned, constrained by women's refusal of this work that involved heavy sacrifices, for example, renouncing maternity, and by struggles for emancipation. At the same time, precisely as a result of the struggles for emancipation, housework has become more and more visible and waged. The 1970s was also the decade in which, riding the wave of the feminist movement, the United Nations' global conferences on the condition of women began.

The first UN conference was held to celebrate the International Year of the Woman in Mexico City, in 1975. On December 18, 1979, the General Assembly of the UN adopted the Convention on the Elimination of All Forms of Discrimination against Women, which came into effect in 1981. However, we had to wait until 1993, when the UN Conference on Human Rights was held in Vienna, to see women's fundamental rights recognized as an integral part of human rights, and to have the Declaration on the Elimination of All Forms of Violence against Women. This was a problem that had already been denounced in all its seriousness and in the various forms it took across the world at the Nairobi Conference of 1985, held at the end of the first UN Decade on Women. In the same conference it was also stipulated in the final document[10] that "the contribution, remunerated and unremunerated, that women make to all aspects and sectors of development should be recognised, and that this contribution should be measured and included in economic statistics and the Gross National Product (GNP)." While there is a lot of skepticism about the efficacy of these charters, undoubtedly the planetary dimension of the policy debate has strengthened the power to decide what is just and what is unjust in traditions and legislations and to go beyond the constraints of both to affirm new principles and new norms.

Second Act

The 1980s marked the advent of neoliberalism, which would fully unfold with the neoliberal globalization of the 1990s. In various countries this involved years of normalization and repression after the great struggles of the previous decade. These were also the years of the deepening of international debt and the ever more drastic application of structural adjustment programs,[11] officially adopted to enable the indebted countries to pay at least the interest on their debts. These policies actually aimed to lower standards of living and expectations, so that the new forms of production premised on rendering labor cheaper and more precarious could take off everywhere, thus enabling business to have a competitive advantage in different regions across the planet. Changes to markets and production, now strongly oriented toward export, meant that the type of development that was imposed through the structural adjustment programs could only aggravate the level of debt. During that period a new phase of accumulation was ushered in through the privatization of communal goods like land and water and of public goods like state and parastatal agencies, currency devaluations, the withdrawal of subsidies from basic goods, high subsidies given to modernized and monocultural agriculture, wage cuts, reducing and rendering employment more precarious, cuts to public spending on social services and entitlements, starting with pensions, cutting and restructuring public expenditure with the privatization of health care and education, increases in the fees paid by consumers, and the liberalization of commerce, with the adoption of policies that favored export and import, together representing a *powerful instrument for the underdevelopment of reproduction* at a global level and functional for launching a new phase of accumulation.

This period also witnessed an unprecedented attack on the struggles waged by women not only for the well-being of their families and the improvement of their living conditions but also on women's struggle *to gain a higher level of autonomy.* In the advanced regions this *meant the loss of a 'good job,'* the loss, therefore, of the type of emancipation that this employment guaranteed, and the *immersion into precarity, poverty, and dependence.* In the less advanced areas this meant, above all, that more and more land was expropriated for so-called processes of agricultural modernization or for large and often devastating projects financed by the World Bank, of which the construction of dams is only the best-known example. This poverty, which was caused by the politics of debt rooted in land expropriation, and then, particularly in the 1990s, by the intervention of the permanent politics of war that made the land increasingly unusable because of military operations and war residues, generated *migratory flows* to the advanced countries, and to Europe, above all, of new subjects, of whom a considerable part, *mostly women*, were to do *significant amounts of reproductive work.*

The bellicose politics of neoliberalism are at the origin of a *new division of reproductive labor* worldwide, whereby women coming from the so-called developing countries or countries 'in transition' (transition to democracy in the case of Eastern European countries) increasingly come to do reproductive work in advanced countries. They have left behind a shattered reproductive environment, that of the family first of all, patched up at the cost of greatly increased toil for those remaining, but at least compensated for by the remittances sent by the women who migrated. In order to redefine and deepen the stratification of the working social body on a planetary level, the reproduction of *the areas considered 'more peripheral'* has been *devastated*. It seems clear that the plan is to produce cheap labor power to be employed in the reproductive sector of the more developed regions. In this way, the state avoids having to confront the emerging reproductive problems and, crucially, can avoid taking on the financial burdens that should be its responsibility.

But what were these problems? What were these urgent necessities, which were conspicuous, given that fewer and fewer children were being born? *What caused the expansion of this new need for labor? The emerging problem,* though it was not the only one, *was the care of those among the elderly who were not self-sufficient,* an issue that was to become particularly crucial in the discourse on women's *autonomy*.

Third Act

Since 1990, after a decade of the general application of the politics of debt and the unfolding of neoliberal globalization, migration has become a truly worldwide phenomenon, reaching more than *175 million migrants across the planet* according to United Nations estimates.[12] Italy, traditionally an exporter of labor power, became a net importer in the 1980s and 1990s, attracting laborers from Asia and Africa, and more recently Eastern Europe. During the last decade, an increasing number of women have migrated to Europe. At the end of the 1990s, 45 percent of immigrants to Europe were women, coinciding with a growing demand for domestic workers in southern Europe.[13]

It is in the 1990s that a new figure of the worker begins to take a more precise shape, increasingly embodied by immigrant women who are *caregivers*. She is the one (occasionally, it's a man)[14] who cares for a person who is no longer capable of autonomously handling his/her daily tasks, *generally an elder, male or female, who to a greater or lesser degree is no longer self-sufficient.* The *need* for this new figure of the domestic worker, the demand for this *specific type of care work* stems from *demographic changes* that have seen an increase in both life expectancy and the percentage of the population that is elderly, as women's refusal of maternity has reduced the number of young people to a remarkable degree. This is a trend that affects European countries as a whole not just Italy. It is a *crisis of social reproduction*, because the balance between young and old has broken down, and there is no longer an adequate generational replacement. Because of women's refusal of maternity, the prospect is that in Italy (a country that, according to the ISTAT estimates, has one of the lowest birth rates in the world, namely, the 1.2 ratio mentioned above, recently raised to 1.3 thanks to the newborn to immigrant women) within thirty years one out of three people will be over sixty-five.

The significant fact, one that must be properly interpreted, is that *in Europe the majority of those over sixty-five* (with the exception of those over ninety) *live at home*, not in private or public institutions. This situation is obviously the result of a decision made not only by the elderly, when they are still able to express themselves, but by a younger woman, a relative, generally the daughter, who is aware that this is the most humane option. This decision is made, despite the fact that due to the number of tasks and duties involved it *will heavily condition her life and limit her autonomy*, even with the intervention, whenever possible, of the paid work of other women.

The feminist refusal of unpaid reproductive work, also expressed in the refusal of maternity, has not substantially liberated women from care work, except for that period of their lives when they would have had to raise a child. "Mom Has Gone Out" was the title of an exhibition organized by the Wages for Housework group in Varese.[15] But "She Had to Come Back," we would have to write today, if we were to present that exhibition again. Her time out was brief. The problem of care returned in an even heavier and more complex way with the elderly, who are often not self-sufficient. A fifty- or sixty-year-old woman, or one even older, who participated in the struggles of the feminist movement, who herself needs some rest, and, if retired, needs to enjoy what during her work life she could not, now must face the problem of having parents of a very advanced age, *often over eighty*, with all the *typical old-age ailments*. The burden is on her, and she often has no adult sons or daughters who could at least help out to some degree. After having worked hard to construct her autonomy, this autonomy is again reduced by the problem of the caring for others who are weaker and depend on her, an issue that has not been resolved. The *social body* is precisely that, a body; it is not divisible, and it *reproposes the problem of care in an eternal return*.

It is in this context that we must place the work of the *caregiver*[16] provided by women who migrate to Italy in the wake of the disasters produced in their countries by structural adjustment programs, by wars, and by 'democratizing interventions.' It responds to a need that state policies are still very far from satisfying. The employment of caregivers demonstrates, first of all, that this type of care work has been increasingly subsumed within that *process of the salarization* of housework that I have already mentioned, and that *the problem is such that it is usually necessary to employ a person full-time to deal with it.* But some common notions must be demystified.

The first is that the work of the caregiver liberates the relative from the care of the elder. On the contrary, the work of a caregiver cannot function well if it is not accompanied by the constant guidance, cooperation, and verification of the female relative—work that begins with the presentation of the case situation, which is always shifting and changing and requires constant help, in effect, a division of tasks between the female relative and the paid woman. It is generally the former who must do the shopping, because it is difficult to do it with the person cared for. She is also the one who does the bureaucratic work, handles administration and the financial management of the house, takes the elder to the doctors, and guarantees an immediate presence and intervention in all the emergencies. Precisely because of the loneliness that comes with living every day with an elder, who is often mentally debilitated, the caregiver herself has to be reproduced. Thus, the so-called 'work of love'[17] comes back not only as a real need in the care of the elders, who will be poorly assisted if there is not a real concern for their well-being, but also as a need in the relationship between the employer (often the daughter) and the *caregiver*. The relative has to follow the situation as it evolves and respond in a timely way when the problems become difficult to handle, as well as offering all of the resources and aid necessary to make the work less burdensome. Often, she will have to replace the caregiver to allow her some extra rest during the most demanding times and, above all, pay her more if the situation becomes too intense.

Let's keep in mind that if, given the normal family budget, there is no extra money in the family to pay for another caregiver on Saturdays and Sundays, this type of work being expensive,[18] it will be the daughter and her husband who will care for the elder relative on weekends, which means that their weekly rest and the time that would have been spent shopping, if they still have a job, vanishes. This is how many couples spend their weekends, and the problem arises again when the caregiver takes her month vacation. While a cleaning job can wait or a temporary solution can be found, elders who are not self-sufficient cannot be left alone even for a moment, and they cannot find themselves suddenly faced with people that they do not know and that have not been instructed about how to relate to them and what tasks to perform. Caregiver work does not tend to be precarious work, because it is not convenient for the employer to change caregivers, especially after having done all the work of teaching them what is required, or if a good relationship develops between the caregiver and the person cared for. Precarity intervenes, instead, when work conditions are irregular, and this shows how crucial it is that more substantial economic support be provided by the state to families to enable them to stipulate regular work contracts.

I thought it was important to detail this combination of tasks, those done by the caregiver and those done by the relative to not make the inverse error to the one mentioned above. There was a time following the decline of the feminist movement of the 1970s when the identification of women's emancipation with a job outside the home obscured the role of domestic workers employed by the hour; today, in dealing with the work of the caregivers, the risk is that it will be treated as an '*a solo*,' with no mention of the work done by female relatives.

The employment of immigrant women has highlighted the magnitude of the problem. It is not a form of care work that the female relative, if she does it alone, can combine with other jobs. If today the subjects who take on this task have been forced to do it because of the political circumstances that have devastated their lives, it is desirable that in the future this work may become a normal 'good job' also done by Italian women (in part, this has already started), that the state provide more substantial support for this work, and that the working conditions improve.

There is no question, in fact, that the state should devote more funds to pay for this care work, given that its cost for many families is already unsustainable, and this leads to conditions of irregular employment. Let's keep in mind, however, that this is a terrain where some economic response to *care work* or *domestic work* have already come from the central state or local governments. It is thanks to this response that many families can manage to stipulate an employment contract. First of all, there has been the *assegno di accompagnamento* (attendance allowance), 450 euros a month, paid by the National Social Insurance Office (INPS) directly to the person to be assisted, independent of income levels, when she or he is not physically or mentally self-sufficient. However, it is very difficult to obtain this allowance. It requires a declaration of total and permanent disability from the National Health Service. Many cases, mostly cases of physical rather than mental disability, are not considered serious enough to justify it. There are also other provisions that are provided for on a regional basis, however these require very low income levels and are not an alternative to the attendance allowance. Among them is the *contributo badante* (caregiver grant) of a maximum of 250 euros monthly, given by the Veneto region to those who have hired a *caregiver for at least twenty hours a week.* Then there is the Alzheimer's grant (516 euros monthly) added to what is prescribed by the regional law no. 28 of 1991.[19] There are also specific support services. In order to put an end to the irregular immigration status of many caregivers and the risks connected with the possibility of infiltration by criminal organizations, initiatives have also been taken by the provinces, for example, Bergamo, which has decided to devote 400 euros monthly to families who have already hired a caregiver or need to do so.

Despite the neoliberal tendency to cut public spending on social welfare, we must nevertheless reckon that the terrain of welfare, where some *salaried* care work has occurred, resurfaces as an irreducible terrain of bargaining, starting precisely from policies of this type. The crisis of social reproduction also creates problems for the state. Currently, the minister for family policies, Rosy Bindi, is proposing to oblige banks and foundations to participate in the increasing funding for the elderly. While issuing a warning about the falling birth rate, she is also proposing to give 2,500 euros yearly for every newborn till adulthood. *Wages for Housework*, which was so heavily opposed by the institutional forces during the high phase of the movement, returns articulated in various forms as an irrepressible need. Those who would have preferred that this money be used to support institutional care for the elderly made a mistake. Institutes are appropriate for those extreme cases of elderly people who cannot be cared for at home., but not only is the care they provide of a different quality, but, above all, the elderly do not like these places and prefer to stay at home.

The woman, *through her refusal* to be solely responsible for unpaid reproductive work, no matter what the case and conditions, has made work in this specific sector visible as 'salaried' work. However, *she has also guaranteed—by accepting a limited freedom, that is, a relative autonomy—the preservation of the relative autonomy and the physical and psychological well-being of those, who, in a weakened condition, depend on her.* With her refusal and relative acceptance, she has shown that in the case of care work, refusal alone is a utopia, and that the specific work of eldercare must be supported by increased funding by the state, so that the families can cope with the cost. Furthermore, just as the state must expand the services devoted to this vulnerable sector of the population, the work itself needs to be performed under regular contractual conditions.

Women have also shown that one of the main obstacles to keeping an elder at home or in the home of a relative is the hike in real estate prices and rents, which has reduced the space in the apartments to a minimum, so that often there is not even a room available for the elder or the caregiver. This is a problem that people with children have already faced for years. Increasingly, apartments are holes that do not allow for visits and even less the permanent presence of parents or the arrival of children. Nevertheless, the problem posed by the presence of elders who are not self-sufficient once again raises the question of having children, and of having some economic support to raise them, in addition to different living conditions, so that people can again begin to want to have children and to see having them as possible. In fact, with rare exceptions, nobody but their children will care about keeping elders who are not self-sufficient at home nor will anyone else organize and watch over their reproduction. The problem of eldercare is one that in different ways and in very different situations is present at a planetary level. Thus, the question of economic support by the state for this work must, I believe, take its place on the political agenda as one of the most urgent issues.

If these are the emergent terrains and problems of care work, to argue as some have, that *domestic work, and more broadly reproductive work*, has a tendency in the current period to increasingly become *immaterial work*,[20] or should at least be included in the sphere of immaterial work, indicates a lack of knowledge about this work. The work of reproduction, which is articulated in many ways—here we have considered just one—has always been made up of a lot of material work grafted onto the immaterial work of reproduction, involving psychological, affective relations. Therefore, there is nothing new under the sun. In contrast, to say that today the category of immaterial work better grasps the novelties of reproduction is to do an injustice to this work and the new realities that traverse it, of which the one discussed above is a good example. It is work that is loaded with heavy material tasks. The fact that these tasks might possibly be performed with affection does not make them immaterial. If being an elder who is not self-sufficient is a significant difference, arguing that "women are increasingly burdened with the control of the flows of difference"[21] and articulating this as immaterial work again implies overlooking the reality of work that is burdened with this difference and its problems.

It is equally clear, considering the terrain of eldercare (and similarly childcare), that the work of reproduction *cannot be resolved with communication.*[22] This is particularly so as its problematics are not exhausted by the search for better agreements among the partners, but instead imply that women do many hours of work, do not have sufficient money, risk poverty, and lack of autonomy. These problems cannot be resolved by communication.

It is not a further technological innovation that is necessary. Nor do we need the genial idea of some 'informatics' worker, whose political program would not, it seems to me, be very promising, precisely because it would come from the realm of the immaterial.[23] Genial ideas are not what we need.

What is needed is work, more adequately remunerated and with more free time for all, both women and men. What is necessary is to recognize the materiality of life and of the work that safeguards it, in the house and in the field,[24] and the way it connects to human relations and the land, and this holds true for the work of women and the work of peasants.[25] If anything, women have shown that the autonomy that everyone pursues and desires faces irreducible conditions, whether it be children or the elderly, and if today the difference is between those who are burdened with this work and those who are not, this is a difference that should not be celebrated but demolished, by building a more common responsibility for care work and demanding of the state (since the 'common' does not exhaust the 'public') more substantial and generalized allocations of money and services.

Notes

This paper was presented at the international conference on *"La autonomia posible,"* Universidad Autonoma de la Ciudad de Mexico, October 24–26, 2006.

1   *Il Manifesto,* July 14 and 20, August 4, *Lotta Continua,* July 15 and 21, 1972. See also "L'offensiva," *Quaderni di Lotta Femminista* 1 (Turin: Musolini Editore, 1972), which collects the reports of that seminar and the militant materials that came out concerning that moment of confrontation.

2   There was a particularly strong attempt in recent years by Catholic forces to abrogate law no. 194/78, which authorizes the voluntary interruption of pregnancy. The Veneto Region has proposed a regional bill that would authorize the presence of members of Catholic organizations in the *consultori* (clinics for family counseling) and hospital wards. In response to this, women have decided to make their voices heard and, with the support of the CGIL (Italian General Confederation of Labor), organized a rally in Venice on October 7, 2006, under the banner of "Let's break the silence." It was, in fact, the first time since the 1970s feminist movement that women made their voices heard with such strength. And this time men supported the women and participated in the demonstration.

3   If in Europe the first anti-violence centers, or shelters for women, were formed at the end of the 1970s, in Italy, aside from the initiatives of the feminist movement, we had to wait until the beginning of the 1990s. Significantly, a decade of repression and normalization had to pass before anti-violence centers began to be formed. Today, there are more than eighty, of which a quarter offer their hospitality in

secret apartments, also called shelters. The first four shelters for women who have suffered violence were formed in 1990 and 1991, in Bologna, Milan, Modena, and Rome.

4   This phenomenon is addressed in the article "Ecco la generazione 'No figli,'" *La Repubblica*, August 28, 2006. It reports that very low birth rates are now found not only in Italy but in other countries in Southern, Northern, and Eastern Europe and in the Far East, where in the case of Singapore and South Korea it is a new phenomenon.

5   The minister for family policies, Rosy Bindi, declared on television that the most worrisome lack of growth in Italy is that of birth rates; *Ballaro*, Rai 3, October 3, 2003.

6   I mention here, above all, the journal "*Le operaie della casa*," published by Marsilio Editore of Venice, and also a series of little books for militants edited by the Collettivo Internazionale Femminista and put out by the same publisher. This series includes the following booklets: *8 marzo* (1974); *Le operaie della casa* (1975); *Giornata internazionale di lotta delle donne* (1975) (partial English translation: Wages for Housework Committee of Toronto, *Women in Struggle: Italy Now*, no. 3); *Aborto di Stato: strage delle innocenti* (1976); *Dietro la normalitá del parto: lotta all'ospedale di Ferrara* (1978); Silvia Federici and Nicole Cox, *Contropiano dalle cucine* (1978) (Original text in English: *Counterplanning from the Kitchen* [1975]). See also "L'offensiva," *Quaderni di lotta femminista* 1 (Turin: Musolini Editore, 1972); *Il personale é politico: quaderni di lotta femminista* 2 (Turin: Musolini Editore, 1973).

7   The reform of the Family Code issued in 1942 was sanctioned with the bill no.151, approved on May 19, 1975, stipuating first of all the parity of the partners in the married couple. Other bills were later approved that changed the regulation of other important aspects of the Code.

8   Mariarosa Dalla Costa, "Emigrazione, immigrazione e composizione di classe in Italia negli anni '70," *Economia e lavoro* 4 (October–December 1981).

9   *La Repubblica*, November 9, 2006, 38, reported that from 1995 to 2000, separations grew by 59 percent and divorces by 66.8 percent, and that it is the south that registers the most conspicuous growth.

10 This occurred with the acceptance of the amendment of paragraph 120 of the document "Forward Looking Strategies for the Advancement of Women" proposed by Housewives in Dialogue.

11 The literature on the problematic of international debt is vast. I refer above all to the works of Susan George. Among them: *A Fate Worse Than Debt* (London: Penguin Books, 1988); *The Debt Boomerang* (Boulder, CO: Westview Press, 1992); Mariarosa Dalla Costa, "The Native in Us, the Land We Belong To," *Commoner* 6 (Winter 2003); Mariarosa Dalla Costa and Giovanna Franca Dalla Costa, ed., *Paying the Price: Women and the Politics of International Economic Strategy* (London: Zed Books, 1995); Mariarosa Dalla Costa and Giovanna F. Dalla Costa, ed., *Women, Development and Labor of Reproduction: Struggles and Movements* (Trenton, NJ: Africa World Press, 1999).

12 United Nations Economic Commission for Europe, Census 2000.

13 In Italy, there were 1,512,324 immigrants registered as legal residents in 2002, of whom 45.8 percent were women; Caritas, *Dossier statistico immigrazione 2003* (Rome: Edizioni Nuova Anterem, 2003).

14 It is estimated that in Italy 25 percent of *caregivers* are men and that 73 percent of those who do this job are between thirty to forty years old; *La Repubblica*, October

16, 2006, 16, citing the following sources: INPS, Caritas Ambrosiana, and the CGIL, Lombardia.

15 This is discussed in the homonymous article in the journal *Le operaie della casa* oo (November-December 1975–January-February 1976): 21.

16 It is calculated that half of these workers in Italy are not regularized. Many of the women who do this specific work come from Eastern Europe, particularly Romania, Moldavia, and Ukraine. Again *La Repubblica*, in the article already mentioned in note 16, dedicated to the presence and work of *caregivers* in Italy, reports a growth from 51,110 in 1994 to 142,196 in 2000, 490,678 in 2003, and 693,000 in 2006, of whom 619,000 were foreigners. See also Rossana Mungiello, "Segregation of Migrants in the Labor Market in Italy: The Case of Female Migrants from Eastern European Countries Working in the Sector of Care and Assistance for the Elderly: First Results of an Empirical Study Carried out in Padova," in *Zu Wessen Diensten? Frauenarbeit zwisischen Care-Drain und Outsourcing* (Zurich: Frauenrat für Aussenpolitik, 2005), 72–77.

17 Giovanna F. Dalla Costa, *The Work of Love: Unpaid Housework, Poverty and Sexual Violence at the Dawn of the 21st Century* (Brooklyn, NY: Autonomedia, 2008).

18 For the caregivers who have a regular contract, it stipulates from 750 to 900 euros net, plus 200 euros of contributions by the employer, one month of paid vacation, another month of pay as a thirteenth monthly pay (*tredicesima*), and another again as severance pay. Food is provided by the employer, as is a room in the apartment, a problem that is usually solved by changing the use of another room. The live-in *caregiver* who has a contract for at most eight or nine hours a day, has the right to two or three hours a day free, as well as a day and a half a week, generally Saturday afternoon and Sunday. But there are also part-time contracts, different from those for live-in, and they depend on the conditions of the person to be assisted and what the caregiver is most interested in. Many prefer to work as live-ins for some years, thereby not having expenses for food and rent and being able to send home almost all their salary.

19 Since 2007, these regional policies have been replaced by only one provision: the 'care grant' introduced by the Veneto region for a maximum of 520 euros monthly.

20 Antonio Negri, *Movimenti nell'Impero* (Milan: Raffaello Cortina Editore, 2006), 184, 215, 241.

21 Ibid., 193.

22 See Christian Marazzi, *Il posto dei calzini* (Bellinzona: Edizioni Casagrande, 1994).

23 Negri, *Movimenti nell'Impero*, 184.

24 The emerging networks of peasants in both the south and the north defend sustainable agricultural methods, which are often very traditional, requiring much living labor (which implies jobs for many people) and rest on the availability of very material goods like land, water, and natural seeds, instead of other methodologies that are being imposed on them. Even in the north, it is what peasants say is significant, as they do not refuse technology tout court but prefer not to depend too much on machines, and where it is widely available and makes more senese instead to use the resource of labor. On this point, see José Bové and François Dufour, *The World Is Not for Sale* (London: Verso, 2001). I believe that the new subjectivities that are significant from a political viewpoint emerge from these contexts not from the leading capitalist methodologies.

25 Mariarosa Dalla Costa, "L'indigeno che è in noi, la terra cui apparteniamo," in *Camminare domandando*, ed. Alessandro Marucci (Rome: DeriveApprodi, 1999); Mariarosa Dalla Costa, "Rustic and Ethical," *Ephemera, Theory and Politics in Organization* 7 no. 1 (March 2007), accessed August 2, 2018, http://www.ephemerajournal.org/contribution/rustic-and-ethical; Mariarosa Dalla Costa, *La sostenibilidad de la reproducción: de la luchas por la renta a la salvaguardia de la vida*, in *Trasformaciones de trabajo desde una perspectiva feminista: produccion, reproduccion, deseo, consumo*, ed. Laboratorio feminista, (Madrid: Tierradenadie Ediciones, 2006).

To Whom Does the Body of This Woman Belong? (2007)

Translated by Silvia Federici

The Naples WFH group demonstrates for the legalization of abortion at a December 6, 1975, demonstration in Rome.

My analysis in this essay centers on a fact that I consider fundamental for every other discourse concerning women's autonomy. That is: for women, in every part of the world, the construction of autonomy has meant first of all the reappropriation of their bodies. It has meant a struggle to be recognized as the only owners of their female bodies, an issue that has always been at stake in the relationship and struggle between the sexes. This was true for us at the beginning of the 1970s in Italy, as it was for the Mayan women when they began to draft their law in the early 1990s in Chiapas. In the text that follows I analyze and compare aspects of our shared problematics and struggles, battles that for us in Italy, for the women in Chiapas, and for many other women across the world have achieved many important goals but are far from over.

When I read the Revolutionary Law of the Mayan Women, I was struck by the very close correspondence between the demands presented in it and our own demands at the dawn of the 1970s. We, like them, had to unite as women in a movement in order to lift ourselves out of our pain and impotence. Impotence was the very problem we had witnessed in the lives of our mothers. It was the impotence, principally due to the lack of money, that made any choice, even running away from violent husbands or fathers, impossible. It was the impotence of not knowing our sexuality that made marriages fail, but that was inevitable, because our counterparts were men who also knew nothing about female sexuality.[1]

And, again, it was the impotence of not being able to communicate, as it was a taboo to speak with other women of things that were too intimate. The impotence that came from the stigmatization of life outside of marriage, that forced our still very young mothers to move from their father's house to that of their husband, without ever having a chance to find out who they were and what they wanted. The impotence of finding themselves mothers just nine months after marrying, without ever having known themselves as women—prematrimonial 'virginity' being a social imperative. The impotence of being subjected to violence inside or outside of the family but not being able to speak about it, so as not to expose the family to a scandal and not be guilt-tripped by other men, starting with judges and policemen. The impotence of being subjected to sexual harassment on the job but not being able to afford to lose it. All these are issues that, despite great differences in terms of social contexts and living conditions, stand out clearly in the demands and debates that are developing among Mayan women.

In prioritizing the issues concerning women's sovereignty over their body, we find that women are fighting for the right to their sexuality, and not simply a sexuality orientated solely toward procreation or male satisfaction.[2] They are fighting for the right not to marry, to have the option of a relationship with a partner without being compelled to marry, the right to choose a husband or partner instead of having to accept the husband chosen by their parents. The right to control the number of children they want and can raise and the right to have special attention paid to their health care and nutrition and that of their children. The right to an education, which begins with the right to learn about one's body and the issues concerning 'reproductive health' and the right to have basic services. The right not to be subjected to violence either inside or outside of the family.

Furthermore, they are demanding that housework, which absorbs the entire day of a woman's body, be equally shared with men, as one of the conditions for having more time and energy to pursue their own interests. This too corresponds closely to what we demanded in the 1970s. We never considered a more equal division of domestic work the final objective of our struggle but only as a precondition for struggling to obtain better living and working conditions for ourselves and for other people. Women's struggle over the reproductive work has always created greater well-being and autonomy among the people dependent upon them, in the first instance children and the elderly. As is also well-known, we demanded that this work be remunerated, reduced, and supported by adequate services.

At the beginning of our movement we made a poster of the body of a woman with the caption: "To whom does the body of this woman belong? The Church? The state? The doctors? The bosses? No, It's her own." The answer could not be taken for granted. The need to affirm it derived precisely from the fact that fathers, husbands, doctors, and clerical authorities all competed for the right to control women's sexuality and reproductive capacities. They all claimed the right to decide whether or not to allow women to have a sex life, to have access to contraceptives, to keep a child without being married, or to abort. The conquest of autonomy on this terrain and with regard to these 'authorities,' the reappropriation of our body, compelled us to move on different levels, and above all to build the knowledge of our bodies that women did not have.

To this end it was above all necessary to make and distribute small pamphlets with some illustrations, often small homemade pictures that gave basic information. For example, the structure of women's and men's reproductive organs, what needs are posed by the main events and changes in female biological life (menstruation, contraception, pregnancy, childbirth, nursing, abortion, menopause), what are the most common pathologies, how to recognize them, how to cure them, and how to gain knowledge about and experiment on the terrain of sexuality. In 1974, the famous *Our Bodies, Ourselves*[3] was translated into Italian. It was produced by a women's collective in Boston that had concentrated its efforts on the question of women's health and sexuality. A commitment to women's health and sexuality had characterized the feminist movement in the U.S. since the nineteenth century,[4] and it reemerged as a leading issue in the international feminist movement of the 1970s, triggering the diffusion of 'counterinformation' that exposed the distortions or silences of medical science, aiming to give back to women the knowledge and decision-making power concerning sexuality and procreation that official medicine, from its inception, had violently taken away from them.[5]

It was especially urgent to launch a campaign for the legalization of the voluntary and free interruption of pregnancy, to be carried out in hospitals (we achieved this goal with law no. 194, in 1978), and to mobilize politically around the criminal trials for abortion that women were subjected to. One such trial took place in Padua on June 5, 1973, sparking the struggle on this terrain, due to a set of initiatives that we launched in common with the rest of the feminist movement. It was urgent to make it known that the majority of women who aborted were mothers who already had children and could not afford to have another one. We also wanted to expose the fact that too many women were dying or being severely and permanently injured by clandestine abortions, and that we would not allow any more suffering and death.

On April 7, 1976 a twenty-seven-year-old mother of two died in Padua following an abortion. Her death sparked the occupation of the university buildings where gynecology was practiced and taught. We publicly denounced the many doctors who were conscientious objectors and refused to carry out abortions because of their Catholic beliefs, but in fact conducted a large, illicit business in clandestine abortions. Abortions that were generally carried out using dangerous techniques and without anesthesia, therefore causing the woman atrocious pain.[6] I have learned that in Mexico's rural regions, one in five women has had the same experience, often as a result of sexual violence suffered inside the family.[7] I hope that she does not have to suffer it alone any longer, that she does not have to face the dangers and pains to which Italian women were subjected before the rise of the feminist movement. Above all, I hope that she will soon have access to some means of birth control,[8] and in the case of sexual intercourse with uncertain outcomes, that she will have access to 'the morning after pill,' which allows women to avoid an abortion.

Childbirth[9] also became a moment of significant political mobilization and struggle in the hospitals where women who were giving birth were dying for no reason—three women died in the space of a few months in the obstetrical division of Padua's Civic Hospital. We opposed the excessive medicalization of the event, the imposition on women of a total passivity that turned them into patients, the sadism with which childbirth was treated (for example, stitching without anesthesia), and doctors' authoritarian, arrogant behavior. The response to all these problems was a vast mobilization and a women's movement that called for active childbirth and the restoration of women to their role as protagonists in birth. Furthermore, the movement demanded that the conditions of childbirth be such that women could experience it as something natural, to be held in a serene environment and surrounded by people they trust. It is from that moment that the presence of the husband or another person in the birthing room began. For us, this was a difficult conquest, whereas I have learned that the husbands of the Mayan women are present and cooperate in the birth.

In the following years, some 'birthing centers' were set up in Italy, with a few capable of providing hospital-like assistance in case of need, but above all structured to provide a domestic environment where childbirth can return to being a natural event and not be treated as a disease. The idea was revisited that women could give birth in their homes, but with the guarantee of a quick connection with the hospital if necessary. Birthing positions that women had practiced in the Middle Ages and in ancient times were rediscovered, certainly more natural and comfortable than the one imposed in the hospitals, which is only convenient for the doctors.

Concerning childbirth, I was struck by Guiomar Rovira's report[10] that village midwives in cases of breech delivery were able to turn the child inside the mother's womb. In Italy, too, the old midwives were able to do this. Now almost nobody can, neither doctors nor midwives, creating one more justification for cesarean births. The medical profession obviously does not consider it convenient to preserve this knowledge and skill. Instead, cesarean births have grown exponentially in recent years; in some hospitals they represent 40 percent or more of all births. However, it needs to be acknowledged that it is a surgery and not an alternative way of giving birth. Concerning childbirth, we also denounced the high number of children that were born with disabilities or injuries in some hospitals[11] because of bad practices or an incompetent use of the forceps. In contrast, in Chiapas an infant can die because of bad hygienic conditions or because it lacks what it needs to survive. In both cases, we see the destruction of the woman's long labor of care and hard work and of her and the infant's fundamental rights.

The condition of the unmarried mother, specifically the pregnant unmarried woman, was very punitive before the women's movement. Often, she was chased from the home, as are the Mayan women, without knowing where to go, what to do to continue her pregnancy, or how to find work to support her child. She frequently had to leave her child in an orphanage. There were some organizations for women who were pregnant out of wedlock, but these institutions were rather sad and when we did organizational work with their women guests we discovered that they very often made these women feel guilty.[12] In our international campaign for wages for housework, the figure of the self-supported mother with children was a fundamental one, because all advanced states devoted some funds and facilities to these women. Italy, was a negative exception. The family allowance provided by the state in Britain and the Aid to Families with Dependent Children given to so-called 'welfare mothers' in the United States[13] were among the first concrete forms of remuneration for the work of procreation and child raising that women do. In the analysis and mobilizations we devoted to this female situation, we denounced the Italian state for giving substantial financial support to the institutions that accepted the children these women had to abandon due to lack of means—financial support destined to be dispersed along the meandering paths of the 'clientelism' that permeates political relations. It would have made more sense to give that money to the woman to enable her to raise her child—even less would have been enough.

More broadly, to reappropriate their bodies women questioned and tried to establish a different relationship with every aspect of gynecology. At the time, almost all gynecologists were men; some women, many of them feminists, were just beginning to graduate with specialization in this discipline and would become a key point of reference. The same is true of the male activists that became gynecologists and who, responding to the new awareness that the women's movement had created, took the side of women and provided generous and serious assistance. It was in this medical field in particular that we collected testimonies,[14] as we did in every other field in which we moved. Some of us in Milan conducted an inquiry[15] to verify the functioning of the public health structures in their city, with some women agreeing to pretend to be patients. We found that there was no respect and no delicacy, to say the least. The authoritarianism of the doctors was even more unchecked in this field than average. What we found out about public clinics is significant. Women, besides having to go there very early as a group—which meant that they had to cross the city at dawn—then had to wait for most of the morning (getting an individual appointment was apparently too much to expect); they were also forbidden to speak among themselves, as announced by a sign hanging on the wall. That is, communication was forbidden. Today, this may seem absurd, but it provides a good idea about the despotism of the medical profession at the time. Soon, however, the movement was to break through this compulsory silence.

In 1974, to create an example of a different relationship between doctors and women we built the first self-managed community-based gynecological counselling clinic in Padua, a *consultorio* where both doctors and many women provided assistance. Soon others followed suit in other cities.[16] In these *consultori* women were taught how to conduct a self-examination, how to use a speculum, how to recognize the most common ailments, and how to treat them; they were taught about the diaphragm as a contraceptive that women could manage by themselves without needing to consult a doctor and without any cost. This is perhaps why the diaphragm, as a means of contraception, never particularly spread in Italy. It was a contraceptive that female students discovered on their first trips to England, as it was very common in the Family Planning clinics of Britain; with it they also discovered a sense of autonomy and how cheap it was to use it.

Not long after that, in 1975, bill no. 405 was passed, introducing clinics for family counselling. However, they would always be inferior in numbers to what the law decreed and lacking in the ability to provide information and preventive measures, which was their function. They were certainly a far cry from the exemplary structures we had wanted to build. These deficiencies were obviously a function of the public and private business made off disease. Among the information that we provided was of the existence of the already available epidural injection that could spare women the pain of childbirth. But it was almost impossible to obtain it. The hospitals considered it a waste and hiring the anesthesiologists who could give the injection to the women who requested it an unaffordable expense. Above all, it was inconceivable that women should not have to suffer in childbirth. It was an entrenched belief in the medical profession that women should not have an alternative to suffering in that event. That in spite of the fact that in our pamphlets we asked the obvious question: "Even to treat a cavity one gives anesthesia, why then we should not receive it for labor pains?" The medical adherence to the biblical precept 'you will procreate in pain' remained practically unquestionable.

Only in recent years has this type of anesthesia begun to be more available in Italian hospitals, on account of the privatized character of health care, which creates a fear of competition among the structures that offer this option. This year, finally, the recently appointed minister of health care, Livia Turco, has decided that all hospitals must offer this procedure to women giving birth. This is a turning point in the history of female suffering. The same minister has also decided that 'the morning after pill,' which can allow women to avoid abortion in cases of sexual intercourse with the risk of pregnancy, should be available in all pharmacies and should be sold with a medical prescription. Here too, finally, we have an initiative that recognizes that women have the right to exercise their sexuality—a right that has always been recognized for men—as well as recognizing that sexual relations can in some cases have an uncertain outcome, and that in these cases it is a duty to give women the means available to science today to spare them the pain, in every sense, of abortion. As for the abortion pill RU486, which if taken during the first two months of pregnancy spares women the bloodiest type of surgical abortion, the same minister has authorized its experimental use in the hospitals across Italy. However, since this pill has already been experimented with in other European countries, where it is now for sale, this amounts to its official acceptance among abortion procedures. Here, too, breaking with the commandment that women should suffer the maximum pain, a device has been made available to them that— in the context of a choice that is inevitably dramatic—at least causes less pain. It is nonetheless significant that the Karman method, that is, abortion by vacuum aspiration, a procedure that is also far less bloody than surgical abortion, and one that the feminist movements of the 1970s revamped, had, in the meantime, fallen into disuse.

While procreation and the interruption of pregnancy were events that a number of us had experienced, and which provided the basis for our awareness and determination to change their conditions, we had not, however, had the opportunity to experience how, at an older age, the female body would become the object of new abuses. How, for no good reason, but in the interests of the health care system and the medical profession, the older woman's body would often be mutilated and deprived of the organs that characterize it as a female body. I refer here to the abuse of hysterectomy,[17] a surgical procedure carried out even when not justified by the patient's pathology, or even in the absence of any pathology (accompanied in about half the cases by the surgical removal of healthy ovaries). This surgery has many negative consequences for sexuality, cardiovascular diseases, and the strength of pelvic floor muscles. Despite the negative side effects, in recent decades its abuse has characterized medical practice in many advanced countries. In Italy, one woman out of five can expect to undergo this procedure, while in some regions, like Veneto, where I live, it is one in four.[18]

This is the third great battle that the female body must face after childbirth and abortion. In many regions of the world, advanced or not, the battle is to defend the female body's integrity and the quality of life in mature age, including against the violence and abuse of medical science. The medical approach that sustains this abuse reveals a conception of the woman as a reproductive machine. Many doctors declare that when she has already procreated the number of children she desired, or in any case when she is near (or often, unfortunately, not near) menopause, it is better to take out those organs that are of 'no use' and that could one day contract some serious disease. But these organs, ovaries, and uterus are very important for the health and hormonal balance of women before and after menopause. However, in the eyes of too many gynecologists, the woman, as a person, does not count, the integrity of her body does not count, and even less her sexuality, which often this operation compromises.

Above all, it is profitable for the medical business to carry out many operations. The medical profession benefits from having on its record many of these interventions, which represent the most important type of surgery for gynecology. It is a battle in which the knowledge of one's body, the determination to safeguard it, and far-reaching communication among women are crucial. Recently, several online websites have been created by groups of women to provide information about this operation and a site for many patients who have been subjected to it offer their testimonies.

The year 1974 was particularly important. With other women in the movement, we had won the referendum on divorce.[19] We had guaranteed that divorce—adopted into Italian legislation just a few years earlier—would not be abolished, something that would have condemned women and men to irreversible choices no matter what might happen or what the marriage contract might say. This was a victory that the movement won against a despotic condemnation to a life of suffering without remedy.

The other great theme regarding the female body was violence against both adult and young women. Reading about how, in the Mayan villages, women are often subjected to violence in the family as well as outside of it, I remembered how we discovered the violence that young women were subjected to in the family from reading the compositions they wrote in the elementary schools. The women in the movement who were teachers began to pay special attention to them. Soon they also discovered the extreme impotence of the mother: If she denounced the husband and he went to prison, who would support the family? How would those in the often rural environment in which the family lived react to this? How would the husband react once he returned home? This problematic was very similar to that of the Mayan women. With regard to cases of violence against adult women, there were numerous mobilizations, above all establishing with our combative presence during the trials against those who perpetrated this violence that the victim should not be turned into the defendant by judges, lawyers, or men in general. We decided that it was intolerable, a sign of lack of consideration for the woman as a person, that sexual violence should be classified in the penal code as a crime against public morality and decency and not as a crime against the person, and we worked to ensure that case histories and penalties would be better determined. Many bills were proposed, but none were passed for twenty years.

We had to wait until 1996 for bill no. 66 to be passed before we saw violence against women classified as a crime against the person, rather than against public morality and decency, penalties made more severe, and case histories catalogued with more precision. Meanwhile, our long-term activity and debate led to the emergence of women's associations[20] that awakened a new awareness and determined a different, more respectful attitude among male and female operators at the sites a woman who denounced violence had to pass through (hospitals, police stations, courts). Today, the phone book of some communes, Padua included, offers among its public utility numbers the "Women's Anti-Violence Service." Other communes made up of rural villages object to the idea of women building centers against violence, because they consider it inappropriate that these stories go beyond the domestic walls. As the saying goes, "You wash your dirty linen at home."

Why this domination, this control by others over the body of the woman, and why is it impossible or at least difficult for her to exercise sovereignty over her own body? Why so much inertia on the side of the institutions, even though in some places the movement's intervention has generated initiatives that in some way confront it? The answer lies in another poster that pictures the body of the woman cradled and compressed within the walls of a house with the caption: "Domestic work sustains the world but suffocates and limits the woman." That is, her body must be imprisoned, so that she can provide the unpaid domestic labor that sustains the world and, in this world, men above all. But the answer must be found, first of all, in the representations of the women accused of witchcraft and burned at the stakes that proliferated throughout Europe in the sixteenth and seventeenth centuries, causing the atrocious deaths of hundreds of thousands of women, many of whom were midwives and folk healers, guilty only of possessing knowledge about childbirth, abortion, and contraceptive practices.[21]

The expropriation of women's bodies and their transformation into machines for the reproduction of labor power began five centuries ago, at the dawn of capitalism, when labor power became the most precious commodity and female sexuality was distorted and forced to function for procreation and reproduction of others. At the witches' stakes, not only was a knowledge of gynecology that had always been in the hands of midwives in an egalitarian relation with other women destroyed, but the model of the woman that the family in the developing capitalist society needed was also forged: a woman isolated, sexually repressed, subjected to the authority of her husband, the producer of children, with no economic autonomy, and without any knowledge and decision-making power about sexuality and procreation. Above all, with that homicidal expropriation the state stripped women of their knowledge and, assisted by the mediation of the medical profession that was itself under the control of state and Church, took control of the reproduction of labor power.

The model of the woman forged at the stake remained in place in Italy until the movement began to reject it. In the 1970s, we denounced male domination over the woman's body as a function of extracting from her body the maximum amount of work, above all domestic work, and the satisfaction of the sexual needs of men, who, for their part, did not have to address women's needs (hence the convenience of women's ignorance concerning sex). Violence intervenes as a disciplinary instrument in this work relation to the extent that the disciplinary power of the wage is missing.[22] It intervenes when the man's provision for her 'upkeep,' which is what the woman gains in exchange for her work on the basis of the marriage contract, is not enough to guarantee him access to a certain quantity and quality of her work.

We must, of course, think of domestic work in its complex character as reproductive work, that is, as a combination of material and immaterial activities, to understand how in many cases this violence can explode, especially now when women have in part reappropriated their bodies and desires. It is still significant, however, as reported by members of some anti-violence centers in Italy,[23] that even today male violence against a woman is often unleashed because she refused to do the housework or did not do it as he wanted it done. That is, the woman who is 'not well disposed' or well trained to do housework (certainly much less disposed or trained than in previous generations) is more exposed to the risk of violence. Let us add that today it is more and more difficult to earn a male wage capable of guaranteeing the upkeep of the wife and the children. Instead, it is secured by two precarious wages, his and hers. From this it follows that the woman certainly feels even less obliged to do domestic work.

As for institutional inertia regarding violence against women, which is a worldwide reality and in various Italian regions remains extreme, the reason is largely determined, as we already verified in the 1970s, by the need to offer men a safety valve for the frustrations they experience in their work and their lives, to offer them someone, the woman, over whom they can exercise power. We must add that the male complicity of staff members in the hospitals, police stations, and courts has always been and continues to be a reality, especially in those situations that have not been as immediately touched by policies that have sought to increase institutional awareness of violence against women and professional initiatives to reeducate the staff. Today, I repeat, the situation has improved in many of these places, so that we find more competence and sensitivity, which is also due in part to the higher presence of women, who in the past were either completely absent or present in irrelevant numbers. And, of course, the work of increasing institutional awareness has also had positive effects for the male personnel.

The fact remains that while initiatives have increased that provide women victims of violence some reference point for gaining initial support, and while there has been some work to increase institutional awareness, as well as the training of specific staff members to address the needs of victims, the cases of violence against women have multiplied. The violence has become even more sadistic, with deadly torture, often carried out by a gang or as group violence. As for the violence within couples, a recent TV report[24] stated that from 2000 to 2002, in Italy, 405 such cases resulted in the murder of the woman. While a very high number of women who suffer violence do not report it, the number of those who do is growing.

In a social context where neoliberal policy reduces human life and the physical and social body that contains it to a commodity, women's sexuality remains a commodity that is emerging from a past where it was not recognized as a woman's personal right and can still be robbed with impunity. After all, the woman's body is still seen by too many men not as her own but as belonging to the man who takes it.

In recent months, the competition over who owns the woman's body has emerged in Italy with two dramatic cases, both of which ended in the death of the woman. A young Pakistani migrant woman, who had decided to lead her life in the way she saw other Italian women living, working, and cohabiting with their partners, was killed as the result of a decision made by her father, because she had chosen this life, instead of accepting being given in marriage to a man chosen by her parents.

In the second case, a young Indian widow killed herself by lying on train tracks, because she did not want to be married off to her husband's brother and wanted her two children to be able to remain in Italy, where they had gone to school, begun their formation, and made their first friends. She left a written note praying that the town council to take care of them.

These are two significant examples of how globalization, through the emigration-immigration flows it generates, also sees women engaged in a planetary process of elaboration and comparison of their rights and their own conditions. It sees the growth of a women's determination, cost what it may, to reappropriate their bodies, no longer as a productive machines controlled by others, but as their own bodies with their own desires and subject to their own decisions. What the movements that developed a quarter of a century ago in the advanced countries have won as far as women controlling their own bodies represents a point of comparison and strength for other women who today must confront this difficult battle. The most fundamental rights, control over our own bodies and the emotions and feelings they generate, the right not to be imprisoned once and for all in marriages with men we have not chosen, the right to control the number of children we have or to decide not to have children or not to marry, and to nevertheless be treated with respect in society, to be treated with dignity even if we choose to remain alone, all of this is increasingly nonnegotiable.

It is true that to have money of one's own, to be able to have and inherit land, and to have access to education and basic services are all very important instruments in the construction of women's autonomy. Nevertheless, the battle to reclaim one's body cannot be delayed or subordinated to other deadlines—it must prepare its own instruments to succeed. In this sense, I have started with our little pamphlets from the 1970s and the initiatives that we took at the time to begin to discover and liberate our bodies.

Notes

This paper was presented at the international conference on "The Possible Autonomy," Universidad Autonoma de la Ciudad de Mexico, October 24–26, 2006.

1   A significant book on this topic is Lieta Harrison, *La donna sposata: mille mogli accusano* (Milan: Feltrinelli, 1972).

2   As Guiomar Rovira reports, "men simply 'use' women." It is striking that this is the same verb used in the past in rural environments in Italy. Rovira reports that female sexual pleasure is unknown. The same was true for us before the movement. Sebastiana in the dialogue with the government at the end of 1995 denounced this situation, screaming angrily that women's sexual pleasure "is not accepted, this is the habit"; Guiomar Rovira, *Donne di mais* (Rome: Manifestolibri, 1997), 76. And later, at the dialogue table, she added, "When did we ever feel pleasure in our sexual relations? Never, because they never teach you that, and it is sad that this is not done in our communities; they say that this is the custom, and that it is the same for women everywhere" (174).

3   Boston Women's Health Collective, *Our Bodies, Ourselves* (New York: Simon and Schuster, 1971).

4   Its beginning coincided with the peaking of a popular health movement (1830–1850) that pursued and practiced a type of medicine completely different from that of 'regular' doctors coming out of the universities. Taking a class and feminist perspective, this movement was above all concerned with guaranteeing medical treatment for the lower classes of whatever ethnic origin and with preserving and elaborating upon knowledge that was certainly more valid than that of the pretentious medical science at the Faculty of Medicine.

5   Barbara Ehrenreich and Deirdre English, *Witches, Midwives, and Nurses: A History of Women Healers* (New York: The Feminist Press, 1973) and *Complaints*

and Disorders (New York: The Feminist Press, 1973). The two original pamphlets have been put together in a single Italian book, *Le streghe siamo noi: Il ruolo della medicina nella repressione della donna* (Milan: Celuc Libri, 1975); Silvia Federici Silvia and Leopoldina Fortunati, *Il grande Calibano: storia del corpo sociale ribelle nella prima fase del capitale* (Milan: Franco Angeli, 1984). See also Silvia Federici, *Caliban and the Witch: Women, the Body and Primitive Accumulation* (Brooklyn, NY: Autonomedia, 2004), particularly the chapter on "The Great Witch Hunt."

6   Collettivo internazionale femminista, ed., *Aborto di Stato: strage delle innocenti,* (Venice: Marsilio Editori, 1976).

7   Rovira, *La donna sposata.*

8   It seems appropriate for me to inform women that the pill, the condom, or the dia-phragm are not the only possible contraceptives. Small devices are now available that a woman can administer herself, these are markers that test her saliva, turning one color or another, depending on whether she is a fertile or not on that particular day.

9   Gruppo femminista per il salario al lavoro domestico di Ferrara, ed., *Dietro la nor-malitá del parto: lotta all'ospedale di Ferrara* (Venice: Marsilio Editori, 1978).

10 Rovira, *La donna sposata.*

11 Gruppo femminista per il Salario al lavoro domestico di Ferrara, ed., *Dietro la nor-malitá del parto.*

12 Comitato di Lotta delle Ragazze Madri, *Ragazze madri in lotta: documenti e testimo-nianze delle ragazze madri della Casa della Madre e del Fanciullo di via Pusiano 22* (Milan: self-published, 1973). See also Lotta Femminista a Modena, *Madri in azione,* a mimeograph that reports on the history and the activity of "Mothers in Actions," a collective of unsupported mothers with dependent children, without distinction of race or nationality, present in London since 1967.

13 Mariarosa Dalla Costa, "A proposito del welfare," *Primo Maggio* 9–10 (Winter 1977–1978).

14 Movimento di Lotta Femminista di Ferrara, *Basta tacere: testimonianze di donne: parto, aborto, gravidanza, naternitá* (self-published, undated).

15 L.C. Poggio, *Avanti un'altra. donne e ginecologi a confronto* (Milan: La Salamandra, 1976).

16 Clara Jourdan, *Insieme contro: esperienze dei consultori femministi* (Milan: La Salamandra, 1976).

17 Hysterectomy means the surgical removal of the uterus, while oophorectomy, or ovariectomy, means the surgical removal of the ovaries. I have dedicated a book to the abuse of this operation that includes many testimonies of women and doctors; Mariarosa Dalla Costa, ed., *Gynocide: Hysterectomy, Capitalist Patriarchy, and the Medical Abuse of Women* (Brooklyn, NY: Autonomedia, 2007).

18 In comparison with neighboring France, and on the basis of the type of pathologies for which it is applied, 80 percent of these surgical interventions seem unjustified. In the United States, the country that sadly is the leader as far as the number of these operations, one out three women will undergo this operation before the age of sixty and 40 percent before the age of sixty-four.

19 Lotta Femminista, "Vogliamo decidere noi: donne, referendum, divorzio," *Document* 275 (March 1974).

20 In Padua, the "Centro Veneto Progetti Donna" has conducted this type of activity, as well as organizing support for women who had been victims of violence. This is

an initiative of Lucia Basso, a feminist who was very active in the Padua Committee for Wages for Housework. Together with other women, Basso also created the Gruppo Donne Ospedaliere, which played a very important role in the struggles about women's health care in the hospitals.

21 Silvia Federici and Leopoldina Fortunati, *Il grande Calibano*; Silvia Federici, *Caliban and the Witch*.

22 This theme has been thoroughly analyzed in Giovanna F. Dalla Costa, *The Work of Love: Unpaid Housework, Poverty and Sexual Violence at the Dawn of the 21st Century* (Brooklyn, NY: Autonomedia, 2008).

23 In Europe, the first anti-violence centers, or houses for women who suffered violence, appeared toward the end of the 1970s. In Italy, except for the initiatives organized by the feminist movement of the 1970s, they appeared at the beginning of the 1990s. They are supported by public funds and voluntary work. Today there are more than eighty, of which one-quarter offer hospitality in a secret apartment, or shelter. The first four shelters for women who suffered violence were created in 1990 and 1991 in Bologna, Milan, Modena, and Rome.

24 Channel 5, September 29, 2006, 1:30 p.m.

Workerism, Feminism, and Some United Nations Efforts
(2008)

Translated by Rafaella Capanna

The Padua WFH theater group performs the play *L'identità* at the May 1, 1975, demonstration in Mestre, Venice.

On June 5, 1973, in Padua, a criminal trial against a woman for abortion was transformed into a moment of political mobilization and marked the beginning of the campaign for abortion rights in Italy. Within the context of the ongoing debate on the issue, in which some support the withdrawal of women's self-determination, this essay traces aspects of the various histories of feminism in the 1970s and of the particular political tendency of 'workerism.' It seeks to inscribe this mobilization into the context of struggle that was important in determining major changes in the female condition.

In the 1970s, the feminist movement in Italy basically had two souls identified by two different paths of action. One was 'self-consciousness' based on the formation of small groups in which women, starting from their own experience, analyzed the female condition and its hardships. This was similar to the North American practice of 'consciousness-raising' and was widely practiced in Milan and in relationship to the Parisian group Psychanalyse et Politique (which included Antoinette Fouqué).

The other, which carried out 'political intervention,' and in which Lotta Femminista (Feminist Struggle), later called Movimento per il salario al lavoro domestico (Sld) (the Movement for Wages for Housework [WFH]), was prominent, concentrated instead on interpreting the female condition, with a focus on analyzing capitalist development and changing it through struggle. Thus, this latter was immersed in a practice of intense militancy that aimed to transform the status of women and capitalist development with its own modalities of organization of production and reproduction.

I will discuss this second soul, whose fate it was, in the late 1970s, to encounter a phase of harsh repression that in particular hit the movements that had fought the hardest, including this feminist strand, and which, from the 1980s onward, were wiped out on a cultural level. However, it needs to be noted that without these struggles there would not have been the transformations that deeply changed the status of women in Italy and in many other countries across the world. If today these gains seem obvious, they were not then and are not now in any way secure, as there is always the risk of being forced to retreat. To better explain this second movement, it is necessary to think back to the 1960s and highlight a few key aspects of that period.

The 1950s and 1960s were the years of the great emancipation through work—primarily through industrial work that finally gave a relatively secure wage to subjects such as farmers, laborers, shepherds, and fishermen—subjects who now felt for the first time that they could get out of the poverty and uncertainty of the rural world and migrate to the cities and industrial centers, no longer those in foreign countries but within their own country. The city also allowed one to get away from the overly tight social control of the village, something that was eagerly welcomed by both men and women. The 1960s were also the years of the emergence of the youth as subjects. Toward the end of the decade, however, modernization also revealed its hidden costs and its backward aspects. Workers rose up against the harshness of conditions in the factory, the young against authoritarianism in the university, in the family, and in society and against the costs of studying (including struggles about cafeterias, transport, and housing). It was 1968 and 1969, and the students soon discovered the factory and the workers' movement, which quickly coalesced with the student movement, particularly in Italy.

Even women migrated to the cities in search of an income of their own, and, above all, they were increasingly unlikely to marry men who would not take them to the city.[1] But for the woman there still remained an indisputable 'characteristic of her femininity,' the primary obligation to fulfil her family duties, namely, to guarantee the reproduction of the family, even if she sought and found work outside the home. A woman's place was in the home, and if she did not marry she was a 'misfit.' On the other hand, article 37 of the Italian Constitution, while sanctioning equal pay, stated that working conditions must allow women to fulfil their essential role in the family—in other words, to do the housework, even if at the time it wasn't stated in such an open and blunt way. In 1960 and 1963, the first laws on equal pay were passed.[2] Even within a context in which young men and women were the emerging subjects of the decade, it is worth remembering that the right of the woman to exist as a person was strongly prejudiced not only by her primary family responsibility but also by legislation concerning her condition. As for her status in the family, as Laura Remiddi observes:

Without referring to ancient times but to just before the new reform [1975], the married woman was subject to the authority of her husband, who was the head of the family. She assumed his surname and was obliged to accompany him wherever he chose to fix his abode. The man even had the right to 'correct' his wife, to control her actions, to punish her for her failings; in short, she submitted to actually belonging to her husband, which considerably limited her rights and established a profound legal difference between the status of a married woman and an unmarried woman. Even the freedom and secrecy of telephone conversations and correspondence, rights that are guaranteed to all citizens by constitutions, laws, and international treaties, were often called into question for the married woman, from whom the husband could take away letters and even intercept telephone communications to watch over her behavior (Court of Appeal of Milan, July 9, 1971).

Let's also keep in mind that the 1960s represented a time when women's sexuality had yet to be 'discovered' and affirmed. Female sexuality was basically a service for male sexuality and a means of procreation. Housework and violence also had yet to be 'discovered.' The regulations that defined the status of women in the family were linked to other rules that controlled women's conduct in a highly discriminatory manner with respect to the conduct of men. First of all, the laws relating to adultery, which according to article 559 of the penal code constituted a criminal offense punishable by imprisonment for one to two years, were only applicable to women.[3]

In addition, anyone who wished to marry a woman against her will knew how to force her to do so through a brutal procedure that was practiced in some areas of southern Italy. That was to kidnap and rape the woman, and then, relying on the fact that no other man would want her for his wife after such dishonor, the man would go to her family asking for her hand in marriage. It was precisely the shotgun wedding that under article 544 of the penal code expunged the crime of violence, as well as washing away the shame of the family. This article was repealed by law no. 442, on August 5, 1981. But it was only the heroic rebellion of Franca Viola from Alcamo, Trapani, that put an end to the inevitability of having to accept such violence. After being kidnapped on December 26, 1965, and raped and left for days alone in an abandoned country cottage, she refused the shotgun wedding. It was a historic turning point in the affirmation of the woman as a person and her right to choose her husband. It was a preview of the process for self-determination that would be the motif of the feminism of the 1970s.

Article 587 of the penal code sanctioned 'honor killing,' a crime with a paltry punishment (three to seven years in prison, as compared with twenty-one years as the minimum sentence for murder)[4] that was as such a license to kill[5] for a husband, father, or brother who discovered his wife, daughter, or sister having an illegitimate sexual relationship. It should be noted that while this legislation applied to both spouses, the victim of these crimes was to all intents and purposes the wife. Article 587 of the penal code was also repealed in 1981, when law no. 442, mentioned above, was adopted.

Abortion was prohibited (permitted only in the case of so-called thera-peutic abortion), however, as always, it was practiced by women and often paid for by death or severe injury. There was a ban on advertising contra-ceptives, which was repealed by ruling no. 49 of the Constitutional Court, on March 10, 1971. Incest was not punishable unless it constituted a public scandal (article 564 of the penal code), and the penalty was increased if it led to an incestuous relationship.[6]

Divorce, which began its passage into law in 1965, entered the Italian legal system in 1970 with law no. 898, with the proviso that it be submitted to referendum, which took place in 1974, resulting in a victory for the feminist movement.

Sexual violence against women that was taken to court had little or no chance of an outcome favorable to the woman, and certainly one could not take the violence of a husband against his wife or a pimp against a prostitute to court,[7] or a prostitute's case in general. Furthermore, sexual violence against women was listed in the area of offenses against public morals and decency not against the person.

The rules, written and unwritten, that I have highlighted above illus-trate some of the backward aspects of modernization, as well as demonstrat-ing women's commitment to changing these conditions. The emergence of the workers' and student movement in 1968–1969 also involved numerous women. The chance to attend university, with the opportunity of militancy in the student movement or in extraparliamentary groups that formed in those years, was itself an opportunity for a woman's emancipation from an established role and a predetermined path—going from her father's house to her husband's without ever having had a time or a place to determine who she was and what she wanted.

Above all, in such militancy young women found a free and friendly territory from which to discover and interpret the world and ask themselves how to relate to it. The big difference from the condition of their mothers was primarily that they had a time and place for themselves where they could meet many others, enjoy relationships with their peers, classmates, and companions in struggles that were more egalitarian and free, and experience a social and even sexual life that wasn't dependent on their marital status. This alone marked a big difference from the way the sex lives of women of the previous generation had been denied in marriage itself, not only because of the imperative of virginity before marriage but also because generally the first child, with all the related responsibilities, was born after only nine months of marriage. As well, there had been very few opportunities to meet people and decide to whom to say "I do."

That movement was steeped in Marx. The teachers who were most sensitive to social issues gave regular lectures on *Capital*; the most committed students knew at least chapters 8, 24, and 25 of the first volume. Therefore, it was clear to them that in order to understand the world it was necessary to start with the organization of work. And student militancy, as I said, discovered the factory. In the Veneto Region, the large chemical plant in Porto Marghera was the main place for workers' struggles to quickly make connections with others in the territory. If for students the problems were authoritarianism and the costs of studying, for workers they were despotism, unfairness, and the brutality of working conditions. Wage raises and shorter hours were not the only issues on the table. There was also the determination to do away with the arbitrary nature of a wage level that depended on the foreman or team leader (a large part of the wage was paid by the job); the willingness for more equality and democracy in the factory, which was articulated with the significant request of an increase in the production bonus of five thousand liras a month for everybody; the request to have a month off like office employees instead of just fifteen days; the request for 100 percent sick pay like office employees and not just 60 percent; the request to have elected representatives of each department that actually understood the problems of the work, and who, on the basis of a real mandate, would bring forward departmental requests. Workers denounced and fought against illegal hiring, refused corporate paternalism, which, by facilitating opportunities for study or the holidays of workers' children, tried to gain the approval of the workers, thereby creating divisions in their struggle. They denounced the brutality of working conditions, including workers' exposure to and contact with carcinogenic substances without proper protection.[8] All of this was known to militant students and taken up by them; it was their training course on politics.

The fight, as I said, soon went beyond the confines of a single factory and resulted in political recomposition with other workers[9] and other subjects within the territory that also aimed at improving the conditions of life outside the factory, within the social factory—struggles for homes (against unsanitary housing and high rent), for parks, against the high cost of living and for the autoreduction of utility bills, self-organization to build a sports field (created with the help of Marghera dockers who brought in bulldozers to level the ground), and the occupation of a building to convert it for use as a school. Neighborhood committees were created that promoted improvements to living conditions that at other times would have been carried out by social centers, and in which the role of women was fundamental. In reality the workers' community, factory workers, and housewives already functioned as a social center, as has been observed.[10] A great struggle around reproduction was launched, even if it wasn't yet called that, and even if its key subject, the woman, had not yet revealed her central role and her specific problems.

But it was the very close involvement in this 'political work' that at some point provoked the women who took action to question their own militancy. This was because increasingly women felt uneasy in these relationships; an uneasiness that stemmed from having noticed that they had problems as women that they had not focused on, that they were fighting for everyone but not for themselves.

The feminist movement was forming in Italy. After a few skirmishes in the second half of the 1960s, with Franca Viola's actions a significant example, and after the sporadic formation of some feminist groups[11] at the beginning of the 1970s, those two great souls, which would be referred to as the psychoanalytical and the political, began to define themselves in the movement. If the former didn't much like demonstrations and what it called external deadlines, even sometimes preferring not to participate in crucial initiatives, such as the mobilization for abortion, the latter represented an ever running engine of initiative directed outward. The political soul, strengthened by reading Marx and by the experience of the interventions in the factory and in the neighborhoods carried out within New Left groups or the student movement, intended to do equally militant political work on the female condition. The two souls were united, however, in breaking with the prevalent perspective on emancipation, in their lack of interest in the goal of equality, which was seen as evincing the vice of homologation with men's condition, and in their refusal to have anything to do with the institutions.

'Liberation' not emancipation (in any case a difficult and limited conquest of previous generations) constituted the new flag that constantly took on new meaning as women advanced on their journey and claimed their human rights and fundamental freedoms and their citizenship rights—liberation from male authority, liberation from economic dependence on men, liberation from violence, freedom to determine their own sexuality and procreation, and self-determination in every aspect of their lives. 'Difference' was the other major affirmation, as opposed to the discourse of equality—difference as a specificity of the female condition, difference that needed to come out, and which required specific answers.

The strand of Lotta Femminista that later became the network of groups and committees for Wages for Housework (WFH) and had its first nucleus in Padua among women with a workerist background and the experience of political work in Porto Marghera was a rapidly growing organization. In a short time WFH groups were formed from the northern Italian Trentino region to Sicily. In 1972, the International Feminist Collective was formed to promote debate and coordinate action in various countries. As for Europe, Wages for Housework groups were formed in Germany and Switzerland, as well as in Britain and Italy, and across the Atlantic in the United States and Canada. In addition, the network held regular international conferences.

Lotta Femminista's political perspective highlighted the difference as it appears in the capitalist sexual division of labor. Men's work producing goods was remunerated, while women's work producing and reproducing labor power was not. This was the unbearable contradiction for the woman: being an unwaged worker in a wage economy. This was the difference that created a hierarchy between men and women. This was the insupportable circumstance: being a housewife (Italy at the time had a particularly high rate of housewives) who was continually required to carry out her work of reproducing the entire family, but who remained dependent on the man for support, a dependence that hindered all her life choices.

Breaking through this contradiction meant starting struggles everywhere in order to make housework costly. But it was also a great cultural awakening. The issue of housework dominated the whole feminist movement, taking the place of emancipation through work outside the home, even in those circles that did not share the demand that it be remunerated. Women increasingly rejected a femininity made of infinite willingness to reproduce others for free.

The cornerstones of the matter were: that the family was first and foremost a place of production where labor force was daily produced and reproduced (as opposed to those who saw it only as a place of production of use value, a reserve of labor power, or a place of mere consumption); that the subject whom the capitalist sexual division of labor had saddled with doing this work for free was the woman, thereby defining her condition and compromising her every life choice; that the woman and her work in the house constituted the other pole of production with respect to that of the factory, and around that pole revolved the so-called social factory; and that the work of women constituted the hidden phase of capitalist accumulation that was vital to capital in that it produced its most precious commodity—labor power itself. Consequently, a woman held in her hands a fundamental lever of social power. She could refuse to produce, but in too many cases this would prove to be an impassable road or utopia. The concept of class was expanded to include housewives, who, in the workerist approach, were called *houseworkers*, pointing out that in reality with one salary a boss acquired two employees, the worker and the housewife behind him.[12]

Highlighting how wages actually get not only paid work but also a lot of unpaid work provided a fundamental key to understanding the relationship between the First and Third Worlds, as well as for analyzing how in the current globalization of the economy, both old and new subjects do substantial reproductive work, a situation that applies both in advanced capitalist regions and in rural and urban areas in the 'developing countries.'

If the leftist proposal to women had always been emancipation through work outside the home, which did not really free them from their first job within the home, the novelty of the issue taken up by Lotta Femminista lay in the claim for remuneration for housework, together with the request for a more adequate network of services and a reduction of workday hours for everyone, male and female. So not only was the demand for wages for housework advanced by organizing demonstrations and other events but most of all by actions carried out to make this work, which was considered a free obligation, stand out and cost at every workplace—beginning, above all, with the quota regarding childrearing. In this regard, almost all European and North American countries had some form of remuneration for housework where young children were present, especially for single mothers (the welfare payments for welfare mothers in the United States, the family allowances in England, the allowances destined to unmarried women with children in France). Italy was a very negative exception, in that it was willing to provide substantial funds to institutions for abandoned children, funds that were usually scattered around the maze of political patronage, but did not directly support a mother in difficulty.

The pressure applied to the wage by other subjects in the struggle, not only the workers but also the students who demanded a pre-wage, gave further impetus to the decision to claim wages for housework. Once the full breadth and complexity of the material and immaterial work of psychoaffective reproduction that housework involved had been revealed, it was imperative to demand remuneration, to want economic recognition, because in economic terms it substantially conditioned the life of the woman (who was not only discriminated against but also engaged in self-discrimination to bear the family burden—a horse arriving on the labor market already exhausted). On the other hand, the totalizing militancy that had been experienced in factory intervention would continue, characterizing the feminist action of this movement. The other very important element was that the women activists self-financed all of their activity, including renting their headquarters in Piazza Eremitani no. 26, in an odd one-story building, a kind of fortress overlooking the old church, with its frescoes by Mantegna. They didn't occupy a building, because they felt they would end up wasting too much time and would always be in a precarious situation (nor did they think to ask City Hall, because at that time it was inconceivable). They were more interested in having a stable home where they could gather and plan their actions. Lotta Femminista published a newspaper, *Le operaie della casa* (The Houseworkers), and produced many small pamphlets for militant purposes. In addition to these materials, more analytical works on fundamental issues were produced, building a body of theory that has continued to be developed over time.

Considering the type of practices involved, it should be noted that, as far as Italy was concerned, the regions that saw a more widespread presence of the groups and committees for Wages for Housework were the Triveneto and Emilia Romagna. But there were also very active WFH groups in Milan, Varese, Florence, Rome, Naples, and Gela. Furthermore, often groups emerged spontaneously and were not registered in any way, not even in the address roster, such as the San Donà di Piave branch, which, among other things, published an interesting pamphlet on the issue of health entitled

The Power of Well-Being. At first glance, one could indicate roughly four main areas of feminist struggle[13] and intervention: work, sexuality, health, and violence. But on closer inspection, considering how a woman's sexuality had been distorted into the procreative reproductive work of others, these areas were all closely intertwined. Women's sexuality constituted the central task of housework, and violence was the disciplinary instrument par excellence for such work, being as it was free labor.[14]

Sexuality, childbirth, and abortion were very important terrains of struggle. For example, great struggles were carried out in hospitals. But these terrains also constituted the ground of considerable analytical commitment. Just think of the reinterpretation of the witch hunts[15] within the macroprocesses of the original accumulation, which showed that it was no coincidence that midwives were among the primary victims, since obstetrics was to become a male profession. In fact, the state assumed control over the reproduction of labor power, taking this knowledge away from women and relying upon the nascent medical profession, itself under the control of the state and the Church. The witch hunts served to redefine the social role of the woman, who, in the family under capitalism, had to be subjected to her husband's authority, sexually repressed, stripped of economic autonomy, and, above all, deprived of knowledge and decision-making power about sexuality and procreation. In response to the female body having since been transformed into a machine for reproducing labor power, there was a determination to return to the woman that knowledge and that power. The need for women to know their own bodies was one of the traits characterizing the origins of the feminist movement, and not just in Italy.

Abortion, as I said, was forbidden. Injury and often death were the costs women paid for having clandestine abortions carried out by doctors who, while they officially objected to the procedure used to perform the curette without anesthesia and the intense pain it caused the woman, made large and ill-gotten profits from it. In some cases, midwives used knitting needles and parsley. In 1973, a woman in Padua was arrested and accused of getting an abortion. The decision was taken to transform her trial, which started on June 5, 1973, into political mobilization in which the entire movement participated. This case was the beginning, kickstarting the mobilization that would lead to the legalization of the voluntary termination of a pregnancy in Italy.

At the Burlo Garofalo Children's Hospital in Trieste there was a case in which a woman, already the mother of three, was refused a therapeutic abortion (the only kind permitted by law at the time) in the third month of pregnancy. Her only remaining option was a clandestine abortion. A mobilization of women forced the hospital to perform the abortion.[16] It was important that the movement had brought to light that the women who most frequently had abortions were not so much girls but mothers of families, who were already bringing up children and could not afford to have another one. After years of struggle and mobilization law no. 194 was passed in 1978.

Childbirth also experienced a profound transformation, becoming hospitalized and overly medicalized. In this transformation the woman was rendered totally passive and treated as a patient by doctors who were often arrogant and at times sadistic (suturing without anesthesia, leaving women in labor without any assistance, etc.). The struggle against St. Anna's Hospital in Ferrara remains famous. Here women denounced, among other things, babies injured at birth due to poor practices, in particular the improper use of forceps. The action taken by women was duly documented in the book *Dietro la normalità del parto: lotta all'ospedale di Ferrara.*[17]

More generally, women wanted childbirth to once again be natural and not a pathological event and to return the role of protagonist to the woman. She should be able to experience that moment beside a trusted person, whether the husband or someone else. Thus, the discussion on childbirth centers began and the *active birth movement* took off, including the ANDRIA network,[18] gynecologists who focus intensely on this issue. Part of this network made its voice heard years later when it was necessary to denounce another medical abuse of the female body, the unnecessary hysterectomy.[19] Various other actions were conducted in a variety of hospitals. One significant and successful action was taken against the Padua hospital to defend a student nurse named Marlis from an accusation of abuse of her profession, a charge leveled at a weak sector of the hospital hierarchy, when the real issue was the deficiencies of the structure itself.

In addition to the struggles in the hospitals there were investigations in public clinics. Authoritarianism and medical arrogance were, in fact, the object of numerous investigations by women in the movement. The most widely used method was to check on treatment in these clinics by pretending to be a patient. Another popular method was to collect women's testimonies. One of the nicest pamphlets recounting these testimonies is *Basta tacere* (Stop Being Silent).[20]

Another area of intervention was work outside the home, where women wanted to make the job of reproduction visible and costly using forms of struggle that ranged from taking their children to the office to refusing to carry out tasks that replicated domestic duties and were required just because they were women.

A particularly important year was 1974. On the one hand, the entire movement won the divorce referendum, thereby managing to maintain the institution of divorce in the Italian legal system. A very significant initiative on sexuality and women's health was also launched that year: the first self-run women's clinic was opened and would be followed by others in other major cities.[21] Various doctors generously volunteered their services for free. But above all, in an equal relationship between women and with no hierarchy between the male doctor and the female patient, many women began that journey of knowing their own bodies and their biological deadlines and potentials, which were a prerequisite for healthy sexuality and motherhood. The following year, 1975, law no. 405 on clinics was passed, but the clinics would always remain undersized compared to what the law provided for and far from able to effectively provide the information and preventive medical assistance that they were responsible for.

New family legislation was also passed in 1975. It hinged on equality between spouses, an element more consonant with the greater presence and mobility of women in the labor market. That was also the year that the United Nations called for the first Decade for Women, organizing a conference in Mexico City, where there was some contention around the priorities of women in the North versus women of the South, who placed the problem of poverty in the foreground.

Violence was the other important area that always found the overall feminist movement united and determined, with a general agreement among groups on this issue. The movement gathered at the International Tribunal on Crimes against Women conference in Brussels on March 4–8, 1976. About two thousand women from different regions of the world convened to denounce the various forms of violence they suffered. During the conference's final general assembly, a resolution submitted by activists in the WFH network from Italy, Canada, the United States, and Great Britain was almost unanimously accepted. It read:

> [U]nwaged housework is robbery with violence; this work and wage-lessness is a crime from which all other crimes flow; it brands us for life as the weaker sex and delivers us powerless to employers, government planners and legislators, doctors, the police, prisons and mental

institutions, as well as to men, for a lifetime of servitude and imprisonment. We demand wages-for-housework for all women from the governments of the world. We will organise internationally to win back the wealth that has been stolen from us in every country and to put an end to the crimes committed daily against us all.[22]

On the issue of violence, there were some major trials that marked a turning point in the way that the victim was humiliated and treated like the accused, something that discouraged any woman from denouncing the violence they suffered. One was a Verona trial addressing the violence suffered by Cristina Simeoni, a sixteen-year-old girl who was raped, and the Circeo trial for the torture and murder of Rosaria Lopez and the torture of Donatella Colasanti, who survived by pretending to be dead. The movement not only maintained a strong presence at the trials but also rejected the perverse logic by which the victim was transformed into the accused. It also promoted a new bill that, to begin with, presented sexual violence against women as a crime against the person and not as an offense against public morality and decency. The result was an increase in the penalties for sexual violence that better addressed its various forms. And, above all, the movement eschewed humiliating interrogations as irrelevant. About twenty years would go by before a new law on sexual violence would pass in 1996, law no. 66.

Meanwhile, the UN General Assembly adopted the Convention on the Elimination of All Forms of Discrimination against Women (CEDAW), on December 18, 1979. It came into effect in 1981 and was binding for all of the signatory states, including Italy. The CEDAW Committee, which oversees the application and interpretation of this convention through two General Recommendations (GR), no. 12 of 1989 and no. 19 of 1992 (interpretative recommendations), reiterated that the convention implicitly included violence among the forms of discrimination and bound the states to take any and all steps necessary to combat it. Above all, the signatory states had to include in their own legal codes all the forms of violence indicated (GR 19 of 1992 listed fifteen forms, including those in the context of armed conflict). After CEDAW was passed in 1985, the UN Nairobi Conference took place, with the problem of violence in all the forms it assumed throughout the world being denounced. This would be followed by the Declaration on the Elimination of Violence against Women in 1993, the same year as the Congress of Vienna on Human Rights, where it was recognized that women's rights are an integral part of human rights. Violence, according to the 1992 GR, and its corresponding definition in the Declaration of 1993, includes even the threat of violence.[23]

Another very important area of attention and commitment was prostitution. In the mid-1970s, in various countries, prostitutes found themselves under particular attack by the police and were often deprived of their children. This was the case in the United States, for example, where on the basis of the 1976 Loitering Bill prostitutes were frequently rounded up. In Lyon, France, in 1975, yet another prostitute was killed. Her death was the spark that got prostitutes organized into a movement. Determined to reaffirm their rights, primarily to be free from violence with impunity, they decided to occupy churches.[24] At that time, violence against a prostitute was seen at a social level as a natural risk for those who chose that life, not as a fact worthy of note. In Italy, if the 1958 Merlin Law[25] abolishing brothels had restored to a woman the possibility of dignity and eliminated her exploitation by the state, the figure of the prostitute nonetheless remained in the shadows, without a face or a voice.

It should be noted that the delegation of women from the United Nations who came to Rome and made contact with members of the Italian Parliament played an important role in Senator Lina Merlin's initiative to end the regulation of prostitution through the system of brothels. They pointed out that Italy and Spain were the only remaining nations in Europe that had such regulations and needed to abolish this system if they aspired to join the UN. To do so, they were obliged to respect the rights of human beings as defined by the Universal Declaration of 1948, which was followed in 1949 by the Convention for the Suppression of the Traffic in Persons and of the Exploitation of the Prostitution of Others, requiring the signatory states to implement UN provisions with regard to human trafficking and the exploitation of prostitution.[26]

In the 1970s feminist movement there were two positions on prostitution: one rejected such work, while the other argued that it was necessary to recognize a woman's self-determination and her right to judge for herself what work was most acceptable among the limited choices. Those who held the latter position thought it important to remove the debate from an arena of morality and to highlight the working aspect of prostitution. Since then, *sex workers* has become the term used to indicate prostitutes, with women's right to freely choose being reaffirmed and the battle for civil rights of prostitutes sustained. The first meeting of prostitutes in France was held at the Maison de la Mutualité theater in Paris, on June 16, 1976. In Italy, the Committee for Civil Rights of Prostitutes was formed as a nonprofit organization in 1983, in Pordenone, the city that hosted the Prostitution in the 1980s: Marginalization or Social Issue? conference on February 19–20 of that year. This was the first conference organized by prostitutes in Italy. The same committee organized the Prostitution: Conditions and Constraints, Rules and Freedom conference at the Teatro Comunale in Treviso, on March 16, 1985. Across the Atlantic, in the United States, the PUMA and COYOTE networks of prostitutes had already taken a stand in favor of wages for housework in the 1970s.

Prostitutes had come out of the shadows. They had acquired a face and a voice and publicly expressed their problems, thoughts, and demands. The result was that in 1970s the rights of *sex workers* became an issue that began to receive support.[27]

After the 1970s, the profile of prostitution would change again. In the 1980s, the increasingly drastic global application of structural adjustment programs and neoliberal globalization and the process of proletarianization that it induced, as well as the spread of war policies, would represent a lethal attack on the possibility of human reproduction and on women's work to ensure some gain for themselves and some autonomy. More and more women with no other chance of survival, migrating from other countries or remaining in their country of origin, would willingly sell sex or be forced to do so by criminal organizations. In a tough competition they would lower their prices, set aside their rights, take fewer precautions, and once again be exploited by others.

Nevertheless, the battle begun in the 1970s by prostitutes to have their work recognized as a job would be reflected in the laws of some states. Switzerland adopted a law that recognized prostitution as a legal activity provided it is freely exercised by those who have reached the legal age of majority and observe the canton and city rules governing it. It also amended the Federal Law on Residence and Domicile of Foreigners. Prostitution is subject to taxation and the payment of contributions that entitle a person to access Swiss welfare programs. Among the structures designated to legally host such activities are the "bar-hotels." These places provide a certain security to women practicing prostitution who go home after work. And these structures are located and managed so as to not be in conflict with the territory. Legal prostitution is also organized in other ways, and there is still a wide scope of illegal prostitution, but since the new law came into effect, many women are trying to take advantage of it.

Germany, which is considered one of the countries with the largest number of prostitutes, half of whom are foreigners, also adopted a law on January 1, 2002, recognizing prostitution as a legal activity in all respects, subject to taxation in exchange for the enjoyment of the benefits of the German welfare system: retirement pension, unemployment, sickness, and social assistance. In Germany, too, there are various types of structures where prostitutes work, returning home afterwards, thereby separating their professional and private lives. Veronica Munk, who heads a group that provides assistance to foreign women in Hamburg, argues that if prostitution is now recognized as legal work, entry visas should be granted to foreigners who want to come and practice this trade.

We have only given two examples, albeit significant ones, of sex workers' struggles from the 1970s to today: from refusing to be invisible, victimized, or ghettoized to deciding to speak openly in the first person, to self-organize to defend their civil rights, and to demand recognition of their work as a job. As for states, as we have seen, in some cases they went from a lack of response to the formulation of policies legalizing this work, a crucial aspect given the poverty and the paucity of choices that neoliberal globalization has imposed on an increasing number of women, forcing them to depend on and often be blackmailed by criminal organizations. How to explore other choices in life for which one does not pay the price of poverty or dependence remains a problem that continues to trouble women's lives.

Notes

This text is the re-elaboration of materials presented at conferences I hosted at the Faculty of Economics, University of Calabria, in January 2008 and in April of the same year at three locations in Buenos Aires, Brazil: the University of Caxias do Sul, Rio Grande do Sul, University of Buenos Aires; Faculty of Political Science, at the Instituto de Desarrollo Economico y Social, Universidad Nacional de General Sarmiento; the Feminist Philosophy Debate feminista seminar at the Libreria de Mujeres.

1   I analyze this behavior within a reading of the processes initiated by women since World War II to build their own autonomy in "Reproduction and Emigration," included in this volume.

2   The agreement of 1960 on equal pay in industrial work, followed in 1963 by other measures relative to other economic sectors, introduced a system of contractual framing no longer formulated on the basis of a separate classification for men and women, but which defined remunerative parameters differentiated according to the criterion of skill. The reasons for the systematic subframing of the female labor force with respect to the male labor force remained uninvestigated let alone discussed; see Maria Vittoria Ballestrero, *Dalla tutela alla parità: la legislazione italiana sul lavoro delle donne* (Bologna: Il Mulino, 1979).

3   This article was repealed under ruling no. 126 of the Constitutional Court, December 19, 1968.

4   See Laura Remiddi, *I nostri diritti: manuale giuridico per le donne* (Milan: Feltrinelli, 1976).

5   As defined in Remiddi, *I nostril diritti*, commenting on article 587 of the penal code.

6   For some hypotheses on the reasons for this strange law, see Giovanna Franca Dalla Costa, *The Work of Love: Unpaid Housework, Poverty and Sexual Violence at the Dawn of the 21st Century* (Brooklyn, NY: Autonomedia, 2008).

7   In June 1977, radio news reported on a prostitute denouncing her pimp for violence, an "incident happening for the first time in Italy"; G. Dalla Costa, *The Work of Love*, 101n21.

8   See the interviews with some of the protagonists of the workers' struggles of the period on the DVD Manuella Pellarin, *Porto Marghera—gli ultimi fuochi* (Veneto: Autonomia operaia nel Veneto, 2004).

9   The main stages and objectives of the struggles in Porto Marghera were brought to the attention of the workers of Montedison in Crotone, Calabria. On the history of this factory and its working class, see Antonino Campennì, *L'egemonia breve: la parabola del salariato in fabbrica a Crotone* (Soveria Mannelli: Rubbettino, 2002).

10 Pellarin, *Porto Marghera*.

11 Anna Rita Calabrò and Laura Grasso, ed., *Dal movimento femminista al femminismo diffuso* (Milan: Franco Angeli, 1985); Piera Zumaglino, *Femminismi a Torino* (Milan: Franco Angeli, 1996).

12 Mariarosa Dalla Costa and Selma James, *The Power of Women and the Subversion of the Community* (Bristol, UK: Falling Wall Press, 1972) was the book that defined this analysis and, translated into several languages, promoted international debate on wages for housework.

13 Mariarosa Dalla Costa, "To Whom Does the Body of This Woman Belong?" *Commoner* 13 (2009), accessed September 22, 2018, http://www.commoner.org.uk/wp-content/uploads/2010/10/dallacosta_mexico_paper.pdf; Mariarosa Dalla Costa, "Women's Autonomy and Remuneration of Care Work in the New Emergencies," Commoner 13 (2009), accessed September 22, 2018, http://www.commoner.org.uk/wp-content/uploads/2010/10/dallacosta_mexico_paper2.pdf.

14 This is the main thesis put forward and developed in G. Dalla Costa, *The Work of Love*.

15 Silvia Federici and Leopoldina Fortunati, *Il grande Calibano: storia del corpo sociale ribelle nella prima fase del capitale* (Milano: Franco Angeli, 1984); Silvia Federici, *Caliban and the Witch: Women, the Body and Primitive Accumulation* (Brooklyn, NY: Autonomedia, 2004).

16 Coordinamento Nazionale dei Gruppi e Comitati per il Sld, *Lotta delle donne per la salute* (Rome: Institute of Psychology, 1978); Coordinamento Nazionale dei Gruppi e Comitati per il Sld, *Lotta delle donne per la salute*, Reports from the National Feminist Conference April 29–May 1, 1978 (mimeograph) (Rome: Institute of Psychology, 1978).

17 Gruppo Feminista per il Sld di Ferrara, ed., *Dietro la normalità del parto: lotta all'ospedale di Ferrara* (Ferrara: 1978).

18 ANDRIA is the national coalition of gynecologists and obstetricians. Their mouthpiece is the magazine *Istar*.

19 Mariarosa Dalla Costa, ed. *Gynocide: Hysterectomy, Capitalist Patriarchy, and the Medical Abuse of Women* (Brooklyn, NY: Autonomedia, 2007).

20 Movimento di Lotta Femminista di Ferrara, *Basta tacere: testimonianze di donne. parto, aborto, gravidanza, maternità* (self-published, nd).

21 See Clara Jourdan, *Insieme contro: esperienze dei consultori femministi* (Milan: La Salamandra, 1976). For a significant historical analysis of the relationship of women and medicine, see Barbara Ehrenreich and Deirdre English, *Complaints and Disorders: The Sexual Politics of Sickness* (New York: The Feminist Press, 1973); Barbara Ehrenreich and Deirdre English, *Witches, Midwives, and Nurses: A History of Women Healers* (New York: The Feminist Press, 1973).

22 ISIS Women's International Information and Communication Service, "Document 01467," *International Bulletin*, International Tribunal on Crimes against Women, Brussels, March 4–8, 1976.

23 According to the Declaration of 1993, "'violence against women' means any act of gender-based violence that results in, or is likely to result in, harm or physical, sexual or psychological suffering for women, including threats of such acts, coercion, or arbitrary deprivation of liberty, whether occurring in public or private life." This definition is also echoed by the Beijing Platform in article 113, paragraph D, which indicates the strategic objectives and actions related to the area of violence against women.

24 For information on the prostitutes' movement, see G. Dalla Costa, *The Work of Love*, chapter 6.

25 This is law no. 75, passed on February 20, 1958, after a parliamentary procedure lasting ten years.

26 Anna Maria Zanetti, ed., *La senatrice: Lina Merlin, un "pensiero operante"* (Venice: Marsilio, 2006). In France, the activist and former prostitute Marthe Richard was instrumental in closing the brothels in 1946.

27 Among the texts of those years, see Kate Millet, "Prostitution: A Quartet for Female Voices," in *Women in Sexist Society*, ed. Vivian Gornick and Barbara K. Moran (New York: Basic Books, 1971); Judith Belladona, *Folles femmes de leur corps: la prostitution* (Fontenay sous Bois: Recherches, 1977); *Ulla par Ulla* (Montréal: Editions Sélect, 1977).

Capitalism and Reproduction (1994)

February 11, 1975, demonstration in Padua for the legalization of abortion.

Today, the sphere of reproduction reveals all of the 'original sins' of the capitalist mode of production. Reproduction must be analyzed from a planetary perspective, with specific attention paid to both the changes that are taking place among the ever increasing lower social strata in advanced capitalist countries, as well as in an increasing proportion of the so-called 'Third World' population. We live in a planetary economy, and capitalist accumulation still draws its lifeblood for the continuous valorization of both waged and unwaged labor, the latter consisting first of all of the labor involved in social reproduction,[1] in advanced countries, as well as in the Third World.

We find that the social 'misery' or 'unhappiness' that Marx[2] considered to be the "goal of the political economy" has largely been realized everywhere on the planet. However, setting aside the question of happiness for the time being, though certainly not to encourage the myth of its impossibility, let me stress how incredible it now seems, Marxist analysis aside, to claim that capitalist development in some way brings a generalized well-being to the planet.

Today, social reproduction is more beset and overwhelmed than ever by the laws of capitalist accumulation: the continual and progressive *expropriation*, beginning with the 'primitive' expropriation of the land as a means of production dating from the sixteenth to eighteenth centuries in England, to the expropriation, then as now, of all the individual and collective rights that ensure subsistence; the constant *division* of society into *conflictual hierarchies* of class, sex, race, and nationality that pit the free wageworker against the unfree unwaged worker, the unemployed worker, and the slave laborer; the constant production of *inequality and uncertainty*, with the woman as reproducer facing an even more uncertain fate than any wageworker, and if she is also a member of a race or nation facing discrimination, she suffers yet further injustice; the continual *polarization* of the production of ever more concentrated *wealth* and of increasingly widespread poverty.

As Marx writes in *Capital,* vol. 1:

> The law, finally, that always equilibrates the relative surplus population, or industrial reserve army, to the extent and energy of accumulation; this law rivets the labourer to capital more firmly than the wedges of Vulcan did Prometheus to the rock. It establishes an accumulation of misery, corresponding with accumulation of capital. Accumulation of wealth at one pole is, therefore, at the same time accumulation of misery, agony of toil slavery, ignorance, brutality, mental degradation, at the opposite pole, i.e., on the side of the class that produces its own product in the form of capital.[3]

This process of accumulation is true not only for the population overwhelmed by the Industrial Revolution of the nineteenth century but is even more accurate today, whether capital accumulation passes through the factory, plantation, dam, mine, or the carpet weaving workshop, where it is by no means rare for children to be working in slavery conditions.

Indeed, capitalist accumulation spreads through the world by extracting labor for production and reproduction in conditions of stratification that end in the reestablishment of slavery. According to a recent estimate, slavery is the condition in which over 200 million persons are working in the world today.[4] Those macroprocesses and operations through which economic forces supported by political power unfolded during the period of primitive accumulation in Europe, processes that aimed to destroy the individual's value in relation to his/her community in order to turn him/her into an isolated and valueless individual, a mere container for labor power, which s/he is obliged to sell to survive continue to mark human reproduction on a planetary scale.

The indifference to the very possibility of labor power's reproduction shown by capital in the first phase of its history was only very partially (and today increasingly precariously) redeemed centuries later by the creation of the welfare state. In addition, the major financial agencies, the International Monetary Fund and the World Bank, have redrawn[5] the boundaries of welfare and economic policies in both advanced and developing countries. For example, the economic, social welfare, and social insurance measures recently introduced in Italy correspond precisely to the various 'structural adjustment' programs being applied in many Third World countries. The result is that increasingly large sectors of the world's population are destined to extinction because they are believed to be redundant or inappropriate to the valorization requirements of capital.

At the end of the fifteenth century, the bloody legislation against the expropriated[6] led to the mass hanging, torturing, branding, and chaining of the poor. Whereas today the surplus or inadequately disciplined populations of the planet are exterminated by freezing to death or dying of starvation in Eastern Europe and various countries of the advanced West (with 'more coffins and fewer cradles in Russia'),[7] they suffer death by hunger and epidemic in Africa, Latin America, and elsewhere. Deaths also result from formally declared war, from directly or indirectly authorized genocide, and from military and police repression. The other route toward extinction is an individual or collective decision to commit suicide because there is no possibility of survival. It is significant that, according to Italian media reports in 1993–1994, many cases of suicide in Italy were due to unemployment or to the fact that the only work on offer was to join a criminal gang. In India, the 'tribal people' in the Narmada Valley have declared themselves ready to die by drowning if work continues on a dam that will destroy their habitat and, hence, the basis of their survival and cultural identity.[8]

A recent and monstrous twist to this campaign of extinction comes from the extreme example of resistance offered by those who sell parts of their body, a useless container of a labor power that is no longer saleable. In Italy, where the sale of organs is banned, there were media reports in 1993–1994 in which people explicitly said that they were willing to break the ban in exchange for money or a job. For those impoverished and expropriated by capitalist expansion in the Third World, however, this is already a common way for obtaining money. There have been reports about criminal organizations with perfectly legal outlets flourishing on the basis of trafficking in organs, sometimes obtained by kidnapping the victims (often women or children) or through false adoptions.

An enquiry was recently established at the European Parliament on the issue of trafficking in human body parts,[9] and various women's networks are trying to highlight the issue and oppose these crimes. This is where capitalist development, founded on the negation of the individual's value, celebrates its triumph. The individual owner of redundant or, in any case, superfluous labor power is literally cut to pieces in order to rebuild the bodies of those who can pay the criminal or non-criminal sectors of capital that profit from it for the right to live.

During the era of 'primitive' accumulation, when the free wageworker was still being shaped in England, the law still authorized slavery.[10] By treating the vagabonds created by the feudal lords' violent and illegal expropriation of the land as 'voluntary' perpetrators of the crime of vagabondage and ordaining that if anyone should refuse to work, he would be "condemned as a slave to the person who denounced him as an idler."[11] If this reduction of the poor to slavery remained on a relatively limited scale in England, capital soon after launched slavery on a much vaster scale, emptying Africa of the equivalent of Europe's population through the transatlantic slave trade to the Americas and the Caribbean.

However, slavery, far from disappearing, has remained one of capitalism's unmentioned and concealed constants. The poverty imposed on a large part of the planet by the major financial agencies confines entire families to work in conditions of slavery, often so they can pay their creditors. Workers are forced to work in slavery conditions on livestock farms and in plantations and mines. Children are made to work in slavery conditions in carpet workshops. Women are kidnapped or coerced into working in the sex industry. However, these are only a few examples, and it is significant that the problem of slavery was also raised by many NGOs at their forum in Vienna in June 10–12, 1993, which preceded the UN World Conference on Human Rights on June 14–25 of the same year.

In the period of primitive accumulation, during which free wage labor was being born from the great expropriations, there was the greatest example of sexual genocide in history. The great witch hunts, together with a series of other measures directed expressly against women, contributed in a fundamental way to forging the unfree and unwaged woman worker in the production and reproduction of labor power.[12] Deprived of the means of production and subsistence typical of the precapitalist economy and also largely excluded from craftwork or access to the new jobs that manufacturing was offering, women were essentially faced with two options for survival: marriage or prostitution. Even for women who found some form of income external to the home, prostitution remained a way of supplementing low family income or the low wages paid to women. It is interesting that prostitution first became a trade exercised by women on a mass level during that period. One can say that during the manufacturing period the individual proletarian woman was basically born to be a prostitute.[13]

From this insoluble contradiction in the feminine condition of being an unwaged worker in a wage economy[14] emerges not only mass prostitution in that period but also, in the context of current economic policies, the reoccurrence of the same phenomenon today on a vaster scale, in order to generate profits for owners and managers of one of the most flourishing industries at the world level, the sex industry. This led the World Coalition against Trafficking in Women to hold the first World Convention against Sexual Exploitation in May 1993, in Brussels. The women in the coalition agreed to work for the UN's adoption of the convention and its ratification by national governments. Internationally, in fact, the sexual exploitation of women by organized crime is increasingly alarming. These organizations have already brought men and women from African countries and Eastern Europe to work in Italy as prostitutes. The tricks used to cover up exploitation in prostitution—for example, wife sales by catalogue or 'sex tourism' in exotic destinations—are widespread and well-known. According to the coalition's charges, various countries already accept forms of 'sex tourism' as a planned component of national income. Thanks to the efforts of individual women campaigners and nongovernmental organizations, research into direct government involvement and responsibility in forcing women to serve as prostitutes for soldiers during World War II has also begun.

Woman's condition in capitalism is born of violence, just as the free wageworker is born of violence. It is forged on the witches' pyres and is violently maintained.[15] Within the current global context of the population's reproduction, the woman continues to suffer the violence of poverty, since her unpaid responsibility for the home makes her the weak contracting party in the external labor market. Because of her lack of economic resources, she also suffers the further violence of being drawn increasingly into forms of sex work that are exploitative and have terrible working conditions. The warlike visage that development increasingly assumes simply worsens women's condition still further and magnifies the practice and mentality of violence against women.[16] A paradigmatic case is the war rape exercised as ethnic rape in the former Yugoslavia.

I have mentioned only a few of the social macro-operations that allowed the capitalist system to 'take off' during the period of primitive accumulation. Just as important were a series of other operations[17] that have been left unmentioned here for the sake of brevity, but which could also be highlighted as aspects of the continual refoundation on a world scale of the class relationship on which capitalist development rests. In other words, the perpetuation of the stratification of workers that begins with the separation and counterposition imposed through the sexual division of labor.

These considerations lead to one fundamental thesis: capitalist development *has always been unsustainable* because of its *human impact*. To understand the point, all one needs to do is to take the viewpoint of those who have been and continue to be killed by it. A presupposition of capitalism's birth was the sacrifice of a large part of humanity—mass exterminations, the production of hunger, misery, slavery, violence, and terror. Its continuation requires the same presupposition. Particularly from the *woman's* viewpoint, capitalist development has always been unsustainable because it places her in an *unsustainable contradiction*, making her an unwaged worker in a wage economy and, hence, denying her the right to an autonomous existence. If we look at subsistence economies—continually besieged, undermined, and overwhelmed by capitalist development—we see that capitalist development continually deprives women of the land and water that are the fundamental means of production and subsistence for sustaining the entire community.

The expropriation of land leaped to the world's attention in January 1994 with the revolt of the indigenous people in Chiapas, Mexico. The media could hardly avoid reporting on the revolt largely because of the crucial role of Mexico's alignment with the Western powers through the North American Free Trade Agreement. The perversity of producing wealth by expropriation and the production of misery was there for all to see. It is significant that the dramatic consequences of expropriation of the land led those involved in drawing up the Women's Action Agenda 21 in Miami in November 1991 to make a forceful appeal for women to be guaranteed land and access to food. At the same time, the process of capitalist expansion—in this case, the Green Revolution—led many people to practice the selective abortion of female fetuses and female infanticide in some areas of the Third World: from sexual genocide to preventive annihilation.[18]

The question of the unsustainability of development has become ever more topical with the emergence of evidence of various environmental disasters and forms of harm inflicted on the ecosystem. The earth, the water running in its veins, and the air surrounding it have come to be seen as an ecosystem, a living organism of which humans are a part—to be able to live we depend on the life and equilibrium of the ecosystem. This is in opposition to the idea of nature as humanity's 'other'—a nature that is to be dominated and whose elements are to be appropriated as though they were potential commodities waiting in a warehouse.

After five centuries of expropriation and domination, the earth is returning to the limelight. In the past it was sectioned, fenced in, and denied to the free producers. Now, it is itself having its reproductive powers expropriated, being turned topsy-turvy, vivisectioned, and made a commodity. These extreme operations like the 'banking' and patenting of the genetic codes of living species belong to a single process whose logic of exploitation and domination has brought such planetary devastation in human and environmental terms as to provoke disquieting questions about the future possibilities and modalities of human reproduction.

Environmental destruction is united with the destruction wrought on an increasingly large proportion of humanity. The destruction of humans is necessary for the perpetuation of capitalist development today, just as it was at its origins. To stop subscribing to this general destruction, and hence to approach the problem of 'sustainable development,' means, above all else, taking into account the struggles that oppose capitalist development in the metropolises and the rural areas. It also means finding the ways and defining the practices to set capitalist development behind us by elaborating a different approach to knowledge.

In interpreting and taking into account the various anti-capitalist struggles and movements, a global vision must be maintained of the many sections of society rebelling in various forms and contexts across the planet. To give priority to some and ignore others would mean adopting the same logic of separation and counterposition that has constituted the soul of capitalist development. The cancellation and annihilation of a part of humanity cannot be treated as a foregone conclusion. In the metropolises and the advanced capitalist countries in general, many no longer have a waged job. At the same time, the welfare measures that contribute to ensuring survival are being cut back. Human reproduction has already reached its limits: the woman's reproductive energy is increasingly dried out like a spring whose water has been used for too much land. Water, says Vandana Shiva,[19] is finite; it cannot multiply.

Human reproduction is crushed by the general intensification of labor, by the overextension of the workday, amid cuts in resources whereby the lack of wage work becomes a stress-laden work of looking for legal and/or illegal employment, on top of the laborious work of reproduction. There is not space to give a more extensive description of the complex phenomena that have led to the drastic reduction in the birth rate in the advanced countries, particularly in Italy where the fertility rate is 1.26 and population growth zero. However, it should be remembered that women's refusal to function as machines for reproducing labor power—demanding instead to reproduce themselves and others as social individuals—represents a major moment of women's resistance and struggle.[20] The contradiction in women's condition—whereby women are forced to seek financial autonomy through wage work outside the home, yet on disadvantageous terms in comparison to men, while they also remain primarily responsible for labor power's production and reproduction—has exploded in all its unsustainability. Women in the advanced countries have fewer and fewer children. In general, humanity in the advanced countries less and less desires to reproduce itself.

Women's great refusal to reproduce also demands an answer to the overall question being discussed in this essay. It demands a *new type of development* in which human reproduction is not built on an *unsustainable sacrifice by women*, as part of a conception and structure of life that is nothing but labor time within an *intolerable sexual hierarchy*. The 'wage' struggle, in both its direct financial and indirect social provisioning aspects, does not only concern 'advanced' areas as distinct from 'rural' ones, for there are very few situations in which survival rests solely on the land. To sustain the community, the wage economy is most often interwoven with resources typical of a subsistence economy, whose overall conditions are continually under pressure from the political and economic decisions of the major financial agencies such as the IMF and the World Bank.[21] Today, it would therefore be a fatal error not to defend wage levels and income guarantees—in money and goods and services. These are working humanity's rights, since the wealth and power of capitalist society has been accumulated on the basis of five centuries of its labor. At the same time, land, water, and forests must remain available for those whose subsistence comes from them and to whom capitalist expropriation offers only extinction. As different sectors of humanity seek and demand a different kind of development, the strength to demand it grows to the extent that no one accepts their own extinction or the extinction of others.

The question of human reproduction posed by women's rejection of procreation is now turning into the demand for another type of development—one that seeks completely new horizons by breaking down the walls of the concept of well-being. The demand is now for happiness. The demand is for a formulation of development that guarantees the satisfaction of the basic needs on whose suppression capitalism was born and has grown. The need for time against a life consisting solely of labor. The need for physical life and sexuality—with one's own and other people's bodies, with the body as a whole not just the functions that make it more productive and against the body as a mere container for labor power or a machine for reproducing labor power. The need for collectivity and not just with other men and women but also with the various living beings who can only be encountered now after a laborious journey out of the city and against the isolation of individuals in the body of society and living nature as a whole. The need for public space and not just the public parks and squares or the few other areas permitted, and against the enclosure, privatization, and continual restriction of available space. The desire to find a relationship with the totality of the earth as a common space, as well as the need for play, indeterminacy, discovery, amazement, contemplation, and emotion.

Obviously, the above makes no pretense of 'defining' fundamental needs, but it registers needs whose systematic frustration by this mode of production has certainly not served human happiness. I think one must have the courage to pose happiness as a problem. This requires rethinking the notion of development, in order to think again 'in the grand manner' and to reject the fear that raising the question of happiness may appear too daring or too subjective. Rigoberta Menchú[22] spoke of how the mothers in her community teach their girls from the start that the they face a life of immense toil and suffering. She wondered why, and she found very precise, capitalist reasons: "We started to reflect on the roots of the problem, and we came to the conclusion that its roots lay in possession of the land. We did not have the best land, the landowners did. And every time we clear new land, they try to take it from us or to steal it in some way."[23] Rigoberta has raised the problem of how to change this state of affairs; she has not cultivated the myth of human unhappiness. The Christian teachings she has used alongside the Mayan traditions has offered various lessons, including that of the Old Testament's Judith.

It is no coincidence that in the last twenty years, the women's question, the question of the indigenous populations,[24] and the question of the earth have assumed growing importance, for they are linked by an especially close synergy. The path toward a different kind of development cannot ignore them. There is still much knowledge in civilizations that have not died but have managed to conceal themselves. Their secrets have been maintained thanks to their resistance to the will to annihilate them. The earth encompasses so many powers, especially its power to reproduce itself and humanity as one of its elements. These powers have been discovered, preserved, and enhanced more by women's knowledge than male science. It is

crucial, then, that this other knowledge—of women, of indigenous populations, and of the earth—whose 'passiveness' is capable of regenerating life[25]
should find a way of emerging and being heard. This knowledge appears
now as a decisive force that can lift the increasingly deadly siege capitalist
development imposes on human reproduction.

Notes

This chapter originally appeared in Werner Bonefeld, John Holloway, and Kosmas
Psychopedis, ed., *Open Marxism*, vol. 3: *Emancipating Marx* (London: Pluto Press, 1995).
It was presented at the seminar Women's Unpaid Labour and the World System, organ-
ized by the Japan Foundation, Tokyo, April 8, 1994, as part of the Foundation's European
Women's Study Tour for Environmental Issues.

1   See Mariarosa Dalla Costa and Selma James, *The Power of Women in the Subversion
    of the Community* (Bristol, UK: Falling Wall Press, 1972).
2   Karl Marx, "Economic and Philosophical Manuscripts of 1844," in *Early Writings*
    (Harmondsworth: Penguin Books, 1975), 286.
3   Karl Marx, *Capital: A Critique of Political Economy*, vol. 1 (Harmondsworth: Penguin
    Books, 1976), 799.
4   *The Economist*, January 6, 1990.
5   See Mariarosa Dalla Costa and Giovanna Franca Dalla Costa, *Paying the Price:
    Women and the Politics of International Economic Strategy* (London: Zed Books,
    1995).
6   Cf. Marx, *Capital,* vol. 1, chapter 28.
7   *La Repubblica*, February 16, 1994.
8   The protest over the Narmada dam has received extensive coverage in interna-
    tional publications and the international media. For a critical interpretation of the
    proliferations of dams in the world, see Vandana Shiva, *Staying Alive: Women and
    Survival in India* (London: Zed Books, 1990).
9   See *La Repubblica*, September 16, 1993.
10 See Marx, *Capital,* vol. 1, chapter 28.
11 Ibid., 897.
12 See Silvia Federici, "The Great Witch-Hunt," *Maine Scholar* 1, no. 1 (1988).
13 See Leopoldina Fortunati, *L'arcano della riproduzione: casalinghe, prostitue, operai
    e capitale* (Venice: Marsilio, 1981); Leopoldina Fortunati, "Sesso come valore d'uso
    per il valore," in Leopldina Fortunati and Silvia Federici, *Il grande Calibano: storia
    del corpo sociale ribelle nella prima fase del capitale* (Milan: Franco Angeli, 1984), 209.
14 See M. Dalla Costa and James, *The Power of Women.*
15 See Giovanna Franca Dalla Costa, *The Work of Love: Unpaid Housework, Poverty and
    Sexual Violence at the Dawn of the 21st Century* (Brooklyn, NY: Autonomedia, 2008).
16 Currently, there is a wide-ranging debate on this issue. A. Michel, "La donna a
    repentaglio nel sistema di guerra," *Bozze* 2 (April–March 1987) remains a good
    reference-point.
17 See Marx, *Capital*, vol. I, chapters 26–33.
18 See Shiva, *Staying Alive.*
19 Ibid.
20 See M. Dalla Costa and James, *The Power of Women.*

21 See Dalla Costa and Dalla Costa, *Paying the Price*.
22 Elizabeth Burgos, *Mi chiamo Rigoberta Menchú* (Florence: Giunti Editore, 1990).
23 Ibid., 144.
24 As was stressed by the Working Group on Indigenous Peoples at the NGO Forum in Vienna, June 10–12, 1993, these peoples have worked especially hard during the last two decades to have their voices heard, to make progress on questions concerning them, the question of land, above all, to obtain greater respect for and a formalization of their rights in written form. Significant stages in the process have been the Kari Oca Declaration, the Land Charter of the Indigenous Peoples, and the International Labour Organization's Convention on Indigenous and Tribal Peoples (lLO Convention no. 169). This growing liaison and promotion of their demands was a major factor in the speedy expressions of solidarity from the North American indigenous populations during the rebellion of the indigenous peoples of Chiapas.
25 See Shiva, *Staying Alive*.

The Door to the Garden (2002)

Translated by Fulvia Serra

May 1, 1976, women's torchlight procession demonstration in Naples for wages for housework.

The door to the garden creaked
And a footstep rustled the sand . . .
—Giacommo Puccini, *Tosca*

I t's often said that the most typical languages of femininity are silence and emotions. I will not use the first one because the factory of militancy doesn't yet have the tools to understand it. On the other hand, you will have to put up with me using a bit of the second one.

That said, I'm grateful to the authors of *Futuro Anteriore* for successfully taking on the hard work of clearing the path of remembrance for many thinkers coming from the tradition of workerism, myself included. I did not contribute to the book, not for lack of interest but because at that moment I didn't have the time to do so. I was, in fact, in the process of defining a strategy for what I consider, after birth and abortion, to be the third big battlefield between women's bodies and the medical body: the abuse of the hysterectomy. I will briefly talk about this later and give it precedence over the other issues, because it is the one that most closely interfered with the possibility of me contributing to this book. It required, in fact, all of my attention and prevented me from confirming my intention to contribute in due time.

First of all, though, I need to explain where I'm coming from. By the way, I just finished reading the book the other day. It had been presented to me as a study of subjectivity, but it obviously ended up including, in the course of its development, other important themes that I didn't have the time to think about as much as I would have liked. I'm sorry then if my lecture is out of focus regarding some of the issues that I find very important for the school of feminism that derived from workerism.

However, I'm very happy to participate in this conversation. How come I'm still here after thirty years? The answer is simple: this is my home. I was born here. Here is where I was first politicized and, most importantly, this is the experience I had been looking for, the one capable of answering my urge for understanding as well as for action. You can't ever forget your roots, and I never wanted to. This is where my thinking fits. Here I find the people who speak my language, even if it is a language I had to modify slightly to be able to communicate with other people. Other than this, there was no other home for me. There was only a long road, along which I identified the few issues that I will present to you today and where I fought various battles.

Besides its successes and its failures (personally I participated in Potere Operaio, Veneto), workerism has had the considerable power to determine my life journey, and not only mine, it seems, since many of us are gathered here today. It would therefore be useful to investigate further this profound sense of belonging that workerism produced in so many of us. I have the feeling, in fact, that we would have at our disposal more tools than we think, taking into consideration only the efficacy of the political discourse of the past.

First of all, workerism gave us a method, together with the determination and the passion to act to engender a transformation in the existing order of things. These are only three of the foundational elements I can identify in that experience, but I relied on all of them when traversing other territories in the following years. From 1967 to 1971, I was active in Potere Operaio and then in the feminist movement. The area of the feminist movement that I contributed to promoting and organizing, Lotta Femminista and Wages for Housework, is, without a doubt, a child of Potere Operaio.

Mixing my memories with the current conversation, I would like to call your attention to *three topics*, all pertaining the sphere of reproduction. *First, the abuse of the hysterectomy, which I consider a form of devastation of the flower and vegetable garden of reproduction inside women's bodies:* the destruction of the places for the generation of life and pleasure. *Second, reproductive work meant as the work capable of producing and maintaining life:* a problem that was left unanswered. *Third, the expropriation of the land and the destruction of its reproductive powers, seen as the devastation of the flower and vegetable garden of reproduction outside of our bodies,* because the land is not only our source of nourishment, but it is from the land that bodies gather meaning, sensations, and imagination: here too, then, expropriation and destruction of the land are equivalent to the devastation of the places for the creation of life and pleasure. This issue was central on the radical fringes of political debate during the 1990s and had its origin in the struggles that were organizing in the so-called 'Third World' countries during the 1980s. Of course, those struggles have a story that spans five centuries of capitalism. It is an ancient story.

Let's start then with the devastation of the flower and vegetable garden inside the female body through the *abuse of the hysterectomy*, traditionally performed together with the *ovariectomy* of healthy ovaries. It has not been at all easy to deal with this issue, since I had to dig through it alone and build for myself a knowledge of the relative pathologies, together with their possible remedies, the plausible as well as the implausible ones. However, I am inclined to solitary excavation and the full contact fight with the monster that comes out. A confrontation with doctors soon followed.

Delving into an issue, even by yourself, if there's nobody else available at that moment, uncovering it and building new knowledge to then circulate it and inform the public: this, I think, is the method that more and more *vittattivisti*,[1] those who operate in the sphere of the production and reproduction of life, will have to undertake. At stake is the ability to stand up against the multiplying attacks that, in the grip of a pressing siege, are jeopardizing the integrity and the well-being of our bodies, by undermining the power and the inner workings that regulate the reproduction of life. Of course, I'm available for a deeper discussion of this issue, which I have been committed to for years, together with women and doctors, should the occasion arise. I decided that today I would provide at least a few numbers, considering the extreme seriousness of the abuse, one that both women and men should be aware of. When a man needs surgery, in fact, there are usually women to help him gather information, advise him, and assist him. In the case of this procedure, on the other hand, women are often left alone to make a decision with the doctor. When their partners give them advice, it is often wrong, due to either misinformation or an attempt to appease them: "Come on, get rid of that uterus. You don't need it anymore anyway!"

In Italy hysterectomies increased from thirty-eight thousand a year in 1994 to sixty-eight thousand a year in 1997, so that one in every five women are at risk of being subjected to it, one in every four in some regions, including Veneto. Not even the black plague had as many fatalities. In 1998 and 1999, we have almost reached seventy thousand.

This procedure has serious negative consequences on the physical, emotional, and relational level. In 50 percent of the cases there are complications that can be fatal to one or two women (depending on the procedure) per one thousand (a considerable risk, therefore). For these reasons, it should be considered only for those few pathologies that do not allow an alternative healing approach. It is also very important to have full knowledge of the different procedures available today, because safeguarding a woman's body and her future quality of life could depend on the choice made. If we compare the statistics on the use of hysterectomy in Italy with those of our neighbor France and analyze closely the instances in which this procedure is used, even for those pathologies that present the possibility of an alternate route, 80 percent of them, as I reported to the Department of Public Health, seems to be unfounded.

In France, one woman in every twenty is at risk of being subjected to a hysterectomy, one in every twenty-five in Paris and surroundings areas, and the tendency is toward a further decrease in its use. Therefore, in Italy and other countries, USA first of all, we are witnessing a gratuitous and massive amputation of women's bodies. The necessity to defend the integrity of our bodies (many relationships inside the family or the couple are damaged or even destroyed as a consequence of this procedure) is essential and campaigning, including through movement initiatives, could contribute to creating awareness and knowledge, as well as a support network. At stake is the scientific ideology that invests us with the interests of the medical associations and the further deformations produced in the field of public health by the pressure of big financial corporations that, in keeping with the neoliberal paradigm, commodify our life and the physical and social body that contains it. Reclaiming basic medical knowledge is essential to resisting and opposing not only this particular procedure but an array of aggressive medical practices that generate morbidity, disability, and unhappiness, as well as poverty, as a result of the increasing dependency on the market-laboratory and to the detriment of our vital creative energies and economic resources. Hence the scarcity of health and the privatization of the mechanisms that reproduce it, operated as they are by our medical system.

It is important that I take advantage of this venue to raise awareness around what's happening to women's bodies. Let's look at what's going on with the practice, which is widespread in Italy, of *prophylactic surgery*, the *preventive amputation of both healthy breasts and the removal of healthy ovaries*, performed on those women who, as carriers of the BRCA1 or BRCA2 chromosomes, are considered at high risk of developing breast and/or ovarian cancer: even doctors recognize that there is no certainty that these women will indeed develop those forms of cancer or that they won't, in spite of such mutilations.

The second topic concerns *reproductive work*, also referred to as domestic work, even though reproductive work includes a lot more than what we commonly think of as domestic. On this subject, I'd like to call attention to thirty years of literature produced by workerist feminists or derived from their work. It is worthwhile here to recall a few key points. During the 1970s, in Italy, there were two different schools of feminism: consciousness-raising feminism and the workerist feminism of Lotta Femminista, which later evolved into the groups and committees of Wages for Housework. Lotta Femminista spread nationally, especially in the regions of Veneto and Emilia, but less in cities like Milan, where self-awareness feminism was predominant, or Rome, where we nonetheless had two groups. We were even present as far south as Gela, Sicily, where we had a group. Most importantly, starting in 1972, when we founded the Collettivo Internazionale Femminista to promote both debate and actions in other countries, we created a large international network, especially in the USA and Canada, and were also present in a few European countries, particularly Britain, Germany, and Switzerland. We often held international conferences so that we could organize actions in concert. African American women were also part of our network. They said that the presence of Italian women made it conceivable for them to join the network, because Italian women have little power (sort of like women from the Third World in their eyes). Had there been only white American or English women, they would not have participated.

I remember traveling, beginning in the early 1970s, through the United States and some major cities in Canada to spread our view on housework from the Atlantic coast to the Pacific coast (I was even robbed of the little money I had in El Paso). My budget for travel, by plane and often by bus, was made up of one-dollar contributions provided by our North American comrades. At the same time various universities, many of which would then adopt *Women and the Subversion of the Community* as a feminist classic, invited me to talk. In this way I was able to make some additional money to travel. One particular university in New York offered me a teaching position, and I even had an interview with a board of professors so that I could start teaching at the beginning of the coming semester. Once back in Italy, though, I wrote to them and turned down the offer. I could not possibly give up my political work. Lotta Femminista was still too young and I couldn't leave it. They did not understand my position and got really angry. I have subordinated all my other life choices to this work and political research. In this also I bore the mark of Potere Operaio: I have always been a militant.

How was it that some women left Potere Operaio to form Lotta Femminista?
When I joined Potere Operaio an older comrade, Teresa Rampazzo, asked
me, "What made you join Potere Operaio?" and then answered her own
question: "You had thirst for justice, right?" "Yes" I said. She had guessed.
The answer seemed obvious to me as well.

If, on the other hand, I had to say why I left Potere Operaio, working
together in June 1971 with the group of women who would then form the
first core of Lotta Femminista, I would have to say: "A thirst for dignity." The
relationship between men and women at that time, especially among our
intellectual comrades, was on a level that I did not consider sufficiently
dignified. So I wrote and circulated a pamphlet that, with a few revisions,
became *Women and the Subversion of the Community*, the little book that
the international feminist movement basically immediately adopted and
translated into six languages.

Thus, I co-founded the first chapter of an autonomous organization
together with women coming from the workerist tradition. Soon, others
from different backgrounds joined us, including some women with no
political background, evidently because things between men and women
were not going well on any level.

Another reason for establishing Lotta Femminista had to do with what
was then called the need for self-identification. Women were starting to
define themselves by constructing their own identity, no longer through
the eyes and the expectations of men. I remember a document coming from
the United States with the weird title "Woman-Identified Woman," along
with many more with the same tone. After we saved our dignity and our
identity (in more of an emotional than temporal sense) we started thinking
and wondering about the evil origins of our discomfort and our condition
and about the origins of the exploitation and oppression of women. We
found it in reproductive work, the unpaid domestic work that was ascribed
to women in the capitalist division of labor. This didn't mean that some of
us, driven by the need to go further back and track the ancient origins of
the misfortunes of women, didn't also study the relationship between men
and women in prehistory, focusing on matriarchal vs. patriarchal societies—these studies are still around. The urgency, however, was to provide an
analysis that would be useful for immediate action (in the perfect workerist
tradition) and that made us focus almost exclusively on the capitalist era.
We unveiled the mystery of reproduction, investigating how the production and reproduction of the labor force constituted the hidden phase of

capitalistic accumulation. We unveiled the arcane but not the secret. In fact, I must say, all reproduction hides a secret. We expanded the concept of class so that it would include women as producers and reproducers of labor power. We were mostly interested in working-class women.

Behind the closed doors of their houses, women work without any compensation, schedule, or time off at a job that occupies all of their time. It is a job made up of material and immaterial tasks, and it conditions all of their choices. We defined the family as a site of production because of its daily production and reproduction of labor power. Up to then, others had maintained or continued to maintain that the family was exclusively a place for consumption and the production of use value or a mere reservoir of labor power. We asserted that a job outside the house cannot eliminate or substantially transform domestic work, that it merely adds a new master to the existing one: the job the husband already has. For this reason, entering the job market was never our goal. Neither was equality with men.

To whom are we to be equal, burdened as we are with work men do not have to do? Besides, at a moment when the debate around the refusal of work took center stage, why would we have aimed at something that men were rejecting? From inside the Fordist society of those years, we revealed that production sprang essentially from two sources, the factory and the home, and that women, exactly because their work produces the most important commodity for capitalism, labor power, had at their disposal a key factor to leverage social power: they could refuse to continue producing. This makes women central figures in the process of 'social subversion,' as we called it back then, a struggle that could potentially end in the radical transformation of society.

In spite of the profound transformations that production underwent, the core responsibility that women continued to have for reproduction and the impervious nature of reproductive work remain unsolved problems, indicating the persistence of a fundamental duplicity. This duplicity, however, especially between masculine and feminine, is, I think, inscribed in the universe. Maybe we should observe it in order to understand it better, rather than considering it a dying phenomenon, and, at the same time, invest ourselves in trying to fix its inner injustice.

As previously mentioned, we targeted mainly working-class women. However, reproductive work is the foundational aspect of the female condition in general. Fighting against this condition required first of all the refusal of this work as unpaid and as primarily ascribed to women. It also meant opening up negotiations with the state to obtain part of the wealth produced, both in the form of financial retribution and the social services made available. It meant demanding that reproductive work be assigned a specific time, instead of pretending that it was an option, easily combinable with a job outside the house. The refusal, of course, concerned both the material and the immaterial reproductive work. Essentially, women were replacing a femininity characterized by the care of others, by the enormous willingness to live in function of others, with a femininity in which all of this took second place, making room for the reproduction of themselves. Indeed, the issue of domestic work was closely connected with that of sexuality, which had been distorted by the function of procreating/reproducing. Struggles around work, sexuality, health, and violence were thus closely intertwined. About this, some of our comrades carried out very incisive research.[2] Bodies are in question in reproductive work, and therefore so are relationships and emotions.

We took our struggle to the neighborhoods (a beautiful and victorious campaign for housing, our first one and the only one that was not documented), hospitals, schools, and factories. In Padua, on June 5, 1973, we started a campaign for abortion rights, jumpstarting a political mobilization around the trial of a woman who had had an abortion. After years of mobilizations, in 1978, along with the entire feminist movement, we won approval for law no. 194, which recognized women's right to terminate any pregnancy and to do so in proper medical facilities. Again in Padua, in 1974, we organized the Center for Women's Health, a self-managed feminist clinic, the first in Italy, followed by similar ones in other cities. This experience was intended both to set an example and to gain momentum for the redefinition of the relationship between women and medicine, particularly in the field of gynecology, especially considering that law no. 405 for the establishment of family clinics was about to be approved, going into effect in 1975. We led major campaigns inside many of the ob-gyn units in hospitals, the so-called 'maternity lagers.' I best remember Padua, Milan, and Ferrara.

Among the campaigns organized inside the factories, the one at Solari (which then became a model for the struggle in other factories) was exemplary, with the women workers demanding paid time off and medical coverage for routine gynecological care, so that they did not have to choose between losing workdays and taking care of themselves. We also organized an important campaign in a town in Veneto against a factory that released terrible fumes and polluted the water.

As I was saying, we had a national and an international network but the amazing thing was that we could do all of it with such an extremely small budget. Our means of communication were basically flyers and a newspaper that was called, in true workerist fashion, *Le operaie della casa* (The Houseworkers). The rhythm of so much activism was so intense and totalizing that there was no room left for anything else in our lives. Our attitude toward militancy certainly derived from the experience of militancy in Potere Operaio, but, I guess, in other groups the situation was very similar and even more extreme for those of us who had a leading role.

By the end of that decade we were worn-out. All our reproduction margins had been erased and they were already notoriously much smaller than those that men normally enjoyed, including our comrades. After so many struggles and so much time spent organizing, we couldn't detect even the outline of a transformation of our society. Not one radical enough to meet the demands for which we had struggled, or able to contain the sweeping change of the female individuality that our political journey had brought about. We could no longer fit into the mold for relationships or the organization of society offered by capitalism.

It's also important to keep in mind that the women who participated in the feminist movement at the beginning were not young girls. Often in their thirties, or even older, they were women who had left crippling marriages in order to reclaim the right to feel again. I remember many of them telling me that what they had mostly been missing with their husbands and pre-school children was not so much sexual freedom, but rather the possibility of falling in love. Thinking back, I realize that the premarital youth of those women had probably been miserable as well.

Really, at that point, we would have needed to come up with a project capable of generating an effective transformation of society, as well as the people necessary to carry it out, since it would have been impossible for us to do so alone. This had always been the weakest part of the general discourse, as well as of our discourse, the one we couldn't even pinpoint, because the strategy was to be determined by the power of our struggle itself. In the end, it didn't happen that way, and we didn't have the strength to fight anymore. I remember, however, that the problem of identifying an outlet, 'the transition,' had been on my mind for years, since Potere Operaio, but when I mentioned it to one of my comrades, Guido B., his answer had been vague, as if it were impossible to even outline a solution. I just thought that maybe I didn't have enough experience, that I wasn't yet ready to tackle such an important problem. The reason I posed the question in the first place, however, was that I couldn't imagine spending the rest of my life getting up at four in the morning to canvass Porto Marghera or the Montedison in Crotone in the attempt to generalize the struggle. Till when, till where? And then what? I would, of course, encounter the same dilemma in the feminist movement and again be unable to find anybody to share it with.

After about ten years, the biological clock in our bodies started ticking—even militants have a body, as negated as it often is. There were women who wanted a child and felt that it was already getting late. They had to decide with whom they wanted it and in what kind of context they wanted to raise it.

In the absence of a transformation of our society radical enough to integrate the new subjectivity of women, we started to give up. Many had to capitulate. To what extent depended on how much money these women had at their disposal, how much free time they could count on, and what kind of job they were able to find. The old problem of women's lack of financial means, around which we had organized so much, came to light in all its gravity.

Right at that moment, the repression started and, with it, the total erasure of our feminist current, its struggles, and its accomplishments, mostly the work of leftist women in the fields of sociology and history. Me and Polda,[4] however, documented all of the struggles and all of the campaigns, as well as the issues that came to light during our debates, in booklets meant for activists, in pamphlets, and in the newspaper, sacrificing Saturdays, Sundays, and holidays. During the 1980s, the years of repression and normalization, the feminism of the great struggles was replaced by a fundamentally cultural current of feminism, with the function of controlling and filtering the demands and the voices. We were blacklisted. With great difficulty, considering the circumstances, some of our comrades completed works of theory or historical research. These works had been conceived in the 1970s as parts of an overall project that was never realized. Their circulation was ostracized, to use a euphemism. They basically disappeared (except when I used them in my teaching), submerged within a hostile political climate and by the proliferation of studies on the female condition from a different perspective. What we had produced was also co-opted and domesticated. Institutions turned out to be very supportive of the study of the female condition, investing money and creating networks and research grants, all of them carefully managed. They created sham foundations and projects.

The problem of reproductive work remained unanswered. The discourse on wages for housework was blacklisted as well. The problem of reproductive work would eventually find a partial and false solution with the introduction of migrant workers who would themselves leave behind tragedies of reproduction. For instance, young children left with the grandparents didn't want to go and live with parents they didn't recognize anymore, and the grandparents would go crazy with grief when, having been left to raise their grandchildren, their children came back to take them away forever.

At a certain point during the dark 1980s, when, by the way, I had some personal problems (even activists have a life, although removed), I felt the need to reevaluate the previous years and test them through the infallible filter of emotions. I had to recognize that during my activism, first in Potere Operaio, and then in the feminist movement, I didn't experience even a single moment of joy. I remember just an immense sense of fatigue. A fatigue that was necessitated in Potere Operaio by a need for justice and in the feminist movement by a sense of dignity and by the urge to acquire an identity. Of course, through the experience of Potere Operaio I acquired some important tools for the interpretation of reality, while, along with interpretive tools the feminist movement gave me and many other women a strength, a solidity, and an equilibrium that no man could ever again shatter. It put the land under our feet. I remember many comrades saying that the feminist movement had saved them from insanity. Yet I couldn't remember a single moment of joy, only a lot of suffering in both experiences. How come?

Regarding the feminist movement, I tried to take everything into account, even the melancholy caused by the shattering of a sense of belonging; after all, as I was saying, I was born and raised in Potere Operaio, and the complete separation of the debate hurt me. The male comrades, who didn't know anything about the issues that were central to the theories we were developing, were left behind, and when we crossed paths with them, they could only articulate very primitive answers. At the same time, we were left in the dark about their internal debate, while we should have had a common discussion about themes that were of increasingly pressing importance. At least I had this need. It would have been important, while maintaining our autonomy, to have some level of common discussion. I don't know how and to what extent it would have been possible in those years in Italy, but I never had any problems communicating with the American comrades, those at *Midnight Notes*, for example. *Midnight Notes* was formed after the emergence of Wages for Housework in the United States and had redirected the debate about and understanding of the development of capitalism across the world on the basis of the centrality of reproductive work. As such, they had already been exposed to our feminist analysis and knew it very well. These comrades are still doing compelling research and organizing significant political actions.

While I was looking for the reasons behind my lack of joy, I was forced to admit that my field of struggle during the 1970s, outside of factories or inside women's houses, failed to move me deeply or let my vital energy flow. These were in fact mainly struggles around the dual problem of *time/money*, even when extended to the issue of the harm done by factories or, within the feminist movement, to the struggles in the hospitals about the conditions of giving birth and about abortion, sex work, violence, and much more. That's why I didn't experience joy (and don't feel it even now, while struggling against the medical abuse of women's bodies). What was missing was something capable of moving me in a positive way, of inspiring a strong imagination capable of unveiling different landscapes. I needed to encounter *different questions and new actors* who longed for and were effectively able to imagine a different world. So for part of the 1980s I went on migrating from room to room in the house of reproduction. Then finally I found *the door that opened into the flower and vegetable garden*: I realized the importance of the *question of the land*. That door was thrown open for me by the new actors I was looking for, the protagonists of indigenous rebellions, the farmers, the fishermen, the people fighting against dams or deforestation, the women of the Global South (but luckily also more and more men and women in industrialized countries). They were all treating the land as a central issue. They were all fighting against its privatization and exploitation and against the destruction of its reproductive powers via the Green Revolution (of which GMO represents the most recent phase), the White Revolution, and the Blue Revolution that all destroy the reproductive flower and the vegetable garden outside of our bodies.

These were the people I was looking for. They were in tune with my research and my feelings, moved me, and gave me joy, because they let me have *a glimpse of a different world, starting from the ways in which life is produced and reproduced; the life of plants, animals, and humans.* The land is not only our source of nourishment, but from the land our bodies gather meaning, sensations, and imagination. Here I crossed path with the voices and actions of Rigoberta Menchú, Vandana Shiva, and Marcos. In 1996, in Rome, working with the Via Campesina network, we organized a conference on food alternatives to that of the United Nations Food and Agriculture Organization (FAO), with Vandana Shiva, Maria Mies, Farida Akter, and many others. It was our first counter-summit, and it was followed by a second one just a few days later.

The third question, therefore, that of the land, finally gave me some joy, emotion, and inspiration. In those years I often travelled to various so-called 'Third World' countries, many times to Africa, finally coming to directly understand what it meant to live there, not only in terms of the harshness of the living conditions but also in the presence of a power capable of evoking a different world. I found that world, because I needed it, because I was looking for it.

The question of the land overwhelmingly forced us to rethink that of reproduction. The reproduction of all of humanity, if we want to think in global terms. In industrialized countries reproduction happens essentially through the work of managing money, not the money of reproductive labor's own remuneration, which was never granted, but the money coming from the husband's paycheck or, in more post-Fordist terms, from the two precarious paychecks of his and her jobs outside of the house. In Third World countries, on the other hand (and they remain Third World even when they enter the First World or vice versa), reproduction happens first of all through the work in the fields. In other words, through farming for sustenance or local consumption, according to a system of collective ownership or small property holdings.

In order to appreciate this issue in all its gravity, both regarding the privatization and the exploitation and destruction of the reproductive powers of land, we need to reconsider what happened during the 1980s. While there's no doubt that in Italy those were years of repression and normalization, in Third World countries they were years of draconian adjustment dictated by the International Monetary Fund (IMF). The adjustment involved all countries, Italy included, but in Third World countries the IMF implemented particularly drastic measures. For instance, the cuts to subsidized staple foods and, most importantly, the strong recommendation to put a price on land, thus privatizing whatever remained of the commons (much of the land in Africa), effectively making self-sustenance agriculture impossible.

I would argue that this measure (made even more dramatic in those years in the context of other typical IMF adjustments) is the major cause of world hunger and of the creation of overpopulation to the extent that the population is increasingly made landless, as also happened five centuries ago. *The more severe the implementation of the adjustment programs of the 1980s became, the more reproduction regressed at a global level.* This project of undermining reproduction was the preparatory phase for neoliberalism. Specifically, by creating poorer living conditions, fewer life expectations, and a level of poverty without precedent, *it provided the prerequisites for the launch of the new globalized economy and for the deployment of neoliberalism worldwide.* This preparatory phase required workers to sacrifice so that corporations can better compete on the global market, the endorsement of new models of productivity with smaller salaries and deregulated working conditions, and the stabilization of an international hierarchy of workers with an ever larger and more dramatic gap, both in the fields of production and reproduction. A wave of suicides among farmers in India started in the 1980s, reaching twenty thousand cases in the last three years. None of them could pay back the debt they had been forced to take on to buy seeds and pesticides. This constitutes nothing less than a genocide! Mass suicides give us a measure of the amount of hunger and death brought upon people by the Green Revolution and by IMF policies.

The 1980s also saw the rise of struggles against these policies (from South America to Africa and Asia), specifically against the expropriation and poisoning of the land and against the distortion and destruction of its reproductive power. The protagonists of these struggles created networks, organizations, and movements that surfaced again in the 1990s as components of the worldwide antiglobalization movement, which was called, not accidentally, "the movement of movements." I believe that the first moment of unification of these different entities, and with it, the launch of the antiglobalization movement, happened at the end of July and beginning of August 1996 in Chiapas, when the Zapatistas called for an intercontinental meeting for "humanity against neoliberalism." The central demand of the Zapatista insurrection was that of the land. There was also the issue of the revision of the article 27 of the Mexican Constitution, as well as the NAFTA provisions. I always say about Marcos that his mere appearance in 1994 freed the horses and opened the fence that kept the Western debate confined and unable to see or take into consideration the question of the land. Activists from all over the world went to Chiapas to offer their cooperation, because Marcos had freed their imagination: he was a man on a horse with a balaclava the color of the earth and grass under his feet. Besides, he could talk poetically.

The land, men, and animals, separated and counterposed in the capitalistic *mechanization* of nature, in the industrialization of agriculture and animal farming, were reunited again, thus unveiling a different landscape.

•

These brief considerations about the centrality of the question of the land within the conversation about reproduction have implications for the issues that we are today coming back to. First of all, any discourse about so-called *'political recomposition,'* if it is to relate to the new global economy, needs to recognize the *centrality of this problem* and find ways to *relate to existing struggles*, because the expulsion of great masses of people from their land is what makes possible the *continuous restoration and reestablishment of a hierarchy inside the working class of the global economy*. Evidently, in fact, only a small portion of these expropriated people will be able to find a job, more often than not an under-the-table job offering minimal compensation. The vast majority are destined to be wiped out by wars, harsh economic conditions, starvation, the spread of contagious diseases, or police and military repression. It is almost like all the political work done all over the world is being continuously thrown into a bottomless pit. We need to start thinking about how to seal that pit.

I started dreaming about the change in the stratification of work that would take place if a considerable portion of the expropriated multitudes were to reclaim their land, and about what would happen to capitalism then. After all, capitalism started with the expropriation of land. That's why I don't understand the criticism of Third Worldism or of Third Worldist tourism. I always tell my students that they should travel to Third World countries, even if only as tourists. Tourism is better than nothing. It is an essential step if we want to understand the relationship between development and underdevelopment in capitalism.

When it comes to militancy, on the other hand, it is very important that we start projects of serious political cooperation, *vitattività*[5] (while also recognizing that there are enough projects for cooperation in Third World countries that are not serious). Serious projects of political cooperation in Chiapas, for instance, led to the construction of an electric turbine and various hospitals. It goes without saying that you need to stay alive in order to fight and not die or be weakened by diseases that would be curable with the proper medical care. Being serious also means showing the locals how to maintain these structures in an uncomplicated and timely manner, so that, once the comrades leave, the structure doesn't become unusable, as happens regularly with less serious cooperative projects. During this work, knowledge is transmitted and hybridized, but most importantly relationships are created that go beyond any single project. It's a part of that political recomposition that, in different ways, is creating opportunities for organization, networks of communication, and cooperation. These are the building blocks of a project, of a cluster of projects that could effectively make a different world possible. It is possible that we are just seeing a glimpse of light coming in, but it's at least something.

Another myth that we need to bust is that 'we should never look back.' Which is like branding as inadequate or backward everything that has been produced, thought, and planned before the most recent evil deeds of capitalism. That is to play the game of the evildoers: they do the deed and we are left with no option but to act in extremely ambivalent conditions. Particularly, when it comes to the question of land and water, this point of view, that you can never go back, doesn't hold. The struggle in Cochabamba, Bolivia, is an exemplary expression of the opposite tactic of standing up and creating a counterpower to reclaim the commons that have been deviously stripped away. To oppose the privatization of water approved by the government to the advantage of a company that was going to have an exclusive monopoly, the *coordinadora* of the city fought hard and won: not only was the water reinstated as commons, but it was reinstated as collectively managed, restoring the organization that the Incas had perfectly devised, which had been maintained up until the attempt at privatization. In the same way, the farmers' organizations in Colombia were able to take back a great amount of land and to recover many species of beans and edible plants, the memory of which had almost been lost. They reactivated ancient farming and culinary traditions, going back to recuperate their spirit and life, as well as opposing the destructive logic of capitalist production. The network of farmers across the continents acting in a unified direction continues to grow.

These are the strong protagonists who have decided to change the world, starting from that essential and too often ignored question: How can we live?
An initiative that was able to meet these demands better than others, even though, in this case, it came from official institutions, was the restitution of the forest to its community in Nepal through a system of state concessions. It turned out to be the best solution to the problem of poverty, because it reinstated that relationship between humans and land that guarantees the

possibility of a sustainable life for both. During the 1980s, there were many actions organized to reclaim the forest as a source of livelihood. Even before then, there was the Green Belt Movement (which reconstituted stretches of forest around cities, where there had previously only been empty spaces). It was started in 1977 by the Kenyan Wangari Maathai, with the idea of 'reforestation for life.'

I welcome the discussion about our need to imagine an alternative science and different machines. I've been thinking the same thing for some time. The ones we use are such carriers of death that it's impossible to be 'against them from the inside.' At this moment, of course, I'm referring basically to farming technology. Right here in Veneto, farmers in the Steiner tradition were able to obtain, through biodynamics and interbreeding, a species of wheat that produces taller sheaves with more grains, which demonstrates yet again that it's possible to create great agricultural progress without resorting to genetic manipulation and thus endangering public health. Many farms are following suit and finding that it's even financially viable.

I have emphasized many times that the problem of the *land* relates to the *destruction of its reproductive powers*. This is a crucial aspect for Third World countries, as well as for us. *It compels us to reopen and redefine the conversation about reproduction. What are we going to do with a paycheck if everything we can buy is toxic?* What will guarantee the continuation of life on earth, money or the access to healthy land and, therefore, its reproductive capacity? What level of extortion and lack of freedom for humanity would be required for us to depend only and exclusively on money for survival? Are the times ripe for starting to make a connection between a guaranteed salary, the availability of *land*, and the safeguarding of its reproductive powers?

A great process of organization has started all over the world, a process in which many questions (like those related to the Green, the White, and the Blue Revolutions and to the expropriation of land and the way it's used) require the demolition of falsehoods and the promotion of truth about the new and continuous monstrosities-miracles. These questions require both collective and solitary work in order to bring the monsters out into the light of day, unmask them, and get rid of them. At the same time, they require a willingness to discover or recover alternative knowledge and a different kind of technology. The big changes, in my opinion, are being set in motion by the strong protagonists who are figuring out how life is produced and reproduced: by the movements of farmers, fishermen, and indigenous people, by networks of women who pose the problem of the relationship with the land as central, and by new inventors. We are not dealing with isolated campaigns anymore, with people struggling to connect and be heard, as was the case several years ago, because of a certain deafness or a stale default way of dealing with these issues on the part of the left and militants in industrialized countries. On the contrary, intercontinental communication and an interconnection between industrialized and nonindustrialized countries have been established with a convergence of themes and an efficacy on a planetary level. Against the expropriation and devastation of the land, rivers, and oceans, the new protagonists said *ya basta* and are devising *key points* for an *alternative project*, for the establishment of a different kind of relationship with the flower and vegetable gardens of earth.

Notes

Lecture given during the seminar organized at the occupied Rialto, June 1–2, 2002, for the launching of Guido Borio, Francesca Pozzi, and Gigi Roggero, ed. *Anteriore* (Rome: DeriveApprodi, 2002).

1   Translator's note: I left this term in the original Italian because in English it would be something like *life activists*, which in the specific UK/American context sounds like a reference to the pro-life movement. The word, as explained by Dalla Costa within the text, is used to describe activists "who operate in the sphere of the production and reproduction of life."

2   This research is available for consultation at the *Archivio di Lotta Femminista per il salario al lavoro domestico: donazione Mariarosa Dalla Costa*, at the Civic Library in Padua, accessed August 6, 2018, http://www.padovanet.it/sites/default/files/attachment/C_1_Allegati_20187_Allegato.pdf.

3   Leopoldina Fortunati.

4   Life-bringing activities.

Bibliography

AA. VV. *Donne e diritto*, Milan: Gulliver, 1978.

Abbà, Luisa et al. *La coscienza di sfruttata*. Milan: Mazzotta Editore, 1972.

Bacchet, D. "Indagine sul lavoro degli stranieri in Italia con particolare riferimento alla Lombardia e al Veneto." PhD diss., University of Padua, 1978–1979.

Ballestrero, Maria Vittoria. *Dalla tutela alla parità: la legislazione italiana sul lavoro delle donne*. Bologna: Il Mulino, 1979.

Belforte, Silvia, and Martino Ciatti. *Il fondo del barile*. Turin: La salamandra, 1980.

Berti, L. et al. *Crisi delle politiche e politicize nella isi*. Naples: Pironti, 1981.

Beynon, Huw. *Working for Ford*. Harmondsworth: Penguin Books, 1973.

Biermann, Pieke. *Wir sind Frauen 'wie andere auch'! Prostituierte und ihre Kämpfe*. Reinbek: Rowohlt, 1980.

Bock, Gisela. "Frauenbewegung und Frauenuniversität: Die politische Bedeutung." In, *Frauen und Wissenschaft*. Edited by Gruppe Berliner Dozentinnen. Berlin: Courage Verlag, 1977.

Bock, Gisela, and Barbara Duden. "Arbeit aus Liebe—Liebe als Arbeit: Zur Entstchung der Hausarbeit im Kapitalismus." In *Frauen und Wissenschaft*.

Bologna, Sergio. *Irrompe la quinta generazione operaia*. In "Dossier Lavoro."

———. *La tribù delle talpe*. In Primo Maggio, *La tribù delle talpe*.

Boone, Gladys. *The Women's Trade Union Leagues in Great Britain and in the United States of America*. New York: AMS Press, 1968 [1942].

Borio, Guido, Francesca Pozzi, and Gigi Roggero, ed. *Anteriore*. Rome: DeriveApprodi, 2002.

Boston Women's Health Collective. *Our Bodies, Ourselves*. New York: Simon and Schuster, 1971.

Bové, José, and François Dufour. *The World Is Not for Sale: Farmers against Junk Food*. Translated by Anna de Casparis. London: Verso, 2001.

Burgos, Elisabeth. *Mi chiamo Rigoberta Menchú*. Florence: Giunti, 1990.

Calabrò, Anna Rita, and Laura Grasso, ed. *Dal movimento femminista al femminismo diffuso*. Milan: Franco Angeli, 1985.

Campennì, Antonino. *L'egemonia breve: La parabola del salariato in fabbrica a Crotone*. Soveria Mannelli: Rubbettino, 2002.

"Car Plants without Mass Disaffection." *Financial Times*, March 12, 1973.

Caritas. *Dossier statistico immigrazione 2003*. Rome: Edizioni Nuova Anterem, 2003.

Castels, Stephen, and Godula Kosack. *Immigrant Workers and Class Structure in Western Europe*. London: Oxford University Press, 1973.

Chafe, William Henry. *The American Woman: Her Changing Social, Economic, and Political Roles, 1920–1970*. 2nd Edition. New York: Oxford University Press, 1974.

Cipriani, Franca. "Proletariato del Maghreb e capitale europeo." In Serafini, *L'operaio multinazionale in Europa*.

"City Opens Computer Center to Check on Eligibility of Welfare Recipients." *New York Times*, February 28, 1975.

Clark, Alice. *Working Life of Women in Seventeenth Century England*. London: Frank Cass Co., 1968.

Cleaver, Harry. "Learning, Understanding and Appropriating." Accessed July 26, 2018. https://la.utexas.edu/users/hcleaver/Appropriation.htm.

———. "On Schoolwork and the Struggle against It." Accessed July 26, 2018. https://www.google.com/search?q=Schoolwork+and+the+Struggle+Against+It&oq=Schoolwork+and+the+Struggle+Against+It&aqs=chrome..69i57j0l2.432j0j4&sourceid=chrome&ie=UTF-8.

———. *Reading* Capital *Politically*. Austin: University of Texas Press, 1979.

———. "Self-valorization in Mariarosa Dalla Costa's 'Women and the Subversion of the Community.'" Accessed July 26, 1018. https://la.utexas.edu/users/hcleaver/357k/HMCDallaCostaSelfvalorization2.htm.

Clough, Shepard Bancroft. *The Economic History of Modern Italy*. New York: Columbia University Press, 1964.

Collettivo internazionale femminista. ed. *Aborto di stato: strage delle innocenti,* Venice: Marsilio Editori, 1976.

———, ed. *8 marzo 1974: giornata internazionale di lotta delle donne*. Venice: Marsilio Editori, 1975.

———. *Le operaie della casa*. Venice: Marsilio Editori, 1975.

Comitato di Lotta delle Ragazze Madri. *Ragazze madri in lotta: documenti e testimonianze delle ragazze madri della Casa della Madre e del Fanciullo di via Pusiano 22*. Milan: self-published, 1973.

Coordinamento Nazionale dei Gruppi e Comitati per il Sld. *Lotta delle donne per la salute*. Reports from the National Feminist Conference, April 29–May 1, 1978 (mimeograph). Rome: Institute of Psychology, 1978.

Courrière, Yves. *La guerre d'Algérie, Tome II: Le temps des léopards*, Paris: Fayard, 1969.

Cox, Nicole, and Silvia Federici. "Counterplanning from the Kitchen." *Wages for Housework: A Perspective on Capital and the Left*. Bristol, UK: Falling Wall Press, 1969.

D'Agostino, F., ed. *Operaismo e centralità operaia*. Rome: Editori Riuniti, 1978.

Dalla Costa, Giovanna Franca. *The Work of Love: Unpaid Housework, Poverty and Sexual Violence at the Dawn of the 21st Century*. Brooklyn, NY: Autonomedia, 2008.

Dalla Costa, Mariarosa. "Emergenza femminista negli anni '70 e percorsi di rifiuto sottesi." In Guizzardi and Sterpi, *La società italiana*, 363–75.

———. "Emigrazione, immigrazione e composizione di classe in Italia negli anni '70." *Economia e lavoro* 4 (October–December 1981).

————. *Family Welfare and the State: Between Progressivism and the New Deal.* Brooklyn, NY: Common Notions, 2015.

————, ed. *Gynocide: Hysterectomy, Capitalist Patriarchy and the Medical Abuse of Women.* Brooklyn, NY: Autonomedia, 2007.

————. "The Native in Us, the Land We Belong To." *Common Sense* 23 (Winter 1998).

————. *Our Mother Ocean: Enclosure, Commons, and the Global Fishermen's Movement.* Brooklyn, NY: Common Notions, 2014.

————. "Percorsi femminili e politica della riproduzione della forza lavoro negli anni '70." *La Critica Sociologica* 61(1982): 50–73.

————. "A proposito del welfare." *Primo Maggio* 9–10 (Winter 1977–1978).

————. "Quartiere, scuola e fabbrica dal punto di vista della donna." In *L'Offensiva.* Turin: Musolini, 1972.

————. "Riproduzione e emigrazione." In Serafini, *L'operaio multinazionale in Europa.*

————. "'Rustic and Ethical,' Immaterial and Affective Labor: Explored." *Ephemera: Theory and Politics in Organization* 7, no. 1 (March 2007).

————. "La sostenibilidad de la reproducciòn: de la luchas por la renta a la salvaguardia de la vida." In Laboratorio feminista, *Transformaciones del trabajo desde una perspectiva feminista: producciòn, reproduccion, deseo, consumo.*

————. "To Whom Does the Body of This Woman Belong?" *Commoner* 13 (2009). Accessed September 22, 2018. http://www.commoner.org.uk/wp-content/uploads/2010/10/dallacosta_mexico_paper.pdf.

————. "Women's Autonomy and Remuneration of Care Work in the New Emergencies." *Commoner* 13 (2009). Accessed September 22, 2018. http://www.commoner.org.uk/wp-content/uploads/2010/10/dallacosta_mexico_paper2.pdf.

Dalla Costa, Mariarosa, and Monica Chilese. *Our Mother Ocean: Enclosures, Commons and the Global Fishermen's Movement,* Brooklyn, NY: Common Notions, 2014.

Dalla Costa, Mariarosa, and Giovanna Franca Dalla Costa, ed. *Paying the Price: Women and the Politics of International Economic Strategy.* London: Zed Books, 1995.

————, ed. *Women Development and Labor of Reproduction: Struggles and Movements,* Trenton, NJ: Africa World Press, 1995.

Dalla Costa, Mariarosa, and Dario De Bortoli. "For Another Agriculture and Another Food Policy." *Commoner* 10 (Spring–Summer 2005).

Dalla Costa, Mariarosa, and Leopoldina Fortunati. *Brutto ciao: direzioni di marcia delle donne negli ultimi 30 anni.* Rome: Edizioni delle donne, 1977.

Dalla Costa, Mariarosa, and Selma James. *The Power of Women and the Subversion of the Community.* Bristol, UK: Falling Wall Press, 1972.

de Fréminville, Bernard. *La ragione del più forte.* Milan: Feltrinelli,1979.

Del Boca, D., and M. Turvani. *Famiglia e mercato del lavoro.* Bologna: Il Mulino, 1979.

Domenighetti, G., and A. Casabianca. "Rate of Hysterectomy Is Lower among Female Doctors and Lawyers' Wives." *Lancet,* December 24–31, 1988.

Domenighetti, G., P. Luraschi, A. Casabianca, F. Gutzwiller, A. Spinelli, and F. Repetto. "Effect of Information Campaign by the Mass Media on Hysterectomy Rates." *Lancet*, December 24–31, 1988.

Donnison, Jean. *Midwives and Medical Men*. New York: Schocken Books, 1977.

"Dossier Lavoro." Supplement in *Il Manifesto* 248.

Doubleday, Thomas. *The True Law of Population*. London: Effingham Wilson, Royal Exchange, 1842.

"Ecco la generazione 'No figli.'" La Repubblica, August 28, 2006.

Edmond, Wendy, and Suzie Fleming, ed. *All Work and No Pay: Women, Housework and the Wages Due*. Bristol, UK: Falling Wall Press, 1975.

Ehrenreich, Barbara, and Deirdre English. *Complaints and Disorders: The Sexual Politics of Sickness*. New York: The Feminist Press, 1973.

——. *Witches, Midwives, and Nurses: A History of Women Healers*. New York: The Feminist Press, 1973.

Federici, Silvia. *Caliban and the Witch: Women, the Body and Primitive Accumulation*, Brooklyn, NY: Autonomedia, 2004.

——. "The Great Witch-Hunt." *The Maine Scholar* 1, no.1. (1988).

——. *Wages against Housework*. Bristol, UK: Falling Wall Press, 1975.

Federici, Silvia, and Leopoldina Fortunati. *Il grande Calibano: storia del corpo sociale ribelle nella prima fase del capitale*. Milan: Franco Angeli, 1984.

"Les femmes au foyer." *Le Nouvel Observateur*, April 10, 1973.

Ferrari Bravo, L., and A. Serafini. *Stato e sottosviluppo*. 2nd edition. Milan: Feltrinelli, 1979.

"Fiat 1980." *Quaderno di Controinformazione* 3. Supplement in *Controinformazione* 19, 1980.

"Fiat: robotizzazione ristrutturazione e riformismo." *Magazzino* 2 (May 1979).

Fleming, Denna Frank. *The Cold War and Its Origins*. New York: Doubleday, 1961.

Fleming, Suzie. *The Family Allowance Under Attack*. Bristol UK: Falling Wall Press, 1973.

Fortunati, Leopoldina. *The Arcane of Reproduction: Housework, Prostitution, Labor and Capital*. Brooklyn, NY: Autonomedia, 1995.

——. "La famiglia verso la ricostruzione." In M. Dalla Costa and Fortunati, *Brutto ciao*.

——. "Sesso come valore d'uso per il valore." In Federici and Fortunati, *Il grande Calibano*.

Gambino, Ferruccio. "Alcuni aspetti della erosione della contrattazione collectiva in Italia." In Guizzardi and Sterpi, *La società italiana, crisi di un sistema*.

George, Susan. *The Debt Boomerang*. Boulder, CO: Westview Press, 1992.

——. *A Fate Worse Than Debt*. London: Penguin Books, 1988.

Gobbi, Romolo. *Operai e resistenza*. Turin: Musolini, 1973.

Goode, William J. *World Revolution and Family Patterns*. New York: The Free Press, 1970.

Gornick, Vivian, and Barbara K. Moran, ed. *Women in Sexist Society*. New York: Basic Books, 1971.

Graziosi, Andrea. *La ristrutturazione nelle grandi fabbriche, 1973–1976*. Milan: Feltrinelli, 1979.

Gruppo femminista per il salario al lavoro domestico di Ferrara. *Dietro la normalitá del part: lotta all'ospedale di Ferrara.* Venice: Marsilio Editori, 1978.

Guizzardi, Gustavo, and Serevino Sterpi, ed. *La società italiana, crisi di un sistema.* Milan: Franco Angeli, 1981.

Hands Off Our Family Allowances, What We Need Is Money. London: Crest Press, 1973.

Harrison, Lieta. *La donna sposata: mille mogli accusano.* Milan: Feltrinelli, 1972.

Her Majesty's Stationery Office, Sixth Report from the Expenditure Committee, Session 1972–73: The Employment of Women.

Homze, Edward L. *Foreign Labor in Nazi Germany.* Princeton, NJ: University of Princeton Press, 1967.

IRER. *Lavoro femminile e condizione famigliare.* Milan: Franco Angeli, 1980.

ISIS Women's International Information and Communication Service. "Document 01467." *International Bulletin.* International Tribunal on Crimes against Women, Brussels, March 4–8, 1976.

Issoco. "Emigrazione nell'Europa del Mec," Rome, July 10, 1973.

ISTAT (lstituto Centrale di Statistica). *Annuario Statistico Italiano.* Rome: Italian National Statistics Institute, 1972–1985.

Joint Economic Committee. *Studies in Public Welfare.* Paper no. 12, part 1, "The Family, Poverty and Welfare Programs: Factors Influencing Family Instability." Washington, DC: U.S. Government Printing Office, 1973.

Jourdan, Clara. *Insieme contro: esperienze dei consultori femministi.* Milan: La Salamandra, 1976.

Keynes, John Maynard. *Essays in Persuasion.* New York: W.W. Norton & Co., 1963.

———. *The General Theory of Employment, Interest, and Money.* New York: Harcourt, Brace and World, 1964.

———. "Saving and Spending." In *Essays in Persuasion.*

Kindleberger, Charles P. *Lo sviluppo economico europeo ed il mercato del lavoro.* Milan: Etas Kompass, 1968.

Kremen, Bennett. "Lordstown—Searching for a Better Way of Work." *New York Times,* September 9, 1973.

Laboratorio feminista. *Transformaciones del trabajo desde una perspectiva feminista: producciòn, reproduccion, deseo, consumo.* Madrid: Terradenadie Ediciones, 2006.

Lantier, François. "Le travail et la formation des femmes en Europe: Incidences de la planification de l'éducation et du changement technologique sur l'accès aux emplois et aux carriers." *La Documentation Française, Bibliothèque du Centre d'Études et de Recherches sur les Qualifications* 4 (October 1972).

Lanzardo, Liliana. *Classe operaia e partito comunista alla Fiat: la strategia della collaborazione, 1945–1949.* Turin: Einaudi, 1971.

Latilla, N. *Il lavoro domestico.* Rome: Buffetti, 1980.

"Il lavoro a domicilio." *Quaderni di rassegna sindacale* 11, no. 44–45 (September–December 1973).

"Lavoro donna/donna lavoro." *Il Manifesto,* June 1980.

Lavoro femminile e condizione famigliare. Milan: Franco Angeli, 1980.

Livi Bacci, Massimo. "Il declino della fecondità della popolazione italiana nell ultimo secolo." *Statistica* 25, no. 3 (1965).

Lotta Femminista. "Vogliamo decidere noi: donne, referendum, divorzio." *Document* 275 (March 1974).

M'Rabet, Fadéla. *Les Algériennes*. Paris: Maspero, 1969.

Marazzi, Christian. *Il posto dei calzini*. Bellinzona: Edizioni Casagrande, 1994.

Marshall, Alfred. *Principles of Economics*. London: Macmillan & Co., 1920.

Marx, Karl. *Capital: A Critique of Political Economy*. Vol. 1. Harmondsworth: Penguin Books, 1976.

———. "Critique of Hegel's Philosophy of the State." In *Writings of the Young Marx on Philosophy and Society*. Edited and translated by Loyd D. Easton and Kurt H. Guddat. Garden City, NY: Doubleday, 1967.

———. *Economic and Philosophic Manuscripts of 1844*. Moscow: Progress Publishers, 1959.

Masry, Yussef El. *Il dramma sessuale della donna araba*. Milan: Edizioni di Comunità, 1964.

Mattera, Philip. "National Liberation, Socialism and the Struggle against Work: The Case of Vietnam." *Zerowork: Political Materials* 2 (Fall 1977): 71–89.

Mauro, Vincenzo. *Lotte dei contadini in Calabria*. Milan: Sapere, 1973.

May, M. Pia. "Mercato del lavoro femminile: espulsione o occupazione nascosta femminile." *Inchiesta* 3, no. 9 (January–March 1973): 27–37.

Il mercato del laboro comunitario e la politica migratoria italiana 23–24 (1971).

Merli, Stefano. *Proletariato di fabbrica e capitalismo industrial: il caso italiano, 1880–1900*. Florence: La Nuova Italia, 1973.

Michel, A. "La donna a repentaglio nel sistema di guerra." *Bozze* 2 (March–April 1987).

Millett, Kate. "Prostitution: A Quartet for Female Voices." In Gornick and Moran, *Women in Sexist Society*.

Milwaukee County Welfare Rights Organization. *Welfare Mothers Speak Out: We Ain't Gonna Shuffle Anymore*. New York: W.W. Norton & Co., 1972.

Ministère de la Santé. *Tableaux d l'economie algerienne*. Algiers: 1970.

Montaldi, Danilo. *Militanti politici di base*. Turin: Einaudi, 1971.

Mortara, Giorgio. "L'Italia nella rivoluzione demografica, 1861–1961." *Annuali di Statistica*, anno 94, serie VIII, vol. 17 (1965).

Moudjahid, July 22, 1972.

Mouriaux, Marie-Françoise. *L'emploi en France depuis 1945*. Paris: Librairie Armand Colin, 1972.

Movimentodi lotta femminista di Ferrara. *Basta Tacere: testimonianze di donne: parto, aborto, gravidanza, maternità*. Self-published, nd.

Moynihan, Daniel. *The Politics of a Guaranteed Income*. New York: Vintage Books, 1973.

Mungiello Rossana. "Segregation of Migrants in the Labor Market in Italy: The Case of Female Migrants from Eastern European Countries Working in the Sector of Care and Assistance for the Elderly: First Results of an Empirical Study Carried Out in Padova." In *Zu Wessen Diensten? Frauenarbeit zwsischen Care-Drain und Outsourcing*. Zurich: Frauenrat fur Aussenpolitik, 2005.

Negri, Antonio. *Dall'operaio massa all'operaio sociale*. Milan: Multhipla Edizioni, 1979.

———. *Movimenti nell'impero*. Milan: Raffaello Cortina Editore, 2006.

———. *Le Pouvoir constituant: Essai sur les alternatives de la modernité*. Paris: Presses Universitaires de France, 1992.

———. *The Savage Anomaly: The Power of Spinoza's Metaphysics and Politics*. Minneapolis: University of Minnesota Press, 1991.

Nevins, Allan. *Ford: The Time, the Man, the Company*. New York: Charles Scribner's Sons, 1954.

"L'offensiva." *Quaderni di Lotta Femminista* 1. Turin: Musolini Editore, 1972.

Le operaie della casa oo (November-December 1975–January-February 1976).

Organisation for Economic Cooperation and Development. *Labour Force Statistics*. Paris: 1970.

Pellarin, Manuela. *Porto Marghera—gli ultimi fuochi*. Veneto: Autonomia operaia nel, 2004.

"Il personale è politico." *Quaderni di Lotta Femminista* 2. Turin: Musolini Editore, 1973.

Petroli, Eleanora, and Micaela Trucco. *Emigrazione e mercato del lavoro in Europa occidentale*. Milan: Franco Angeli, 1981.

Piaggio, L.C. *Avanti un'altra: donne e ginecologi a confronto*. Milan: La Salamandra, 1976.

The Population Council. "Country Profiles: France." New York, May 1972, 8.

Porta, Carla. *Senza distinzione di sesso, guida pratica al nuovo diritto di famiglia*. Milan: Sonzogno, 1975.

Pressat, Roland. *Population*. Harmondsworth: Penguin Books, 1973.

Primo Maggio. *La tribù delle talpe*. Edited by Sergio Bologna. Milan: Feltrinelli, 1978.

Ramirez, Bruno. "Interview with Guido Viale." *Radical America* 7, no. 4–5 (July–October 1973): 131–92.

Re, Gigliola, and Graziella De Rossi. *L'occupazione fu bellissima*. Rome: Edizioni delle donne, 1976.

Remiddi, Laura. *I nostri diritti: manuale giuridico per le donne*. Milan: Feltrinelli, 1976.

Riasanovsky, Nicholas Valentine. *A History of Russia*. New York: Oxford University Press, 1963.

Romeo, Rosario. *Breve storia della grande industria in Italia*. Bologna: Cappelli, 1973.

Romita, Giuseppe. *Dalla monarchia alla Repubblica*. Pisa: Editore Nistri-Lischi, 1954.

Ross, Heather. *Poverty: Women and Children Last*. Washington, DC: Urban Institute, 1976.

Rovira, Guiomar. *Donne di mais: voci di donne dal Chiapas*. Rome: Manifestolibri, 1997.

Sadler, Michael T. *The Law of Population*. London: C.J.G. and F. Rivington, 1830.

Schopenhauer, Arthur. "On Learning and the Learned." In *Parega and Paralipomena: Short Philosophical Essays*. Vol. 2. Oxford: Clarendon Press, 1974.

————. "On Reading and Books." In *Parega and Paralipomena: Short Philosophical Essays.* Vol. 2.

Serafini, Alessandro, ed. *L'operaio multinazionale in Europa.* Milan: Feltrinelli, 1974.

Shiva, Vandana. *Staying Alive: Women, Ecology and Survival in India.* London: Zed Books, 1990.

Smuts, R.W. *Women and Work in America.* New York: Schoken Books, 1959.

"Social Security Numbers Will Track Runaway Fathers." *New York Times,* April 7, 1976.

"Studi Emigrazione." *Regioni e migrazioni* 22 (1971).

Sullerot, Evelyne. *La donna e il lavoro.* Milan: Etas-Kompass, 1973.

————. *Histoire et sociologie du travail féminin.* Paris: Editions Gonthier, 1968.

Sutton, C. "Hysterectomy: A Historical Perspective." In Baillière's Clinical Obstetrics and Gynecology. London: Baillière Tindall, 1997.

Thomas, Marlo, and Friends. *Free to Be . . . You and Me.* Bell Records, 1972.

Thomson, David. *Europe since Napoleon.* New York: Alfred A. Knopf, 1957.

"Les travailleurs immigrés parlent." *Les Cahiers du Centre d'Études Socialistes* 94–98 (September–December 1969).

"A Twisted Attack on Day Care." *Newsday,* January 30, 1976.

Ulla par Ulla. Montréal: Editions Sélect, 1977.

United Nations. "Nairobi Forward Looking Strategies for the Advancement of Women." In *Report of the World Conference to Review and Appraise the Achievements of the United Nations Decade for Women.*

————. *Report of the World Conference to Review and Appraise the Achievements of the United Nations Decade for Women: Equality, Development and Peace, Nairobi, July 15–26, 1985.* New York: United Nations Publications, 1985.

United Nations Economic Commission for Europe, Census 2000.

"Vietnam, la famiglia nel diritto vietnamita." *Donne e politica* 4, no. 19 (October 1973).

Wandersee, Winifred D. *Women's Work and Family Values, 1920–1940.* Cambridge, MA: Harvard University Press, 1981.

"Welfare." *Robert MacNeil Report,* July 7, 1976.

West, Stanley, and Paula Dranov. *The Hysterectomy Hoax.* New York: Doubleday, 1994.

Willis, F. Roy. *Europe in the Global Era: 1939 to Present.* New York: Dodd, Mead & Co., 1968.

"Women's Action Agenda 21." In *World Women's Congress for a Healthy Planet, Official Report, November 8–12, 1991, Miami, Florida.* New York: United Nations, 1991.

Wright, Steve. *Storming Heaven: Class Composition and Struggle in Italian Autonomist Marxism.* London: Pluto Press, 2002.

Yoder, Dale. *Labor Economics and Labor Problems.* New York: McGraw-Hill Book Company, 1933.

Zanetti, Anna Maria, ed. *La senatrice: Lina Merlin, un "pensiero operante."* Venice: Marsilio, 2006.

Zumaglino, Piera. *Femminismi a Torino.* Milan: Franco Angeli, 1996.

Index

"Passim" (literally "scattered") indicates intermittent discussion of a topic over a cluster of pages.

About the Authors

Mariarosa Dalla Costa is an influential Italian Marxist feminist and activist. She is the coauthor, with Selma James, of the classic feminist text, *The Power of Women and the Subversion of the Community* (1972), which launched the "domestic labor debate" in the early 1970s by re-defining housework as reproductive labor necessary to the functioning of capitalism and as work that has been rendered invisible by its removal from the wage relation. A member of Lotta Femminista, Dalla Costa developed her analysis of reproductive labor as an immanent critique of Italian workerism. Her intellectual work and political activity contributed immensely to the international Wages for Housework campaign. Her research has been translated into multiple languages and published in journals, edited collections, and monographs.

Harry Cleaver is an American scholar, Marxist theoretician, and professor emeritus at the University of Texas at Austin. He is best known as the author of *Reading* Capital *Politically* (1979), an autonomist reading of Karl Marx's *Capital*.

Camille Barbagallo is a feminist activist and researcher. She is an organizer with the Women's Strike Assembly—UK. Her research explores how the reproduction of labor power is valued, what it costs, and who pays the bill. She is the coeditor, with Silvia Federici, of "'Care Work' and the Commons," *The Commoner* 15 (Winter 2012).

ABOUT PM PRESS

PM Press was founded at the end of 2007 by a small collection of folks with decades of publishing, media, and organizing experience. PM Press co-conspirators have published and distributed hundreds of books, pamphlets, CDs, and DVDs. Members of PM have founded enduring book fairs, spearheaded victorious tenant organizing campaigns, and worked closely with bookstores, academic conferences, and even rock bands to deliver political and challenging ideas to all walks of life. We're old enough to know what we're doing and young enough to know what's at stake.

We seek to create radical and stimulating fiction and nonfiction books, pamphlets, T-shirts, visual and audio materials to entertain, educate, and inspire you. We aim to distribute these through every available channel with every available technology—whether that means you are seeing anarchist classics at our bookfair stalls, reading our latest vegan cookbook at the café, downloading geeky fiction e-books, or digging new music and timely videos from our website.

PM Press is always on the lookout for talented and skilled volunteers, artists, activists, and writers to work with. If you have a great idea for a project or can contribute in some way, please get in touch.

PM Press
PO Box 23912
Oakland, CA 94623
www.pmpress.org

PM Press in Europe
europe@pmpress.org
www.pmpress.org.uk

FRIENDS OF PM PRESS

These are indisputably momentous times—the financial system is melting down globally and the Empire is stumbling. Now more than ever there is a vital need for radical ideas.

In the years since its founding—and on a mere shoestring— PM Press has risen to the formidable challenge of publishing and distributing knowledge and entertainment for the struggles ahead. With over 300 releases to date, we have published an impressive and stimulating array of literature, art, music, politics, and culture. Using every available medium, we've succeeded in connecting those hungry for ideas and information to those putting them into practice.

Friends of PM allows you to directly help impact, amplify, and revitalize the discourse and actions of radical writers, filmmakers, and artists. It provides us with a stable foundation from which we can build upon our early successes and provides a much-needed subsidy for the materials that can't necessarily pay their own way. You can help make that happen—and receive every new title automatically delivered to your door once a month—by joining as a Friend of PM Press. And, we'll throw in a free T-shirt when you sign up.

Here are your options:

- **$30 a month** Get all books and pamphlets plus 50% discount on all webstore purchases

- **$40 a month** Get all PM Press releases (including CDs and DVDs) plus 50% discount on all webstore purchases

- **$100 a month** Superstar—Everything plus PM merchandise, free downloads, and 50% discount on all webstore purchases

For those who can't afford $30 or more a month, we have **Sustainer Rates** at $15, $10 and $5. Sustainers get a free PM Press T-shirt and a 50% discount on all purchases from our website.

Your Visa or Mastercard will be billed once a month, until you tell us to stop. Or until our efforts succeed in bringing the revolution around. Or the financial meltdown of Capital makes plastic redundant. Whichever comes first.

Revolution at Point Zero: Housework, Reproduction, and Feminist Struggle

Silvia Federici

ISBN: 978-1-60486-333-8
$15.95   208 pages

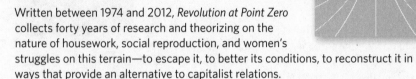

Written between 1974 and 2012, *Revolution at Point Zero* collects forty years of research and theorizing on the nature of housework, social reproduction, and women's struggles on this terrain—to escape it, to better its conditions, to reconstruct it in ways that provide an alternative to capitalist relations.

Indeed, as Federici reveals, behind the capitalist organization of work and the contradictions inherent in "alienated labor" is an explosive ground zero for revolutionary practice upon which are decided the daily realities of our collective reproduction.

Beginning with Federici's organizational work in the Wages for Housework movement, the essays collected here unravel the power and politics of wide but related issues including the international restructuring of reproductive work and its effects on the sexual division of labor, the globalization of care work and sex work, the crisis of elder care, the development of affective labor, and the politics of the commons.

"Finally we have a volume that collects the many essays that over a period of four decades Silvia Federici has written on the question of social reproduction and women's struggles on this terrain. While providing a powerful history of the changes in the organization of reproductive labor, Revolution at Point Zero *documents the development of Federici's thought on some of the most important questions of our time: globalization, gender relations, the construction of new commons."*
—Mariarosa Dalla Costa, author of *Women and the Subversion of the Community*

"As the academy colonizes and tames women's studies, Silvia Federici speaks the experience of a generation of women for whom politics was raw, passionately lived, often in the shadow of an uncritical Marxism. She spells out the subtle violence of housework and sexual servicing, the futility of equating waged work with emancipation, and the ongoing invisibility of women's reproductive labors. Under neoliberal globalization women's exploitation intensifies—in land enclosures, in forced migration, in the crisis of elder care. With ecofeminist thinkers and activists, Federici argues that protecting the means of subsistence now becomes the key terrain of struggle, and she calls on women North and South to join hands in building new commons."
—Ariel Salleh, author of *Ecofeminism as Politics: Nature, Marx, and the Postmodern*

Re-enchanting the World: Feminism and the Politics of the Commons

Silvia Federici
with a Foreword by Peter Linebaugh

ISBN: 978-1-62963-569-9
$19.95   240 pages

Silvia Federici is one of the most important contemporary theorists of capitalism and feminist movements. In this collection of her work spanning over twenty years, she provides a detailed history and critique of the politics of the commons from a feminist perspective. In her clear and combative voice, Federici provides readers with an analysis of some of the key issues and debates in contemporary thinking on this subject.

Drawing on rich historical research, she maps the connections between the previous forms of enclosure that occurred with the birth of capitalism and the destruction of the commons and the "new enclosures" at the heart of the present phase of global capitalist accumulation. Considering the commons from a feminist perspective, this collection centers on women and reproductive work as crucial to both our economic survival and the construction of a world free from the hierarchies and divisions capital has planted in the body of the world proletariat. Federici is clear that the commons should not be understood as happy islands in a sea of exploitative relations but rather autonomous spaces from which to challenge the existing capitalist organization of life and labor.

"Silvia Federici's theoretical capacity to articulate the plurality that fuels the contemporary movement of women in struggle provides a true toolbox for building bridges between different features and different people."
—Massimo De Angelis, professor of political economy, University of East London

"Silvia Federici's work embodies an energy that urges us to rejuvenate struggles against all types of exploitation and, precisely for that reason, her work produces a common: a common sense of the dissidence that creates a community in struggle."
—Maria Mies, coauthor of *Ecofeminism*

Witches, Witch-Hunting, and Women

Silvia Federici

ISBN: 978-1-62963-568-2
$14.00   120 pages

We are witnessing a new surge of interpersonal and institutional violence against women, including new witch hunts. This surge of violence has occurred alongside an expansion of capitalist social relations. In this new work that revisits some of the main themes of *Caliban and the Witch*, Silvia Federici examines the root causes of these developments and outlines the consequences for the women affected and their communities. She argues that, no less than the witch hunts in sixteenth- and seventeenth-century Europe and the "New World," this new war on women is a structural element of the new forms of capitalist accumulation. These processes are founded on the destruction of people's most basic means of reproduction. Like at the dawn of capitalism, what we discover behind today's violence against women are processes of enclosure, land dispossession, and the remolding of women's reproductive activities and subjectivity.

As well as an investigation into the causes of this new violence, the book is also a feminist call to arms. Federici's work provides new ways of understanding the methods in which women are resisting victimization and offers a powerful reminder that reconstructing the memory of the past is crucial for the struggles of the present.

"It is good to think with Silvia Federici, whose clarity of analysis and passionate vision come through in essays that chronicle enclosure and dispossession, witch-hunting and other assaults against women, in the present, no less than the past. It is even better to act armed with her insights."
—Eileen Boris, Hull Professor of Feminist Studies, University of California, Santa Barbara

"Silvia Federici's new book offers a brilliant analysis and forceful denunciation of the violence directed towards women and their communities. Her focus moves between women criminalized as witches both at the dawn of capitalism and in contemporary globalization. Federici has updated the material from her well-known book Caliban and the Witch *and brings a spotlight to the current resistance and alternatives being pursued by women and their communities through struggle."*
—Massimo De Angelis, professor of political economy, University of East London

Birth Work as Care Work: Stories from Activist Birth Communities

Alana Apfel, with a foreword by Loretta J. Ross, preface by Victoria Law, and introduction by Silvia Federici

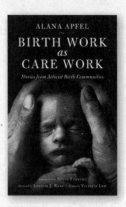

ISBN: 978-1-62963-151-6
$14.95   128 pages

Birth Work as Care Work presents a vibrant collection of stories and insights from the front lines of birth activist communities. The personal has once more become political, and birth workers, supporters, and doulas now find themselves at the fore of collective struggles for freedom and dignity.

The author, herself a scholar and birth justice organiser, provides a unique platform to explore the political dynamics of birth work; drawing connections between birth, reproductive labor, and the struggles of caregiving communities today. Articulating a politics of care work in and through the reproductive process, the book brings diverse voices into conversation to explore multiple possibilities and avenues for change.

At a moment when agency over our childbirth experiences is increasingly centralized in the hands of professional elites, *Birth Work as Care Work* presents creative new ways to reimagine the trajectory of our reproductive processes. Most importantly, the contributors present new ways of thinking about the entire life cycle, providing a unique and creative entry point into the essence of all human struggle—the struggle over the reproduction of life itself.

"I love this book, all of it. The polished essays and the interviews with birth workers dare to take on the deepest questions of human existence."
—Carol Downer, cofounder of the Feminist Women's Heath Centers of California and author of *A Woman's Book of Choices*

"This volume provides theoretically rich, practical tools for birth and other care workers to collectively and effectively fight capitalism and the many intersecting processes of oppression that accompany it. Birth Work as Care Work forcefully and joyfully reminds us that the personal is political, a lesson we need now more than ever."
—Adrienne Pine, author of *Working Hard, Drinking Hard: On Violence and Survival in Honduras*